Keir
Elam

The Semiotics of Theatre and Drama

2nd Edition

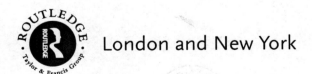 London and New York

First published 1980 by Methuen & Co. Ltd
Reprinted three times

Reprinted 1988, 1991, 1993, 1994, 1997, 2001
by Routledge
2 Park Square, Milton Park, Abingdon, Oxon, OX14 4RN

Simultaneously published in the USA and Canada
by Routledge
270 Madison Ave, New York NY 10016

Transferred to Digital Printing 2010

This second edition first published 2002

Routledge is an imprint of the Taylor & Francis Group

© 1980, 2002 Keir Elam

Typeset in Joanna by RefineCatch Limited, Bungay, Suffolk

British Library Cataloguing in Publication Data
A catalogue record for this book is available from the British Library

Library of Congress Cataloging in Publication Data
A catalog record for this book has been requested

ISBN 0–415–28017–6 (Hbk)
ISBN 0–415–28018–4 (Pbk)

CONTENTS

GENERAL EDITOR'S PREFACE   ix
ACKNOWLEDGEMENTS   xi

1   Preliminaries: Semiotics and Poetics   1
    The semiotic enterprise   1
    How many semiotics?   2
    The material   3

2   Foundations: Signs in the Theatre   4
    Prague structuralism and the theatrical sign   4
    Typologies of the sign   17

3   Theatrical Communication: Codes, Systems and the
    Performance Text   28
    Elements of theatrical communication   28
    Theatrical systems and codes   43
    Theatrical competence: frame, convention and the role
    of the audience   78

4   Dramatic Logic   88
    The construction of the dramatic world   88

Dramatic action and time 105
Actant, dramatis persona and the dramatic model 114

5 Dramatic Discourse 123
Dramatic communication 123
Context and deixis 125
Universe of discourse and co-text 135
Speech acts 142
The said and the unsaid: implicatures and figures 155
Textuality 162
Towards a dramatological analysis 167

6 Concluding Comments: Theatre, Drama, Semiotics 190
Dramatic text/performance text 190
A united enterprise? 191

'POST'-SCRIPT: POST-SEMIOTICS, POSTHUMOUS SEMIOTICS,
   CLOSET SEMIOTICS 193
SUGGESTIONS FOR FURTHER READING 222
BIBLIOGRAPHY 231
INDEX 251

In memory of my mother

GENERAL EDITOR'S PREFACE

No doubt a third General Editor's Preface to New Accents seems hard to justify. What is there left to say? Twenty-five years ago, the series began with a very clear purpose. Its major concern was the newly perplexed world of academic literary studies, where hectic monsters called 'Theory', 'Linguistics' and 'Politics' ranged. In particular, it aimed itself at those undergraduates or beginning postgraduate students who were either learning to come to terms with the new developments or were being sternly warned against them.

New Accents deliberately took sides. Thus the first Preface spoke darkly, in 1977, of 'a time of rapid and radical social change', of the 'erosion of the assumptions and presuppositions' central to the study of literature. 'Modes and categories inherited from the past' it announced, 'no longer seem to fit the reality experienced by a new generation'. The aim of each volume would be to 'encourage rather than resist the process of change' by combining nuts-and-bolts exposition of new ideas with clear and detailed explanation of related conceptual developments. If mystification (or downright demonisation) was the enemy, lucidity (with a nod to the compromises inevitably at stake there) became a friend. If a 'distinctive discourse of the future' beckoned, we wanted at least to be able to understand it.

With the apocalypse duly noted, the second Preface proceeded piously to fret over the nature of whatever rough beast might stagger portentously from the rubble. 'How can we recognise or deal with the new?', it complained, reporting nevertheless the dismaying advance of 'a host of barely respectable activities for which we have no reassuring names' and promising a programme of wary surveillance at 'the boundaries of the precedented and at the limit of the thinkable'. Its conclusion, 'the unthinkable, after all, is that which covertly shapes our thoughts' may rank as a truism. But in so far as it offered some sort of useable purchase on a world of crumbling certainties, it is not to be blushed for.

In the circumstances, any subsequent, and surely final, effort can only modestly look back, marvelling that the series is still here, and not unreasonably congratulating itself on having provided an initial outlet for what turned, over the years, into some of the distinctive voices and topics in literary studies. But the volumes now re-presented have more than a mere historical interest. As their authors indicated, the issues they raised are still potent, the arguments with which they engaged are still disturbing. In short, we weren't wrong. Academic study did change rapidly and radically to match, even to help to generate, wide reaching social changes. A new set of discourses was developed to negotiate those upheavals. Nor has the process ceased. In our deliquescent world, what was unthinkable inside and outside the academy all those years ago now seems regularly to come to pass.

Whether the *New Accents* volumes provided adequate warning of, maps for, guides to, or nudges in the direction of this new terrain is scarcely for me to say. Perhaps our best achievement lay in cultivating the sense that it was there. The only justification for a reluctant third attempt at a Preface is the belief that it still is.

TERENCE HAWKES

ACKNOWLEDGEMENTS

This book has been read in typescript by a number of friends and colleagues, to whom I wish to express my sincere gratitude. Marcello Pagnini, Alessandro Serpieri, Paola Gullì Pugliatti and Patrice Pavis all offered me illuminating criticism and stimulating suggestions, which I have taken into account in putting the book into its final form. I should particularly like to thank Terence Hawkes, the general editor, for his warm encouragement and shrewd advice at every stage of the writing of this work.

Various sections of Chapter 5 reflect my experience, from 1977 to 1978, as a member of a research group, directed by Alessandro Serpieri and sponsored by the Rizzoli Foundation of Milan. I happily acknowledge my debt to my colleagues in the group.

KEIR ELAM 1979

The author and publishers would like to thank the following individuals and companies for granting permission to reproduce material in the present volume:

Indiana University Press for the diagram on p. 35, from Umberto Eco *A Theory of Semiotics* (1976); Professor Ray L. Birdwhistell for the diagrams on pp. 40 and 67 from his book *Kinesics and Context: Essays on Body-Motion Communication*, Penguin (1971); McGraw-Hill Book Company for the table on p. 73 from J. L. Davitz *The Communication of Emotional Meaning* (1964); and Librairie Ernest Flammarion for the reproduction of Souriau's dramatic 'calculus' of roles in *Macbeth* on pp. 114–19, from Etienne Souriau *Les 200,000 situations dramatiques* (1950).

1

PRELIMINARIES: SEMIOTICS AND POETICS

THE SEMIOTIC ENTERPRISE

Of all recent developments in what used to be confidently called the humanities, no event has registered a more radical and widespread impact than the growth of semiotics. There scarcely remains a discipline which has not been opened during the past fifteen years to approaches adopted or adapted from linguistics and the general theory of signs.

Semiotics can best be defined as a science dedicated to the study of the production of meaning in society. As such it is equally concerned with processes of *signification* and with those of *communication*, i.e. the means whereby meanings are both generated and exchanged. Its objects are thus at once the different sign-systems and codes at work in society and the actual messages and texts produced thereby. The breadth of the enterprise is such that it cannot be considered simply as a 'discipline', while it is too multifaceted and heterogeneous to be reduced to a 'method'. It is – ideally, at least – a multidisciplinary science whose precise methodological characteristics will necessarily vary from field to field but which is united by a common global concern, the better understanding of our own meaning-bearing behaviour.

Proposed as a comprehensive science of signs almost contemporarily by two great modern thinkers at the beginning of this century, the Swiss linguist Ferdinand de Saussure and the American philosopher Charles Sanders Peirce, semiotics has since had a very uneven career. This has been marked in particular by two periods of intense and wide-based activity: the thirties and forties (with the work of the Czech formalists) and the past two decades (especially in France, Italy, Germany, the Soviet Union and the United States). The fortunes of the semiotic enterprise in recent years have been especially high in the field of literary studies, above all with regard to poetry and the narrative, (see Hawkes 1977a). Theatre and drama, meanwhile, have received considerably less attention, despite the peculiar richness of theatrical communication as a potential area of semiotic investigation. The main purpose of this book is to examine such work as has been produced and to suggest possible directions for future research in so vital a cultural territory.

HOW MANY SEMIOTICS?

'Theatre' and 'drama': this familiar but invariably troublesome distinction requires a word of explanation in this context, since it has important consequences with regard to the objects and issues at stake. 'Theatre' is taken to refer here to the complex of phenomena associated with the performer–audience transaction: that is, with the production and communication of meaning in the performance itself and with the systems underlying it. By 'drama', on the other hand, is meant that mode of fiction designed for stage representation and constructed according to particular ('dramatic') conventions. The epithet 'theatrical', then, is limited to what takes place between and among performers and spectators, while the epithet 'dramatic' indicates the network of factors relating to the represented fiction. This is not, of course, an absolute differentiation between two mutually alien bodies, since the performance, at least traditionally, is devoted to the representation of the dramatic fiction. It demarcates, rather, different levels of a unified cultural phenomenon for purposes of analysis.

A related distinction arises concerning the actual object of the semiotician's labours in this area; that is to say, the kinds of text which he is to take as his analytic corpus. Unlike the literary semiotician or the analyst of myth or the plastic arts, the researcher in theatre and drama is faced with two quite dissimilar – although intimately correlated – types of textual material: that produced in the theatre and that composed for the theatre. These two potential focuses of semiotic attention will be indicated as the theatrical or *performance text* and the written or *dramatic text* respectively.

It is a matter of some controversy as to whether these two kinds of textual structure belong to the same field of investigation: certain writers (Bettetini and de Marinis 1977; Ruffini 1978; de Marinis 1978) virtually rule out the dramatic text altogether as a legitimate concern of theatrical semiotics proper. The question that arises, then, is whether a semiotics of theatre *and* drama is conceivable as a bi- or multilateral but nevertheless integrated enterprise, or whether instead there are necessarily two (or more) quite separate disciplines in play. To put the question differently: is it possible to refound in semiotic terms a full-bodied *poetics* of the Aristotelian kind, concerned with all the communicational, representational, logical, fictional, linguistic and structural principles of theatre and drama? This is one of the central motivating questions behind this book.

THE MATERIAL

Given the unsettled and still largely undefined nature of the territory in view here, the examination that follows is inevitably extremely eclectic, taking into account sources ranging from classical formalism and information theory to recent linguistic, philosophical, logical and sociological research. The result is undoubtedly uneven, but this is perhaps symptomatic of the present state of semiotics at large. By the same token, the differences in terminology and methodological concerns from chapter to chapter reflect some of the changes that have registered in the semiotics of theatre and drama in the course of its development.

As for the illustrative examples chosen, especially dramatic, the chief criterion has been that of familiarity, a fact which accounts for the perhaps disproportionate number of references to Shakespeare. Exemplifications of modes of discourse (Chapter 5) are taken largely from English language texts in order to avoid the problems presented by translation.

2

FOUNDATIONS: SIGNS IN THE THEATRE

PRAGUE STRUCTURALISM AND THE THEATRICAL SIGN

The Prague School

The year 1931 is an important date in the history of theatre studies. Until that time dramatic poetics – the descriptive science of the drama and theatrical performance – had made little substantial progress since its Aristotelian origins. The drama had become (and largely remains) an annexe of the property of literary critics, while the stage spectacle, considered too ephemeral a phenomenon for systematic study, had been effectively staked off as the happy hunting ground of reviewers, reminiscing actors, historians and prescriptive theorists. That year, however, saw the publication of two studies in Czechoslovakia which radically changed the prospects for the scientific analysis of theatre and drama: Otakar Zich's *Aesthetics of the Art of Drama* and Jan Mukařovský's 'An Attempted Structural Analysis of the Phenomenon of the Actor'.

The two pioneering works laid the foundations for what is probably the richest corpus of theatrical and dramatic theory produced in modern times, namely the body of books and articles produced in the

1930s and 1940s by the Prague School structuralists. Zich's *Aesthetics* is not explicitly structuralist but exercised a considerable influence on later semioticians, particularly in its emphasis on the necessary inter-relationship in the theatre between heterogeneous but interdependent systems (see Deák 1976; Matejka and Titunik 1976; Slawinska 1978). Zich does not allow special prominence to any one of the components involved: he refuses, particularly, to grant automatic dominance to the written text, which takes its place in the system of systems making up the total dramatic representation. Mukařovský's 'structural analysis', meanwhile, represents the first step towards a semiotics of the per-formance proper, classifying the repertory of gestural signs and their functions in Charlie Chaplin's mimes.

During the two decades that followed these opening moves, theatri-cal semiotics attained a breadth and a rigour that remain unequalled. In the context of the Prague School's investigations into every kind of artistic and semiotic activity – from ordinary language to poetry, art, cinema and folk culture – attention was paid to all forms of theatre, including the ancient, the avant-garde and the Oriental, in a collective attempt to establish the principles of theatrical signification. It is inevit-ably with these frontier-opening explorations that any overview of this field must begin.

The sign

Prague structuralism developed under the twin influences of Russian formalist poetics and Saussurian structural linguistics. From Saussure it inherited not only the project for analysing all of man's signifying and communicative behaviour within the framework of a general semiotics but also, and more specifically, a working definition of the sign as a two-faced entity linking a material vehicle or signifier with a mental concept or signified. It is not surprising, given this patrimony, that much of the Prague semioticians' early work with regard to the theatre was con-cerned with the very problem of identifying and describing theatrical signs and sign-functions.

Mukařovský's initial application of the Saussurian definition of the sign consisted in identifying the work of art as such (e.g. the theatrical performance in its entirety) as the semiotic unit, whose *signifier* or *sign vehicle*[1] is the work itself as 'thing', or ensemble of material elements, and whose *signified* is the 'aesthetic object' residing in the collective consciousness of the public (1934, p. 5). The performance text becomes, in this view, a macro-sign, its meaning constituted by its total effect. This approach has the advantages of emphasizing the subordination of all contributory elements to a unified textual whole and of giving due weight to the audience as the ultimate maker of its own meanings. It is clear, on the other hand, that this macrosign has to be broken down into smaller units before anything resembling analysis can begin: thus the strategy adopted later by Mukařovský's colleagues is to view the performance not as a single sign but as a network of semiotic units belonging to different cooperative systems.

Semiotization

It was above all the folklorist Petr Bogatyrev, formerly a member of the Russian formalist circle, who undertook to chart the elementary principles of theatrical semiosis. In his very influential essay on folk theatre (1938b), he advances the thesis that the stage radically transforms all objects and bodies defined within it, bestowing upon them an overriding signifying power which they lack – or which at least is less evident – in their normal social function: 'on the stage things that play the part of theatrical signs . . . acquire special features, qualities and attributes that they do not have in real life' (pp. 35–6). This was to become virtually a manifesto for the Prague circle; the necessary primacy of the signifying function of all performance elements is affirmed repeatedly, most succinctly by Jiři Veltruský: 'All that is on the stage is a sign' (1940, p. 84).

This first principle of the Prague School theatrical theory can best be termed that of the *semiotization of the object*. The very fact of their appearance on stage suppresses the practical function of phenomena in favour of a symbolic or signifying role, allowing them to participate in dramatic representation: 'while in real life the utilitarian function of an

---

[1] In what follows, I shall in general use the term *sign-vehicle* rather than *signifier*, as it seems more appropriate to the nature of the material involved. But there is no essential difference of meaning between the two terms.

object is usually more important than its signification, on a theatrical set the signification is all important' (Brušák 1938, p. 62).

The process of semiotization is clearest, perhaps, in the case of the elements of the set. A table employed in dramatic representation will not usually differ in any material or structural fashion from the item of furniture that the members of the audience eat at, and yet it is in some sense transformed: it acquires, as it were, a set of quotation marks. It is tempting to see the stage table as bearing a direct relationship to its dramatic equivalent – the fictional object that it represents – but this is not strictly the case; the material stage object becomes, rather, a semiotic unit standing not directly for another (imaginary) table but for the intermediary signified 'table', i.e. for the *class of objects* of which it is a member. The metaphorical quotation marks placed around the stage object mark its primary condition as representative of its class, so that the audience is able to infer from it the presence of another member of the same class of objects in the represented dramatic world (a table which may or may not be structurally identical with the stage object).

It is important to emphasize that the semiotization of phenomena in the theatre relates them to their signified classes rather than immediately to the dramatic world, since it is this which allows non-literal signifiers or sign-vehicles to perform the same semiotic function as literal ones (the dramatic referent, the imaginary table, might be represented by a painted sign, a linguistic sign, an actor on all fours, etc.). The only indispensable requirement that is made of the stage sign-vehicle is that it successfully stands for its intended signified; as Karel Brůsák observes in his article on the Chinese theatre, 'A real object may be substituted on the set by a symbol if this symbol is able to transfer the object's own signs to itself' (1938, p. 62).

Stage semiotization is of particular interest and importance with respect to the actor and his physical attributes, since he is, in Veltruský's phrase, 'the dynamic unity of an entire set of signs' (1940, p. 84). In traditional dramatic performance the actor's body acquires its mimetic and representational powers by becoming something other than itself, more and less than individual. This applies equally to his speech (which assumes the general signified 'discourse') and to every aspect of his performance, to the extent that even purely contingent factors, such as physiologically determined reflexes, are accepted as signifying units. ('The spectator understands even these non-purposive components of the actor's performance as signs' (Veltruský 1940, p. 85).) Groucho Marx illustrates the point in his amazement at the scratches on Julie Harris's legs in a performance of *I am a Camera*: 'At first we thought this had something to do with the plot and we waited for these scratches to come to life. But . . . it was never mentioned in the play and we finally came to the conclusion that either she had been shaving too close or she'd been kicked around in the dressing room by her boyfriend' (quoted by Burns 1972, p. 36). The audience starts with the assumption that every detail is an intentional sign and whatever cannot be related to the representation as such is converted into a sign of the actor's very reality – it is not, in any case, excluded from semiosis.

Brechtian epic theatre made great play with the duality of the actor's role as stage sign-vehicle *par excellence*, bound in a symbolic relationship which renders him 'transparent', at the same time that it stresses his physical and social presence. By driving a dramaturgical wedge between the two functions, Brecht endeavoured to expose the very quotation marks that the actor assumes in representation, thus allowing him to become 'opaque' as a vehicle. The gesture of putting on show the very process of semiotization involved in the performance has been repeated and varied by many directors and dramatists since. The Austrian playwright Peter Handke, for instance, has the professed object in writing his plays of drawing the audience's attention to the sign-vehicle and its theatricality rather than to the signified and its dramatic equivalent, that is 'Making people aware of the world of the theatre . . . There is a theatrical reality going on at each moment. A chair on the stage is a theatre chair' (1970, p. 57).

Connotation

Even in the most determinedly realistic of dramatic representations, the role of the sign-vehicle in standing for a class of objects by no means exhausts its semiotic range. Beyond this basic denotation, the theatrical sign inevitably acquires secondary meanings for the audience, relating it to the social, moral and ideological values operative in the community of which performers and spectators are part. Bogatyrev notes this capacity of theatrical sign-vehicles for pointing beyond the denotation to some ulterior cultural signification:

> What exactly is a theatrical costume or a set that represents a house on stage? When used in a play, both the theatrical costume and the house set are often signs that point to one of the signs characterizing the costume or the house in the play. In fact, each is a sign of a sign and not the sign of a material thing. (1938b, p. 33)

It may be, for example, that in addition to the denoted class 'armour' a martial costume comes to signify for a particular audience 'valour' or 'manliness', or a bourgeois domestic interior 'wealth', 'ostentation', 'bad taste', etc. As often as not, these second-order and culturally determined units of meaning come to outweigh their denotative basis.

Bogatyrev's 'signs of signs' are what are generally designated *connotations*. The mechanism of connotation in language and other sign-systems has been much discussed, but the most satisfactory formulation remains that provided by the Danish linguist Hjelmslev, who defines a 'connotative semiotic' as one 'whose expression plane is a semiotic' (1943, p. 77). Connotation is a parasitic semantic function, therefore, whereby the sign-vehicle of one sign-relationship provides the basis for a second-order sign-relationship (the sign-vehicle of the stage sign 'crown' acquires the secondary meanings 'majesty', 'usurpation', etc.).

Every aspect of the performance is governed by the denotation–connotation dialectic: the set, the actor's body, his movements and speech determine and are determined by a constantly shifting network of primary and secondary meanings. It is an essential feature of the semiotic economy of the theatrical performance that it employs a limited repertory of sign-vehicles in order to generate a potentially unlimited range of cultural units, and this extremely powerful generative capacity on the part of the theatrical sign-vehicle is due in part to its connotative breadth. This accounts, furthermore, for the polysemic character of the theatrical sign: a given vehicle may bear not one but n second-order meanings at any point in the performance continuum (a costume, for example, may suggest socio-economic, psychological and even moral characteristics). The resulting semantic ambiguity is vital to all but the most doggedly didactic forms of theatre, and especially so to any mode of 'poetic' theatre which goes beyond 'narrative' representation, from the medieval mystery play to the visual images of the Bread and Puppet Theater.

How strictly the connotative markers are determined depends upon the strength of the semantic conventions at work. In the classical Chinese and Japanese Noh theatres, the semantic units are so strictly predetermined that the denotation–connotation distinction virtually disappears: all meanings are primary and more or less explicit. In the West, the second-order significations of any particular element are less tightly constrained, and will even vary from spectator to spectator, although always within definite cultural limits (the crown in *Richard II* is unlikely to bear the connotation 'divine providence' for any member of a contemporary audience).

Connotation is not, of course, unique to theatrical semiosis: on the contrary, the spectator's very ability to apprehend important second-order meanings in his decoding of the performance depends upon the extra-theatrical and general cultural values which certain objects, modes of discourse or forms of behaviour bear. But Bogatyrev and his colleagues draw attention to the fact that, while in practical social affairs the participants may not be aware of the meanings they attach to phenomena, theatrical communication allows these meanings sway over practical functions: things serve only to the extent that they mean. In drawing upon these socially codified values, what is more, theatrical semiosis invariably, and above all, connotes *itself*. That is, the general connotative marker 'theatricality' attaches to the entire performance (Mukařovský's macro-sign) and to its every element – as Brecht, Handke and many others have been anxious to underline – permitting the audience to 'bracket off' what is presented to them from normal social praxis and so perceive the performance *as a network of meanings*, i.e. as a *text*.

The transformability of the sign

What has been termed the 'generative capacity' of the theatrical sign – the extraordinary economy of communicational means whereby in certain forms of dramatic presentation, from the ancient Greek to

Grotowski's 'poor' theatre, a rich semantic structure is produced by a small and predictable stock of vehicles – is enhanced by a quality variously characterized by the Prague structuralists as its *mobility, dynamism* or *transformability*. The sign-vehicle may be semantically versatile (or 'over-determined') not only at the connotative level but also, on occasion, at the denotative – the same stage item stands for different signifieds depending on the context in which it appears: 'each object sees its signs transformed in the most rapid and varied fashion' (Bogatyrev 1938a, p. 519). What appears in one scene as the handle of a sword may be converted, in the next, into a cross by a simple change of position, just as the set which stands in one context for a palisade is immediately transformed, without structural modification, into a wall or garden fence. This denotational flexibility is complemented, often enough, by the mobility of dramatic functions that a single physical item fulfils: 'Mephistopheles signifies through his cape his submission to Faust, and with the help of the same cape, during Valpurgis night, he expresses the unlimited power which he exercises over diabolical forces' (Bogatyrev 1938a, p. 519).

Jindřich Honzl, a noted director as well as analyst of the theatre, develops this notion in a paper dedicated to what he terms the 'dynamism' of the sign. Honzl's thesis is that any stage vehicle can stand, in principle, for any signified class of phenomena: there are no absolutely fixed representational relations. The dramatic scene, for instance, is not always figured analogically through spatial, architectural or pictorial means, but may be indicated gesturally (as in mime), through verbal indications or other acoustic means (the 'acoustic scenery' of which Honzl writes (1940, p. 75) is clearly essential to radio drama). By the same token, there is no fixed law governing the customary representation of the dramatis persona by the human actor: 'If what matters is that something real is able to assume this function, the actor is not necessarily a man; it can be a puppet, or a machine (for example in the mechanical theatres of Lissitzky, of Schlemmer, of Kiesler), or even an object' (1940, p. 7).

Realistic or illusionistic dramatic representation severely limits the mobility of the sign-relationship: in the Western theatre we generally expect the signified *class* to be represented by a vehicle in some way recognizable as a member of it. This is not the case, however, in the

Oriental theatre, where far more semantic scope is permitted to each stage item, on the basis of explicit conventions. Karel Brušák, in his pioneering semiotic study of the Chinese theatre, describes the 'scenic' functions performed by the actor's strictly codified gestures:

> A great proportion of the actor's routine is devoted to producing signs whose chief function is to stand for components of the scene. An actor's routine must convey all those actions for which the scene provides no appropriate material setup. Using the applicable sequence of conventional moves, the actor performs the surmounting of imaginary obstacles, climbing imaginary stairs, crossing a high threshold, opening a door. The motion signs performed inform the onlooker of the nature of these imaginary objects, tell whether the nonexistent ditch is empty or filled with water, whether the nonexistent door is a main or ordinary double door, single door, and so forth. (1938, p. 68)

The mobility of the sign may be a structuralist principle, but it is by no means a recent discovery. In a metadramatic exposition in *The Two Gentlemen of Verona*, the clown Launce confronts the problem of the semiotic economy of the performance, having to decide which signified dramatis personae he must assign to his paltry set of sign-vehicles (of whom only two are animate and only one human):

> Nay, I'll show you the manner of it. This shoe is my father; no, this left shoe is my father: no, no, this left shoe is my mother; nay, that cannot be so neither: – yes, it is so; it is so; it hath the worser sole. This shoe, with the hole in, is my mother, and this my father. A vengeance on't! there 'tis: now, sir, this staff is my sister; for, look you, she is as white as a lily and as small as a wand: this hat is Nan, our maid: I am the dog; no, the dog is himself, and I am the dog, – O! the dog is me and I am myself; ay, so, so. (II. iii. 15 ff.)
>
> (Line reference here and throughout the book are to the *Complete Works*, ed. W. J. Craig, London, OUP, 1905.)

Even though Launce tries to apply the principle of appropriateness or analagousness between representation and *representatum*, he inevitably discovers that the sign-vehicles are perfectly interchangeable.

The mobility factor – as it were, the 'transformation rule' of stage representation – is dependent not only on the interchangeability of stage elements but still more on the reciprocal substitution of sign-systems or codes (see Chapter 3). The replacement, for example, of scenic indicators by gesture or verbal reference involves the process of *transcodification*: a given semantic unit (say, a 'door') is signified by the linguistic or gestural system rather than by the architectural or pictorial, as often occurs in mime.

Of particular interest in this code- and function-switching semiotic flux is the question – one of Launce's directorial problems – of the dialectic between the animate and the inanimate, or, better, between the subjective and the objective on stage. It is almost unavoidable, when thinking about dramatic representation, to draw a firm and automatic distinction between the active subject, embodied by the actor, and the objects to which he relates and which participate in the action through his agency. This opposition is broken down by Jiři Veltruský, however, and replaced by the more analytic notion of a subjective-objective *continuum* along which all stage sign-vehicles, human and inanimate, move in the course of the representation. While the customary, or automatized, epitome of the dynamic subject is the 'lead' actor, whose 'action force' sets semiosis in motion, and the prime paradigm of the passive object is the prop or element of the set, the relation between these apparent poles may be modified or even reversed.

It is possible for instance, for the action force that the actor bears to fall to a zero level, whereby he assumes a role analogous to that of the prop (in the case, for example, of the stereotyped figure automatically associated with certain functions, like the butler in a typical 1940s drawing-room comedy or, to take Veltruský's example, 'soldiers flanking the entrance to a house. They serve to point out that the house is a barrack' (1940, p. 86. Here the actor functions, effectively, as part of the set.) At the same time, the inanimate stage item is capable of promotion up the objectivity–subjectivity continuum, so acquiring a certain action force in its own right. Veltruský provides the emblematic example of the stage dagger which may move from its purely contiguous role as part of the costume, indicating the wearer's status, through participation in the action as an instrument (as in the murder of Julius Caesar), to an independent association with some act, as when, covered with blood, it comes to connote 'murder' (see Veltruský 1940, p. 87).

At an extreme, of course, it is possible to dispense altogether with the human agent and entrust the semiotic initiative to set and props, which are then perceived as 'spontaneous subjects equivalent to the figure of the actor' (Veltruský 1940, p. 88). It is notable that many of the so-called avant-garde experiments in the twentieth-century theatre have been founded on the promotion of the set to the position of 'subject' of semiosis, with a corresponding surrender of 'action force' by the actor: Edward Gordon Craig's ideal, for example, was a mode of representation dominated by a highly connotative set and in which the actor had the purely determined function of Übermarionette. Samuel Beckett's two mimes, Act Without Words I and II, play with the reversal of subjective-objective roles between actor and prop – the human figure is determined by, and victim of, the stage sign-vehicles around him ('tree', 'rope', 'box', etc.) – while his thirty-second Breath has the set as its sole protagonist.

Foregrounding and the performance hierarchy

From the first, the Prague theorists – following Otakar Zich – conceived of the performance structure as a dynamic hierarchy of elements. Mukařovský's early essay on Chaplin begins by characterizing the object in view as 'a structure, that is, as a system of elements aesthetically realized and grouped in a complex hierarchy, where one of the elements predominates over the others' (1931, p. 342). He proceeds to examine the means whereby Chaplin remains at the apex of this structure, ordering subordinate components of the performance about him. All of the structuralist writers on the theatre emphasize the fluidity of the hierarchy, whose order is not absolutely determinable a priori: 'the transformability of the hierarchical order of the elements which constitute the art of theatre corresponds to the transformability of the theatrical sign' (Honzl 1940, p. 20).

What is of interest in the shifting structure of the performance is, in Veltruský's words, 'The figure at the peak of this hierarchy' which 'attracts to itself the major attention of the audience' (1940, p. 85).

Here a concept first developed in the study of poetic language is applied, *aktualisace* (usually translated as 'foregrounding'). Linguistic foregrounding in language occurs when an unexpected usage suddenly forces the listener or reader to take note of the utterance itself, rather than continue his automatic concern with its 'content': 'the use of the devices of the language in such a way that this use itself attracts attention and is perceived as uncommon, as deprived of automatization, as deautomatized, such as a live poetic metaphor' (Havránek 1942, p. 10).

In terms of the performance structure, the automatized state of affairs, in the Western theatrical tradition, occurs when the apex of the hierarchy is occupied by the actor, and in particular the 'lead' actor, who attracts the major part of the spectator's attention to his own person. The bringing of other elements to the foreground occurs when these are raised from their 'transparent' functional roles to a position of unexpected prominence, i.e. when they acquire the semiotic subjectivity of which Veltruský writes: attention is brought to bear momentarily or for the duration of the performance on a conspicuous and autonomous setting (such as those of Piscator and Craig), or on lighting effects (as in the experiments of Appia), or on a particular and usually instrumental aspect of the actor's performance, for example his gestures (the experiments of Meyerhold or Grotowski).

Aktualisace derives from, and bears a strong family resemblance to, the Russian formalist notion of *ostranenie* (defamiliarization or 'making strange') (see Bennett 1979, pp. 53 ff.). It is not only the granting of unusual prominence or autonomy to aspects of the performance which serves to foreground them, but the distancing of those aspects from their codified functions. When theatrical semiosis is alienated, made 'strange' rather than automatic, the spectator is encouraged to take note of the semiotic *means*, to become aware of the sign-vehicle and its operations. This was, as has been suggested, one of the aims of Brechtian epic theatre; Brecht's noted concept of the *Verfremdungseffekt*, the alienation effect, is, indeed, an adaptation of the Russian formalist principle (see Brecht 1964, p. 99), and Brecht's own definition of the effect as a 'way of drawing one's own or someone else's attention to a thing' which 'consists in turning the object of which one is to be made aware, to which one's attention is to be drawn, from something ordinary, familiar, immediately accessible into something peculiar, striking and unexpected' (Brecht 1964, p. 143) indicates its affinity with the formalist and structuralist principles.

Theatrical foregrounding may involve the 'framing' of a bit of the performance in such a way as, in Brecht's words, 'to mark it off from the rest of the text' (p. 203). This can amount to an explicit pointing to the representation as an event in progress – Brecht's '*gestus* of showing' – as when the actor stands aside in order to comment upon what is happening, or a rendering opaque of representational means through a range of devices such as freezes, slow-motion effects, unexpected changes in lighting, etc. Much experimental theatre of the 1960s and 1970s was devoted to the development of techniques for framing and estranging the signifying process. A particularly successful exponent has been the American director-playwright Richard Foreman, whose 'use of visual and aural "framing devices" constitutes a recognizable stylistic feature' of his productions – that is, his inclusion of 'anything that punctuates, frames, emphasizes, or brings into the foreground a particular word, object, action or position' (e.g. his literal framing of an actor's foot in *Vertical Mobility*) (Davy 1976, pp. xiv–xv; see also Kirby 1973).

Despite its origins as a linguistic concept, foregrounding is essentially a spatial metaphor and thus well adapted to the theatrical text. It is, of course, possible for those devices which serve to defamiliarize the linguistic utterance in other contexts also to operate in the drama. This would allow the linguistic sign to be foregrounded in the performance, although never so fully as in literary discourse where no non-linguistic semiotic systems compete for the audience's attention (see Elam 1977). Conspicuous rhetorical figures, highly patterned syntax, phonetic repetitions and parallelisms augment the material presence of the linguistic sign on stage; Havránek (1942, p. 11) suggests that 'we find maximum foregrounding, used for its own sake, in poetic language', although it must be added that in certain periods, such as the Elizabethan, elaborately worked language in the drama has been the automatized norm, so that a multiplicity of rhetorical or poetic devices is not in itself a guarantee of successful linguistic foregrounding. The explicit framing of language, through metalanguage and other forms of commentary (see pp. 140–2 below), has been a very longstanding feature of dramatic dialogue. But what serves most radically to alienate the signifier from its meaning-function and to increase its opacity is actual nonsense, of the kind so richly employed, for example, by Alfred Jarry or, occasionally, by Shakespeare:

FIRST LORD. Throca mouvousus, cargo cargo, cargo.
ALL. Cargo, cargo, villianda par corbo, cargo.
(*All's Well that Ends Well*, iv. i. 70 ff.)

TYPOLOGIES OF THE SIGN

Natural and artificial signs

After the promising charting of the territory by the Prague School structuralists in the 1930s and early 1940s, little work of note dedicated to the problems of theatrical semiosis was produced for two decades. Roland Barthes suggested provocatively in 1964 that the theatre, marked by 'a real informational polyphony' and 'a density of signs', constituted a privileged field of semiotic investigation: 'the nature of the theatrical sign, whether analogical, symbolic or conventional, the denotation and connotation of the message – all these fundamental problems of semiology are present in the theatre' (1964, p. 262). Barthes failed, however, to follow up his own provocation.

It was, instead, the Polish semiotician Tadeusz Kowzan who, in 1968, took up the structuralist heritage. In his essay 'The Sign in the Theatre', Kowzan reasserts the basic Prague School principles, above all that of the semiotization of the object: 'Everything is a sign in a theatrical presentation' (1968, p. 57). He similarly reaffirms the structuralist notions of the transformability and connotative range of the stage sign: in addition, however, he endeavours to found an initial typology of the theatrical sign and sign-systems, i.e. to classify as well as describe the phenomena (on Kowzan's table of sign-systems, see pp. 45 ff. below).

The distinction that Kowzan draws upon in the first instance is the often-made one between 'natural' and 'artificial' signs, whose distinction lies in the presence or absence of 'motivation': natural signs are determined by strictly physical laws whereby signifier and signified are bound in a direct cause-and-effect relationship (as in the case of symptoms indicating a disease or smoke signifying fire). 'Artificial' signs depend upon the intervention of human volition (in the various languages man creates for signalling purposes). The opposition is by no means absolute, since even so-called natural signs require the observer's 'motivated' act of inference in making the link between sign-vehicle and signified. It serves Kowzan, however, in the formulation of a further principle, namely the 'artificialization' of the apparently natural sign on stage:

> The spectacle transforms natural signs into artificial ones (a flash of lightning), so it can 'artificialize' signs. Even if they are only reflexes in life, they become voluntary signs in the theatre. Even if they have no communicative function in life, they necessarily acquire it on stage. (p. 60)

This is, in effect, a refinement on the semiotization law: phenomena assume a signifying function on stage to the extent that their relation to what they signify is perceived as being deliberately intended.

Icon, index and symbol

More promising, at least intuitively, than the simple natural/artificial opposition is the well-known trichotomy of sign-functions suggested by the American logician and founding father of modern semiotic theory, C. S. Peirce. Peirce's highly suggestive tripartite typology of signs – icon, index and symbol – corresponds so effectively to our commonsense perception of different signifying modes that it has received widespread and sometimes uncritical application in many fields, not least theatre study (see, for example, Kott 1969; Pavis 1976; Helbo 1975c; Ubersfeld 1977), although the conceptual basis of Peirce's distinctions is very problematic and has been repeatedly questioned in recent years (see Eco 1976).

Peirce's definitions of the three sign-functions are subject to variation, depending on the context in which they occur, but the differences can be summarized as follows.

The *icon*. The governing principle in iconic signs is similitude; the icon represents its object 'mainly by similarity' between the sign-vehicle and its signified. This is, clearly, a very general law, so that virtually any form of similitude between sign and object suffices, in principle, to establish an iconic relationship:

> An icon is a sign which refers to the object that it denotes merely by virtue of characters of its own, and which it possesses. . . . Anything whatever, be it quality, existent individual, or law, is an Icon of anything, in so far as it is like that thing and used as a sign of it. (Peirce 1931–58, Vol. 2, § 247)

Examples of iconic signs given by Peirce himself include the figurative painting (an icon to the extent that 'we lose the consciousness that it is not the thing' (Vol. 2, p. 363)) and the photograph; he further distinguishes three classes of icon: the image, the diagram and the metaphor.

The *index*. Indexical signs are causally connected with their objects, often physically or through contiguity: 'An Index is a sign which refers to the object that it denotes by virtue of being really affected by that object' (Vol. 2, § 248). The 'natural' cause-and-effect signs considered in the previous section are thus indices, according to Peircean doctrine, but Peirce also includes in this category the pointing ('index') finger – which relates to the pointed-to object through physical contiguity – the rolling gait of the sailor, indicating his profession, a knock on the door which points to the presence of someone outside it, and verbal deixis (personal and demonstrative pronouns such as 'I', 'you', 'this', 'that', and adverbs such as 'here' and 'now', etc.).

The *symbol*. Here the relationship between sign-vehicle and signified is conventional and unmotivated; no similitude or physical connection exists between the two: 'A *symbol* is a sign which refers to the object that it denotes by virtue of a law, usually an association of general ideas' (Vol. 2, § 249). The most obvious example of a symbol is the linguistic sign.

Despite the qualifications which Peirce himself added to his definitions, indicating that there can never be such a thing as a 'pure' icon or index or symbol, it is only too tempting to fall into a naïve absolutism in applying the categories. The theatre appears, for example, to be the perfect domain of the icon: where better to look for direct similitude between sign-vehicle and signified than in the actor–character relationship? The first writer to apply the Peircean concept to the theatre, Jan Kott, accepts the apparent iconicity of the stage sign and identifies the chief element of similarity: 'In the theatre the basic icon is the body and voice of the actor' (1969, p. 19).

There is, in fact, a good case to be made out for the importance of icons to theatrical semiosis. It is clear that a degree of analogousness often arises between, say, representational and represented human bodies, or between the stage sword and its dramatic equivalent (the 'similitude' involved is, in these cases, definitely stronger than in Peirce's example of the portrait). The theatre is perhaps the only art form able to exploit what might be termed iconic *identity*: the sign-vehicle denoting a rich silk costume may well be a rich silk costume, rather than the illusion thereof created by pigment on canvas, an image conserved on celluloid or a description. An extreme assertion of literal iconic identity was the basis for one of the gestures made by the Living Theater in the 1960s: Julian Beck and Judith Malina claimed to be representing on stage precisely themselves, so that the similarity between sign and object became – supposedly – absolute.

Iconism is usually associated by commentators with visual signs, where the similitude involved is most readily apparent. The illusionistic visual resources of the theatre are unrivalled: literal signs apart, the performance can draw upon an unlimited range of simulacra, from elaborate mock-ups to back projection and film. But it would be mistaken to limit the notion to the visual image alone; if theatre depends upon similitude, this must characterize acoustic sign-systems equally and, indeed, the representation at large. Patrice Pavis has suggested that 'the language of the actor is iconized in being spoken by the actor', i.e. what the actor utters becomes the representation of something supposedly equivalent to it, 'discourse' (Pavis 1976, p. 13). In naturalistic performances especially, the audience is encouraged to take both the linguistic signs and all other representational elements as being directly analogous to the denoted objects.

Yet the principle of similarity is less well defined in the theatre than it might appear. The degree of geniune homology operating between the performance and what it is supposed to denote is extremely variable. If one takes the case of Kott's icon *par excellence*, the actor and his physical features, the similitude between the sign and what it stands for begins to break down as soon as one considers, for example, Elizabethan boy actors representing women, the portrayal of gods by Greek actors, or the numerous cases of ageing theatrical stars who continue to adopt the roles of romantic heroes or heroines (not to mention Sarah Bernhardt's impersonation, in old age and complete with wooden leg, of Hamlet). Here the wholly conventional basis of iconism on stage emerges clearly.

Much of the richness of the stage spectacle derives from the interplay of varying degrees of semiotic literalness: young actors portraying, with a degree of verisimilitude, the lovers in a Forest of Arden represented by cardboard cut-out trees. An extreme example of such mixing of the literally iconic with the blatantly schematic in the contemporary theatre might be Robert Wilson's *Ka Mountain* (1972), an epic 168-hour performance given near Shiraz in Iran, where the setting was represented by real mountains, inhabited, for the occasion, in part by actual bodies (human and animal) in various roles and in part by cut-out stereotypes of old men, dinosaurs, Noah's Ark, a notional American suburb and biblical emblems.

Peirce, it will be recalled, subdivided the icon into the three classes of image, diagram and metaphor. If certain forms of theatre – broadly, 'illusionistic' representation – encourage the spectator to perceive the performance as a direct image of the dramatic world, others content themselves with diagrammatic or metaphorical portrayal where only a very general structural similitude exists between sign and object. Thus the actor, in pantomime or surrealist theatre, may impersonate the shape of a table (diagram). Alternatively, similarity may be simply asserted rather than apparent, as in the case of an empty stage which becomes, for the audience, a battlefield, palace or prison cell (metaphor).

Iconism is further conditioned by the law of the transformability of the sign. If one sign-system can do the work usually fulfilled by another, it is clear that direct similarity is quite dispensable. Honzl's 'acoustic scenery' is a notable case in point. In the Elizabethan theatre, language, apart from denoting speech at large, often played a pseudo-iconic descriptive role in figuring the dramatic scene, as in *Measure for Measure* where Isabella describes in detail the location of her rendezvous with Angelo:

He hath a garden circummur'd with brick,
Whose western side is with a vineyard back'd;
And to that vineyard in a planched gate,
That makes his opening with this bigger key . . .
(IV. iv. 30 ff.)

This device, which the classical rhetoricians termed *topographia*, functions according to a purely metaphorical similarity between the verbal representation and the scene described.

The notion of iconism is useful, therefore, provided that two main qualifications are kept in mind. First, the principle of similitude is highly flexible and strictly founded on convention ('to say that a certain image is similar to something else does not eliminate the fact that similarity is also a matter of cultural convention' (Eco 1976, p. 204), allowing the spectator to make the necessary analogy between the standing-for and the stood-for objects, whatever the actual material or structural equivalence between them. Second, even in the most literal iconic sign-functions (mountains representing mountains or Judith Malina herself) the similarity puts into play not a simple one-to-one relationship between analogous objects but a relationship necessarily mediated by the signified class or concept. In Peircean terms, semiosis involves 'a co-operation of three subjects, such as a sign, its object and its interpretant' (1931–58, Vol. 5, § 484) (the 'interpretant' being, roughly, the idea which the sign produces), so that anything which permits the spectator to form an image or likeness of the represented object can be said to have fulfilled an iconic function:

> Not only is the outward significant word or mark a sign, but the image which it is expected to excite in the mind of the receiver will likewise be a sign – a sign by resemblance, or, as we say, an *icon* – of the similar image in the mind of the deliverer. (1931–58, Vol. 3, § 433)

As with icons, indices are not so much distinct entities as functions. Costume, for example, may denote iconically the mode of dress worn by the dramatic figure but, at the same time, stand indexically for his social position or profession, just as the actor's movement across the stage will simultaneously represent some act in the dramatic world and indicate the dramatis persona's frame of mind or standing (the cowboy's swagger or, to repeat Peirce's example, the sailor's gait). The category of index is so broad that every aspect of the performance can be considered as in some sense indexical. The dramatic setting, for instance, is often represented not by means of a direct 'image' but through cause-and-effect association or contiguity. (Consider the first scene of The Tempest, where the storm may, according to illusionistic principles, be suggested by wind machines, stage rain and other technological paraphernalia, or simply by the actors' movements, depicting the tempest's immediate consequences.)

In these cases, the indexical function appears secondary to the iconic, but there are instances where what predominates on stage is a 'pointing to' rather than an imagistic mode of signifying. Gesture often has the effect of indicating the objects (directly represented or not) to which the speaker is referring and thus of placing him in apparent contact with his physical environment, with his interlocutors or with the action reported, commanded, etc. (see pp. 74/75 ff. below). Similarly, lighting changes may serve to indicate or define the object of discourse in an indexical manner: in Samuel Beckett's Play, for instance, the spotlight (the most direct form of technological 'pointing' that the theatre possesses) serves not only to indicate the subject of each monologue, in a manner similar to that of indexical gesture, but to motivate each speaker, provoke him into speech. Here stage indices have the general function of what Peirce terms 'focusing the attention', and are thus closely related to explicit foregrounding devices (which, in this sense, point to the object offered to the audience's attention). The importance of the indexical sign-function in pointing out where the spectator should direct his notice is emphasized by Patrice Pavis: 'The theatre, which must constantly attract the receiver's attention, will thus have recourse to the index' (1976, p. 16).

Verbal deictics are exemplary but problematic forms of indexical signs. Peirce classes them as subindices or indexical symbols, since any linguistic sign is in the first instance conventional and its semantic or meaning-carrying role is prior to its indicating role. Deixis is immensely important to the drama, however, being the primary means whereby language gears itself to the speaker and receiver (through the personal pronouns 'I' and 'you') and to the time and place of the action (through the adverbs 'here' and 'now', etc.), as well as to the supposed physical environment at large and the objects that fill it (through the demonstratives 'this', 'that', etc.). It has been suggested, indeed, that deixis is the most significant linguistic feature – both statistically and functionally – in the drama (see pp. 126 ff. below).

Peirce's exemplary 'symbol', as has been said, is the linguistic sign. It must be emphasized, however, that theatrical performance as a whole is symbolic, since it is only through convention that the spectator takes stage events as standing for something other than themselves. In certain modes of theatre – mime or the Noh theatre – no other sign-systems, especially the gestural or 'kinesic', are quite as strictly governed by semantic conventions as the linguistic. It can be said, therefore, that on stage the symbolic, iconic and indexical sign-functions are co-present: all icons and indices in the theatre necessarily have a conventional basis.

Metaphor, metonymy and synecdoche

As we have seen, in classifying the kind of iconic similarity which is asserted rather than apparent, Peirce employs the rhetorical category of metaphor. In a sentence such as 'she's a real wallflower', the supposed similarity between the signifier 'wallflower' and the signified 'girl who does not dance at parties' is arbitrary and fanciful – at most the two have in common the semantic feature 'clinging to walls'. In theatrical performance the assertion of equivalence between, say, a green back-cloth and the signified 'woodland setting' might be similarly con-sidered a metaphoric substitution on the basis of a single common feature ('greenness').

The linguist Roman Jakobson – a collaborator with both the Russian formalists and the Prague structuralists – advances a highly influential theory according to which metaphoric substitution forms one of the fundamental poles not only of language use but of semiotic and artistic activity in general. The other pole is likewise categorized by means of a rhetorical figure: metonymy, the substitution of cause for effect or of one item for something contiguous to it (for example, the White House comes to stand for the President of the United States, and the umbrella, bowler hat and folded newspaper for the English city gent). Jakobson argues that this distinction is useful in classifying different modes of artistic representation: 'realism', for instance, is largely metonymic in mode while 'symbolism' is primarily metaphoric (Jakobson and Halle 1956; see also Hawkes 1977a, pp. 77 ff.; Lodge 1977).

It is clear that if metaphoric substitution is allied to the iconic sign-function (both are based on the principle of supposed similarity), then metonymic substitution is closely related to the index (each being founded on physical contiguity). Veltruský observes that on stage a given prop, for example, may come to stand for its user or for the action in which it is employed: 'It is so closely linked to the action that its use for another purpose is perceived as a scenic metonymy' (1940, p. 88). In this sense the use, say, of a stage sword in order to shave a beard is a metonymic 'deviation'. Certain stereotyped roles may be so strongly associated with a particular property that the two become synonymous, as in the case of the so-called 'spear-carrier' where the prop indicates the actor's function rather than vice versa.

Jindřich Honzl notes another form of what he regards as metonymic substitution on stage, namely such 'scenic metonymies' as the representation of a battlefield by a single tent or of a church by a gothic spire (1940, p. 77). The structuralists, including Jakobson, consider the kind of substitution at work here, i.e. of a part for the whole, as a species of metonymy, whereas the classical rhetoricians termed it *synecdoche*. It is worth insisting on the difference, since in practice synecdochic replacement of part for whole is essential to every level of dramatic representation.

Taking Honzl's example of scenic synecdoches, it is evident that even in the most detailed of naturalistic sets what is actually presented to the audience's view stands for only part of the dramatic world in which the action takes place. Extensive settings are usually represented by pertinent and recognizable aspects thereof: a castle, for example, by a turreted wall, a prison cell by a barred window and a wood by a given number of stage trees, whether painted or free-standing. The same principle applies to the actors, who represent members of a presumably more extensive society, just as their discourse and actions are taken to occur in a wider context than the immediately apparent situation (the wider context often being named: Rome, Orleans, etc.). When the stage representation of actions is more than purely symbolic or metaphorical – when, for instance, a 'murder' is apparently enacted rather than being reported or suggested by means of conventional symbols – there is always, none the less, an assumption that the audience will agree to take the motions that the actors go through, which do not in themselves add up to anything, as the impersonation of the complete act (the wielding of a stage knife as an assassination). (See pp. 113–14 below.) Finally, as has been emphasized, since objects on stage function semiotically only to the extent that they are, in Umberto Eco's words, 'based on a synecdoche of the kind "member for its class"' (1976, p. 226), it can be argued that the theatrical sign is by nature synecdochic.

Ostension

One final observation may be made about theatrical semiosis which further distinguishes it from the signifying modes of most other arts, particularly literature. Theatre is able to draw upon the most 'primitive' form of signification, known in philosophy as *ostension*. In order to refer to, indicate or define a given object, one simply picks it up and shows it to the receiver of the message in question. Thus, in response to a child's question 'What's a pebble?', instead of replying with a gloss ('It's a small stone worn into shape by water') one seizes the nearest example on the beach or ground and demonstrates it to the child; or, similarly, in order to indicate which drink one desires, one holds up a glass of beer to whoever is doing the ordering. What happens in these cases is not that one shows the actual referent (the 'pebble' or 'beer' being referred to) but that one uses the concrete object 'as the expression of the class of which it is a member' (Eco 1976, p. 225): the thing is 'de-realized' so as to become a sign.

Eco has argued that this elementary form of signifying is 'the most basic instance of performance' (1977, p. 110). Semiotization involves the showing of objects and events (and the performance at large) to the audience, rather than describing, explaining or defining them. This ostensive aspect of the stage 'show' distinguishes it, for example, from narrative, where persons, objects and events are necessarily described and recounted. It is not, again, the dramatic referent – the object in the represented world – that is shown, but something that expresses its class. The showing is emphasized and made explicit through indices, verbal references and other direct foregrounding devices, all geared towards presenting the stage spectacle for what it basically is, a 'display'.

Beyond the sign

The discussion of theatrical signs in this chapter has been concerned not with entities but with functions, some of which (e.g. 'foregrounding', 'indices' and 'ostension') to a considerable extent overlap (they are different ways, as it were, of looking at the same phenomena). The various sign-functions mentioned here are to be considered complementary rather than mutually exclusive, and they certainly do not exhaust the range of signifying modes of which the theatre is capable. All that these semiotic categories indicate is certain ways in which the formidable task of describing and classifying so complex a matter as the production of meaning on stage has been initiated.

One cannot proceed very far in examining theatrical meaning, however, without moving beyond the concept of the sign towards a discussion of the theatrical 'message' or 'text' and the *systems* of signs, or codes, which produce the performance. The semiotics of theatre, in recent years, has been less concerned with signs and sign-functions than with theatrical communication and the rules underlying it, and it is to these broader issues that we now turn.

3

THEATRICAL COMMUNICATION: CODES, SYSTEMS AND THE PERFORMANCE TEXT

ELEMENTS OF THEATRICAL COMMUNICATION

Signification and communication

Theatrical signification is not reducible to a set of one-to-one relationships between single sign-vehicles and their individual meanings. If it were possible to break down the performance text into atomic units of meaning, the task of analysing theatrical semiosis would be elementary, but by the same token the performance itself would be scarcely more than a parade of items to which the audience has merely to assign fixed values. The production of meaning on stage is too rich and fluid to be accounted for in terms of discrete objects and their representational roles. An adequate account must be able to identify the range of sign repertories making up what might be termed the theatrical *system of systems*; to explain the internal (syntactic) relations of each and the *inter*-relations between systems; and to make explicit the kinds of rules which allow meaning to be communicated and received in the performer-spectator dialectic. The semiotician of theatre, in brief, will be equally concerned with modes of *signification* and with the resulting acts of *communication* and will wish to provide a model that accounts for both.

It is clear that accounting for the rules which permit theatrical meanings to be generated and communicated is an all-but-boundless enterprise, since the entire gamut of social and cultural constraints is potentially involved. Here it will be possible only to sketch a basic communication model for the theatre and to indicate some of the more promising areas of research into the rules governing the theatrical system of systems.

Does theatre communicate?

Paradoxically, the effective historical starting-point of research into theatrical communication is denial of its very possibility. In 1969 the French linguist Georges Mounin challenged the classification of the performer-spectator bond as a communicative relationship, on the grounds that genuine communication – of which linguistic exchange is for him the prime example – depends on the capacity of the two (or more) parties involved in the exchange to employ the same code (e.g. the French language) so that 'the sender can become receiver in turn; and the receiver the sender'. This is not the case, he argues, in the theatre, where the information-giving process is unidirectional and the participants' roles fixed: 'There is nothing of all this in the theatre, in which the sender-actors remain always such, as do the receiver-spectators' (1969, p. 92).

Mounin's conception of theatrical performance is in effect a stimulus-response model in which one-way signals provoke a number of more or less automatic reflexes which do not communicate, in turn, along the same axes. This process can be represented thus:

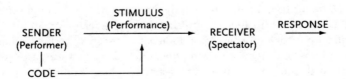

There are several objections to be made to such a scheme. Mounin's view of the actor-audience transaction appears to be based on the weakest forms of bourgeois spectacle where a passive audience may indeed obediently provide predetermined and automatic responses to a predictable set of signals (many a West End or Broadway comedy has operated successfully on this principle). Not only are the audience's signals, in any vital form of theatre, an essential contribution to the formation and reception of the performance text – and indeed various postwar performers and directors such as the Becks and Richard Schechner have extended the bounds of the performance to include the audience explicitly – but the spectator, by virtue of his very patronage of the performance, can be said to *initiate* the communicative circuit (his arrival and readiness being, as it were, the preliminary signals which provoke the performers proper into action; see p. 86 below).

The chief perplexity raised by Mounin's denial of communicative status to the performance concerns his very definitions of communication and of the codes on which it depends: he insists that sender and receiver be in a position equally to *employ* a single code and a set of physical channels, thus transmitting similar signals, while a more generous conception of the communicative process – and one generally accepted today – holds it sufficient that the receiver be *acquainted* with the sender's code and so be able to decode the message. As Franco Ruffini has said, in reply to Mounin's challenge, 'if the sender and receiver know each other's code, it is not at all necessary, in order for communication to take place, that the two codes coincide, nor that they translate each other's messages exactly, nor that the two-way communication occur along the same channel' (1974a, p. 40). A reasonably experienced spectator will be able to understand the performance at least approximately in terms of the dramatic and theatrical codes employed by the performers, and this area of common knowledge or competence is one of the major fields of investigation awaiting the theatrical semiotician.

None the less, the gauntlet boldly thrown down by Mounin should be taken up with care: he furnishes a sober warning regarding the difficulty of defining the actor-audience transaction and, still more, regarding the danger of viewing the performance as a 'language' directly analogous to speech and thus a suitable object for analytic models taken straight from linguistics. It is the business of the semiotician to find a model *specific* to the complexities of theatrical communication.

Towards a simple model of theatrical communication

One can describe the communication process in general terms as the transmission of a signal from a source to a destination. The factors involved in the transmission are represented in the diagram on p. 32 (from Eco 1976, p. 33) of elementary communication.

The initial factor here, the *source* of information, may be in practice an idea or impulse in the mind of the speaker, an actual event (as in the case of journalistic communication) or a state of affairs to be communicated, such as a dangerously high level of water. The *transmitter* set into action by the source may be the speaker's voice, an electric lamp, a computer, a typewriter or telex machine, or anything capable of sending a *signal* (e.g. phonemes, graphic signs, an electric impulse) along a physical *channel* such as an electric wire, light waves or sound waves. During its passage along the channel, the signal is liable to disturbance by *noise*, interference which hampers its proper reception. The signal is picked up by a *receiver* (an amplifier, the eye, the ear) and is thereby converted into a coherent *message* comprehensible to the *destination*.

Formation and understanding (or encoding and decoding) of messages is made possible by the *code*, a preliminary definition of which can be given as the ensemble of rules – known to both transmitter and destination – which assigns a certain content (or meaning) to a certain signal. In linguistic communication the code allows speaker and addressee to form and recognize syntactically correct sequences of phonemes and to assign a semantic content to them. More elementary codes attribute values to, say, the flashing of red, yellow and green lights or the opening and closing of a barrier.

Perhaps the first observation to be made regarding theatrical communication in terms of this simple model is that the performance brings about a *multiplication* of communicational factors. At each stage in the process there arises, rather than a single element, a complex of potential components. One can, for example, identify as the sources of theatrical information the dramatist (the dramatic text, where it exists, being both a *pre*-text and a constituent of the performance text, see

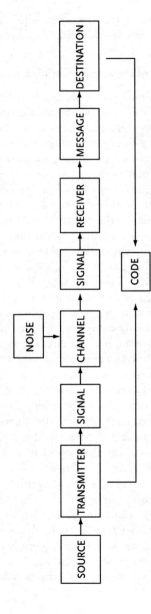

An elementary communication model

p. 191 below); the director, whose decisions and instructions determine to a considerable extent the choice of transmitters, the form that their signals take and the encoding of the messages (in the theatre not only the transmitters but also the sources share the operative codes); together with such auxiliary influences on the performance as the set designer, lighting designer, costume designer, composer, stage manager, technicians and the actors themselves in their capacity as decision-makers, initiative-takers and funds of ideas. None of these potential sources is indispensable, and only in the 'richest' forms of theatre will they all represent significant influences on the performance.

One can continue to locate multiple components all the way along the communicational circuit. The transmitters become, in the first instance, the bodies and voices of the actors, together with their metonymic accessories (costumes, properties, etc.), then elements of the set, electric lamps, musical instruments, tape recorders, film projectors, and so on. The signals transmitted by these bodies – movements, sounds, electrical impulses – are selected and arranged syntactically according to a wide range of sign- or signalling *systems* and travel through any number of the physical channels available for human communication, from light and sound waves to olfactory and tactile means (in modern 'contact' performances smell and touch become significant constraints upon reception of the whole text).

One of the consequences of this multiplication of components and systems is that it is not possible to talk of a single theatrical *message*: the performance is, rather, made up – in the words of the communication theorist Abraham Moles – of '*multiple messages* in which several channels, or several modes of using a channel in communication, are used simultaneously in an esthetic or perceptual *synthesis*' (1958, p. 171). The spectator will interpret this complex of messages – speech, gesture, the scenic continuum, etc. – as an integrated *text*, according to the theatrical, dramatic and cultural codes at his disposal, and will in turn assume the role of transmitter of signals to the performers (laughter, applause, boos, etc.), along visual and acoustic channels, which both the performers and members of the audience themselves will interpret in terms of approval, hostility, and so on. This feedback process and the *inter*communication between spectators is one of the major distinguishing features of live theatre, which can in this sense be seen as a 'cybernetic machine' (Barthes 1964a, p. 261).

There arises a further complicating factor in most forms of theatre, namely the fact that performer-audience communication does not (except in the case of prologues, epilogues, asides or apostrophes) take a *direct* form: the actor-spectator transaction within the *theatrical* context is mediated by a *dramatic* context in which a fictional speaker addresses a fictional listener. It is this dramatic communicational situation which is ostended to the spectator (see pp. 123 ff. below), and this peculiar obliqueness of the actor-audience relationship must be accounted for in any model. A simplified representation of this situation is shown in the diagram below. The model, while undoubtedly reductive and mechanistic, serves at least as an emblem of the multi-levelled character of the theatrical communicational exchange.

Information in the theatre

In setting up even a primitive and reductive theatrical communication model, one inevitably encounters the question of the kind of *information* transmitted in the course of the performance,since every communicative act depends upon the information-value of the message. In its colloquial use, /information/ is generally understood as the 'intelligence given' *about* some topic; this may be called, following a terminological tradition (see Moles 1958, pp. 128 ff.; Eco 1976, p. 267; Lyons 1977, pp. 41 ff.) *semantic* information. This kind of information 'about' is strictly related to the semantic content of the message, and may best be defined as the sum of new knowledge given regarding the state of affairs referred to. In theatrical performance, such knowledge usually concerns the fictional dramatic world set up by the representation (i.e. it appertains to the 'Dramatic Context' box in the model) and so can be designated *dramatic* information, that which the audience learns concerning a set of individuals and events in a particular fictional context.

Dramatic information may be conveyed by any or all of the systems involved, being translatable from one kind of message into another irrespective of the physical qualities of the signs or signals involved: the information 'night falls', for instance, can be conveyed by means of a lighting change, a verbal reference or, in Oriental theatre, gesturally.

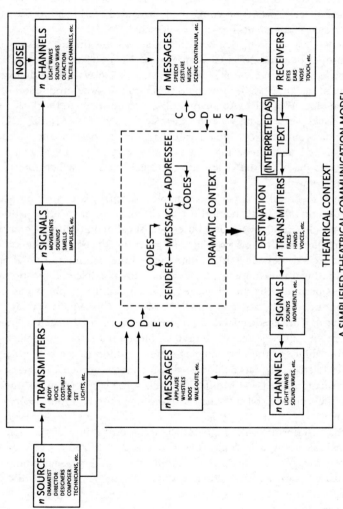

A SIMPLIFIED THEATRICAL COMMUNICATION MODEL

NOISE

n CHANNELS
LIGHT WAVES
SOUND WAVES
OLFACTION
TACTILE CHANNELS, etc.

n MESSAGES
SPEECH
GESTURE
MUSIC
SCENIC CONTINUUM, etc.

n RECEIVERS
EYES
EARS
NOSE
TOUCH, etc.

n SIGNALS
MOVEMENTS
SOUNDS
SMELLS
IMPULSES, etc.

n TRANSMITTERS
BODY
VOICE
COSTUME
PROPS
SET
LIGHTS, etc.

n SOURCES
DRAMATIST
DIRECTOR
DESIGNERS
COMPOSER
TECHNICIANS, etc.

C
O
D
E
S

CODES
SENDER → MESSAGE → ADDRESSEE
                    CODES

DRAMATIC CONTEXT

C
O
D
E
S

(INTERPRETED AS)

TEXT

DESTINATION

n TRANSMITTERS
FACES
HANDS
VOICES, etc.

n SIGNALS
SOUNDS
MOVEMENTS, etc.

n CHANNELS
LIGHT WAVES
SOUND WAVES, etc.

n MESSAGES
APPLAUSE
WHISTLES
BOOS
WALK-OUTS, etc.

THEATRICAL CONTEXT

Theatrical display has traditionally been founded on this informational function: the audience generally expects to receive a more or less coherent set of data concerning the represented world and to become interested in the events reported or depicted.

It is clear, though, that we do not go to the theatre only to be informed of other 'worlds', however powerful a factor this kind of knowledge may be. We may well return to see plays whose dramatic content we know well, or even, at times, to the same production of a given play. 'Why', asks Abraham Moles, 'should we go to the theater to see Hamlet performed if we know the play already?' (1958, p. 127). The fact that our interest in a particular play or performance is not exhausted once the actual 'intelligence given' has been acquired suggests that there are other informational levels on which theatrical messages work.

In its technical acceptance – i.e. in what is usually known as information theory, the mathematical theory of information – /information/ has a far more restricted and purely statistical definition: it comprises the reduction of the equiprobability of signals (i.e. the equal likelihood of their occurrence) that exists at the source of the communication. If one is awaiting a telex message, for example, any possible combination of letters permitted by the language may occur: all the graphic signs and all sequences thereof are equally probable. This equiprobability is reduced with every character in the sequence, so that at the point where the message reads 'The cat sat on the ma–' the probability or predictability of the next letter is extremely high (since proverbially, and so statistically, cats do not usually sit on maps or men). This kind of information based on the differential relations between signs or signals may be termed signal-information (see, for example, Lyons 1977, pp. 41 ff.).

Signal-information is highest where the probability of the sign or signal occurring is lowest: if the telex message quoted above were to end with a /c/, the signal-information-value of the message would be increased (a cat which sits on a plastic mac being very rare statistically). The 'surprise' value of the signal, as it were, is the measure of its information level.

In elementary communication, signal-information is purely functional and remains quite distinct from the semantic content assigned to the message. On stage, however, the physical characteristics of the signs and signals are not only ostended for their own sake (the texture of the costumes or the actors' bodies being major sources of pleasure), together with the formal patterns of their combination, but contribute directly to the production of meaning. Signal-information, that is to say, becomes, in the theatre, a source of semantic information, owing to the ability of the material qualities of the message to connote a range of meanings in their own right. Two performances of, say, *Agamemnon* may give more or less the same dramatic information (regarding the state of Greek society, the course of events in the Trojan Wars, the interaction between the dramatis personae, etc.), but if one performance is austerely 'poor', limited to reproducing the main elements of the Greek stage, and the other lavishly modern in its representational means, the differences in signal-information involved will have drastic effects upon the spectator's decoding of the text (one performance may be understood, say, in terms of universal metaphysical conflicts and the other in terms of personal and material struggles between the participants).

What we may call the *semanticization* of the material qualities of the sign-vehicle or signal – common to all aesthetic texts (in poetry, for instance, the phonetic structure is often all-important) – creates a bridge, as it were, between signal- and semantic information. The (connotative) semantic value of signal-information, unlike dramatic information, is system-specific: it cannot be translated from one kind of message into another since it derives from the ostension of the message itself in its formal and textural composition.

It is possible, at an extreme, for dramatic information to be suppressed altogether, in order to allow a free play of sign-vehicles and signals without stable denotations. The performances of The People Show, for example, or of Meredith Monk, depend very substantially on the continual and varied ostension of gestural, scenic and linguistic messages as material and formal constructs. The production of meaning in this kind of display occurs almost exclusively at the level of the form and substance of the expressive means. Even in directly representational theatre, however, each kind of message will attract attention to itself and to the peculiar characteristics of its channel. It may be an indifferent matter, in terms of the dramatic narrative, as to whether the

murder of Julius Caesar is reported, imitated by actors, enacted balleti-
cally or depicted in a puppet show, but the audience's perceptual
experience of the *showing* will derive from the choice of system and
channel and from the syntactic or syntagmatic relations peculiar to
each kind of message.

This semanticization process extends beyond signal, message and
channel to include the very *transmitters* or even, in certain performances,
the *sources* of communication. The actor's voice and body, considered
as signal-transmitters, are rendered pertinent to the text in their
materiality, since his personal stature, vocal qualities and physical
idiosyncrasies, however incidental to the drama, will influence the
spectator's perception and decoding of messages. Artificial transmitters
may similarly participate as connotative presences in their own right.
Brecht insisted on making the sources of light visible in his theatre in
order to prevent 'an unwanted element of illusion' (1964 p. 141) and
so to underline the (anti-bourgeois) ideological premises of 'epic'
theatre. Richard Schechner has more recently pleaded for an extension
of this gesture to include the lighting technicians themselves – usually
among the unseen pre-textual sources of information – who, he
declares, 'must become an active part of the performance . . . improvis-
ing and modulating the uses of their equipment from night to night'
(1969, p. 164). It is notable, in this respect, that certain contemporary
directors, such as Tadeusz Kantor, appear regularly in their own productions as marginal 'controlling' influences, thus rendering explicit
(and textual) their role as source.

If every material aspect of the performance is capable of
semanticization, there can (in theory) be little 'redundancy' in theatrical communication. In non-aesthetic communication, redundancy –
the reduction of information in the message through repetition,
inclusion of signals not strictly necessary to the transmission of information, etc. – is essential to the unambiguous encoding and decoding
of messages, in order to combat 'noise'. Phonemic, morphemic and
syntactic redundancy in language allows one to understand without
difficulty a newspaper item such as 'The Queen upened Parliament
yesterday', since the misprints may be simply discounted as 'noise'.
Redundancy is reduced in telegrams in order to lower costs ('Arrive
tommorow 10': here a misprint might be disastrous).

Theatrical messages are non-redundant to the extent that, even where the direct semantic information is low, each signal has (or supposedly has) an 'aesthetic' justification, and the reduction of signals will drastically alter the value of the ostended messages and text. Repetitions and leisurely syntagmatic patterns may be the very point of the message in some performances, for instance in the work of Richard Foreman or the Italian director Carmelo Bene where obsessively repeated action constitutes the major kind of information transmitted, since it represents the most original and innovative aspect of the performances in question.

In theory, then, the information-value of the performance is absolute, and this demands of the spectator constant and alert attention, since every signal will have its textual weight. But in practice, of course, the spectator will decide for himself what constitutes redundancy and whether the information he is receiving – dramatic, signal and otherwise – makes the performance worthy of his attention. It may be that he will dismiss the entire text as a predictable and tautological – and thus non-informative – exercise.

Message, discourse and text

How can we best characterize the overall or global 'message' produced by this multi-channelled, multi-systemic communicational system? It is not, clearly, a single-levelled and homogeneous series of signs or signals that emerges, but rather a weave of radically differentiated modes of expression, each governed by its own selection and combination rules. As Christian Metz puts it (with reference to cinema, but the statement is more appropriate to theatre), 'Different, perfectly distinct systems intervene in the same message' (1971, p. 32). At the same time, the interrelation of performance levels is not haphazard but subject to *global* semantic and syntactic constraints whose end is the production of a single unified structure. For this reason, it is legitimate to term the multilinear – but integrated – flow of information theatrical *discourse* and the resulting structure articulated in space and time a *text*.

Synchronically – at any given point in the performance continuum – theatrical discourse is characterized by the 'density of signs' noted by Barthes (see p. 17 above). At each moment the spectator will have to assimilate perceptual data along diverse channels, perhaps conveying identical dramatic information (e.g. simultaneous pictorial and linguistic references to the scene of action) but transmitting different kinds of signal-information. The first characteristic of this discourse is thus its semiotic *thickness*.

Diachronically – in its temporal unfolding on stage – the text is characterized by the *discontinuity* of its various levels. 'Information', as Michael Kirby notes, 'is usually presented in a discontinuous fashion. It comes in sudden bursts or "bits", scattered irregularly through the performance like stars in the night sky' (1976, p. 58). Not all the contributory systems will be operative at every point in the performance: each message and signal will at times fall to a zero level, so that, while theatrical discourse at large is a constant, its actual make-up is subject to continual change. The temporal unnevenness of multi-channel communication can be represented diagrammatically as follows. Channel 1 is the audio-acoustic channel, Channel 2 the visual, Channel 3 the olfactory, etc. (From Birdwhistell 1971, p. 117.).

Time:	T^1	T^2	T^3	T^4	T^5	T^6	T^7	T^8	$T\ldots$
Channel 1	–	—	–	–	–		——		–
Channel 2	——	——	——			——	—		—
Channel 3	——	——		——	——		——		
etc.									

The heterogeneity of theatrical discourse is at once temporal and spatial. As Abraham Moles notes (1958, p. 9), the performance as an integrated ensemble unfolds along three spatial dimensions and a single temporal dimension (on the question of *dramatic* time, see pp. 105 ff. below). Each contributory message, however, has its own spatio-temporal make-up and will not necessarily operate in all the dimensions utilized in the performance as a whole. Linguistic messages, for example, are purely temporal (or, at least, they register only in what Marshall McLuhan terms 'acoustic space' (McLuhan and Carpenter 1960, p. 65)), unless presented in the form of graphic signs as in the projected titles used by Brecht. Movement is spatially three-dimensional and at the same time subject to temporal constraints, although its tempo will be quite different from that of the flow of phonemes. Certain (fixed) elements of the set will not be characterized temporally and may, as in the case of the cut-out, be only two-dimensional. What this suggests is that the global spatio-temporal structure of the text is constructed by the spectator for himself from the uneven bits of perceptual data that he receives (whereas in most other art forms, such as painting or poetry, the text is more homogeneous spatially and temporally).

The performance text, to summarize, is characterized by its semiotic thickness or density, by its heterogeneity and by the spatial and temporal discontinuity of its levels. It is, at the same time, a highly ambiguous text, being at every point semantically 'over-determined' and relatively non-redundant. By the same token, the text is intensely self-focusing (a 'display text' in Mary Louise Pratt's terms (1977, pp. 136 ff.)), being not a mere sum of 'information about' or 'intelligence given' but an event aesthetically ostended as a formal and material structure.

Segmenting the text

It has been the credo of many theatrical semioticians in recent years that the proper object of their analysis is the individual performance in its 'horizontal' unfolding and in its 'vertical' semantic relations (see, for example, Corvin 1971; Ruffini 1974a; Bettetini and de Marinis 1977; de Marinis 1978). But little progress has been made in this direction, owing to the formidable methodological and practical difficulties with which the enterprise is beset.

The dynamism of theatrical discourse – the fact that it must, by definition, remain in progress – makes its effective examination highly problematic. It cannot (unlike, say, film) be interrupted or frozen for purposes of scrutiny and, still more, it is necessarily unrepeatable, since the precise internal relations established in one performance will differ, however subtly, in the next. The text's density poses for the would-be analyst the problem of where to focus his attention, presenting him with an embarrassment of informational riches. Furthermore, the precise *extent* of the performance structure is not always easy to determine, given that such factors as the architectural constraints imposed by playhouse and stage and the effect of audience reception (or even participation) cannot legitimately be excluded as influences upon textual form.

Certain partial solutions have been suggested to these strategic difficulties, such as the use of film to provide a more stable, if radically different, text (or meta-text) for purposes of analysis (see Pagnini 1970). But the chief problem is theoretical and methodological, namely the establishing of agreed analytic *criteria* by which to undertake the semiotic division or *découpage* of the performance. In the words of Marcello Pagnini, 'one immediately comes up against the *punctum dolens* of every research of a semiological nature, namely that of the segmentation of the continuum into discrete units' (1970, p. 128). Is it possible, in short, to define specifically theatrical semiotic units bringing together the elements of *all* simultaneously operative messages, so as to allow a coherent segmentation of theatrical discourse?

Such categories as have been suggested do not encourage optimism regarding the search for discrete theatrical units. Kowzan, working on the principle that the semiotics of theatre necessitates 'first of all the determination of the significative (or semiological) unit of the spectacle', tentatively offers a temporal criterion which cuts through the different levels of the performance: 'the semiological unit of the spectacle is a slice containing all the signs emitted simultaneously, a slice the duration of which is equal to the sign that lasts least' (1968, p. 79). Each segment, then, according to Kowzan's scheme, would be marked off by the intervention or cessation of one of the contributory messages. The main problem with this suggestion – apart from the fact that some signals are more or less permanent (e.g. aspects of the set) – is that the discrete units of each individual message, the linguistic ones apart, are not easily defined in themselves, so that the duration of a given signal is often difficult to determine.

Kowzan's 'slice' has not been found applicable in practice and has produced no textual analyses of note. An alternative approach to the task of segmentation has been adopted by Michel Corvin in his analysis of two productions by Robert Wilson (Corvin 1971). Corvin's rather sketchy anatomy of the two texts is designed to reveal the paradigmatic semantic patterns at work: he takes as his units a number of *semes* or semantic features which recur throughout the performance and which are expressed in various kinds of message (e.g. the semes 'fish', 'infant', 'water'). Such a mode of analysis has the advantage of its flexibility, but does not resolve the question posed by Kowzan of defining multi-levelled units specific to theatrical discourse.

The quest for discrete units rests on the assumption that the performance continuum is subject – like language – to a form of double articulation: that it comprises minimal distinctive units akin to phonemes which in turn make up signifying units analogous to morphemes, lexemes, sentences, and so on. It is only if one considers the performance, in Saussurian terms, as an act of *parole* governed by a theatrical *langue* which stipulates the units involved and establishes rules for their selection and combination (see Hawkes 1977a, pp. 20–1) that one can hope to 'slice up' the discourse continuum into segments which are non-arbitrary.

There is good reason to believe that this approach is an abuse of the 'linguistic model' of the kind that Mounin (1969) warns against. If theatrical discourse were genuinely articulated into cohesive and well-defined units like language itself, then such units would be intuitively recognizable to both performers and audience as the conventional vehicles of communication. The difficulties involved in defining appropriate categories suggest that this is not the case.

It may be that the attempt to slice up the performance across its various levels, like a neatly cohesive layer cake, is not only methodologically misguided but also theoretically premature. We must first endeavour to understand better each of the systems at work and to define *its* rules and units and make explicit the complex of dramatic, theatrical and cultural codes which permit a range of diverse messages to be brought together to the united end of producing a performance text. Until we know more about the levels and rules of theatrical communication, the theatrical 'discrete unit' remains a semiotic philosopher's stone.

THEATRICAL SYSTEMS AND CODES

Code and system

It was observed above (p. 31), with regard to the communication model, that the performance text is dependent for its encoding and decoding both on a flexible number of *systems* and on a set of *codes* more or less common to the sources, performers and audience. The terms /system/ (i.e. of signs) and /code/ are often employed as synonyms, with reference to language and other semiotic mechanisms, in order to indicate at once the ensemble of signs or signals together with the internal rules governing their combination and the rules responsible for assigning semantic content to the units in question. This terminological habit has frequently led to confusion as to the different kinds of rule involved in the production of meaning. In so complex a communicational situation as theatre, it is useful to distinguish between the various kinds of semiotic law at work.

/System/ will be understood here, therefore (following Eco 1976, 1977), as a repertory of signs or signals and the internal syntactic rules governing their selection and combination. A system may be analysed as a formal network of elements having a differential structure (that is, they are defined through mutual opposition, e.g. the colours of traffic lights) and subject to an autonomous syntax, quite independently of the signifying functions that it comes to fulfil. In this sense it is possible, for example, to consider the phonological and syntactic rules of a language as self-sufficient laws, without making reference to the semantic component. The spatial and plastic conventions of painting, similarly, may be viewed independently of its semantic content. But it is further possible to analyse the semantic field itself as another kind of system, arranging conventional cultural units (signifieds) according to its own internal rules.

A *code* is what allows a unit from the semantic system (a signified) to be attached to a unit from the syntactic system. That is to say, it is an ensemble of *correlational* rules governing the formation of sign-relationships. Codes may be extremely simple, comprising perhaps two or three rules (correlating a red light with the signified 'danger' and a green light with 'all clear', for example), or highly elaborate, as in the case of linguistic codes: indeed, a language is in reality a *complex* of codes ranging from denotational correlation rules to dialectal, paralinguistic, rhetorical, pragmatic and contextual rules, all of which go to make up the rich network of constraints regulating utterances and their meanings. Theatrical performance will engage a vast range of correlation rules of this kind – in effect, virtually *all* the codes operative in society are potential factors in the theatre. Certain of these codes (e.g. the kinesic, scenic or linguistic) will be specific to particular systems, while others (theatrical and dramatic conventions and more general cultural codes) will apply to theatrical discourse at large.

The system of systems

Little has been done by way of investigating theatrical systems beyond simply identifying them. Tadeusz Kowzan (1968) provides a preliminary and approximate typology of some thirteen systems, while admitting that 'a much more detailed classification could also be made' (p. 61). He lists language, tone, facial mime, gesture, movement, make-up, hairstyle, costume, props, décor, lighting, music and sound effects (including 'noises off'). It is notable that Kowzan does not include architectural factors (the form of playhouse and stage) and omits occasional technical options such as film and back projection, but he can be said to have identified the principal systemic categories, at least with regard to traditional performances, and no significant modification to his classification has been suggested.

Neither Kowzan nor later commentators have attempted to define the signifying units of each system or to explicate its syntactic and code rules with any degree of rigour. It is clear that some systems – the linguistic and, in certain traditions, the kinesic – are more stable and better articulated than others, with relatively well-defined units and powerful combinational constraints. Certain of Kowzan's divisions are very flexible and open-ended ensembles: it would be difficult to delimit the repertory of items belonging to the 'décor' system, for example, since any object may be brought in to fulfil a 'decorative' function on stage. Boundaries between systems, moreover, are not always so well marked as Kowzan's list suggests: it is often less than easy to distinguish prop from set, just as 'movement', 'gesture' and 'facial mime' are in practice intimately connected and complementary aspects of the general kinesic continuum.

It is doubtful, therefore, that each system is equally accessible to syntactic analysis. While there is no question that selection and combination restrictions do arise, conventionally, with regard to, say, décor (so that a 'drawing-room interior' in the 1940s and 1950s was a more or less obligatory arrangement of a limited and predictable subset of items), these rules are not usually strong or explicit enough to bear analogy with those regulating correct sentence-formation in language.

The present state of our knowledge regarding the internal laws of scenic, costumic, cosmetic and most other systems is too scanty and impressionistic to allow anything resembling formalization. This is undoubtedly one of the more interesting and important tasks awaiting theatrical semiotics, as is, still more, the investigation of the global or trans-systemic syntax of the overall theatrical system (what constraints, if any, govern the combination in a given performance text of kinesic with linguistic and scenic signs?).

Types of code and subcode

If our knowledge of theatrical systems is rudimentary, then our current understanding of contributory codes must be said to be barely nascent, especially since the very concept of the code remains problematic and ambiguous in most of its applications (see Ruffini 1974a). While we are all, as performers or spectators or dramatists, more or less intuitively aware of certain potent dramatic and theatrical conventions ruling the structuring and understanding of plays and performances – we are able to distinguish a tragedy from a comedy and can 'read' bits of stylized action or mime on stage – the precise formulation of the range of rules determining the encoding or decoding of texts is altogether another matter. It is the business of semiotics to make these rules explicit, so as to furnish a model of what we might designate the dramatic and theatrical *competence* exercised by experienced performers and spectators.

One of the initial steps towards such an ambitious and probably utopian end is to determine the broad types or classes of code rule in force. When we enter the theatre and agree to participate in the performer–spectator transaction, we automatically apply those codes specific to the performance – which can be termed *theatrical* codes – that permit us to apprehend it in its own terms and not as, say, a spontaneous and accidental event or a piece of film. We similarly bring into play, where appropriate, our knowledge of the generic, structural, stylistic and other rules – i.e. *dramatic* codes – relating to the drama and its composition. At the same time, however, we cannot leave at home the whole framework of more general cultural, ideological, ethical and epistemological principles which we apply in our extra-theatrical activities. On the contrary, the performance will inevitably make continual appeal to our general understanding of the world.

How do we begin to distinguish the general cultural codes through which we make sense of our lives from the particular theatrical and dramatic norms at work, since these diverse factors will be equally and simultaneously responsible for our understanding of the text? Since theatre draws on the behavioural stuff of social intercourse and its linguistic, kinesic and costumic patterns, in what sense is it legitimate to talk of specifically dramatic and theatrical codes?

A broad answer to such queries is that, while the performance is unquestionably founded on the cultural and systemic norms of society at large, without which it would be incomprehensible, sets of second-ary regulative rules, peculiar to drama and theatre, arise on this basis to produce specific *subcodes*. Thus a production of, say, Sartre's *Huis clos* will inevitably depend on the behavioural, gestural and linguistic patterns characteristic of contemporary French society (or sections thereof), but will also be structured according to prevailing modes of design, posture, across-stage movement, voice projection, etc., which will dis-tinguish it from an impromptu Parisian café scene (just as the written text observes, apart from the constitutive grammatical rules of French, potent rhetorical and structural precepts which qualify it as a 'drama').

Subcodes are generally produced by the process which Umberto Eco terms *overcoding*: on the basis of one (constitutive) rule or set of rules, a secondary rule or set of rules arises in order to regulate a particular application of the base rules (see Eco 1976, pp. 133 ff.). Stylistic maxims or etiquette systems are examples of overcoding (of linguistic and behavioural codes respectively). Such conventions as the aside, the informative monologue, the tragic peripeteia (or reversal) and the marriage at the climax of romantic comedy are clear instances of *dra-matic* subcodes produced by overcoding. *Theatrical* subcodes include the once ubiquitous proscenium arch as an architectural constraint, the rising and falling of a curtain to mark temporal boundaries of the performance, and the use of distinctive kinds of exaggerated move-ment, make-up or voice projection (which in practical terms ensure visibility and audibility but come conventionally to connote 'theatricality').

Overcoding will often mark out as the units of the subcode segments which are more extensive than the base units of the constitutive code. Stylistic rules determining 'heroic', 'naturalistic' or 'expressionistic' dialogic modes apply to entire speeches or exchanges and their syntactic and lexical structure. Scenic subcodes regulating, say, the baroque masque or the bourgeois 'picture frame' set, apply to configurations of scenic items rather than simply the choice of items.

Subcodes produced by secondary rules are frequently bound to fashion and thus often relatively unstable: the histrionic codes ruling Victorian melodrama, for example, survive today only in the form of parodic 'quotation' (i.e. they are still recognized but no longer applicable), just as the dialogic, scenic and kinesic conventions which rendered performances 'realistic' in the early decades of this century would today appear, on the contrary, opaque and factitious. But it is also possible for the norms of a theatrical or dramatic subcode to become so firmly established that they long outlive and out-travel the constitutive cultural codes on which they are originally based. The classical rules of tragic structure outstayed their Graeco-Roman ethical base, influencing dramatic composition in the West for centuries. The conventions of the *commedia dell'arte*, similarly, were reflected in performances well beyond sixteenth-century Naples, and the still-flourishing Japanese Noh and Kabuki theatres are regulated by inviolable laws which originally overcoded a long-defunct chivalric behavioural code.

New and often loosely articulated secondary rules are constantly arising in the theatre, so that audiences may be aware of emerging patterns without being able to identify or formulate them. This was the case, for example, in the 1950s with the work of such dramatists as Beckett, Ionesco, Adamov and Pinter and the innovations in performance which their texts provoked. At first this work was greeted with hostility as an aberrant *breaking* of established dramatic rules. Only later, when certain (fairly loose) common characteristics had been discerned and a general name – 'theatre of the absurd' – had been rightly or wrongly applied to the entire corpus in question, were audiences at large able to accept this mode of theatre. A new subcode had been identified which allowed erstwhile aberrant texts to be 'recuperated'.

The process whereby barely recognized new rules emerge is termed by Eco *undercoding* (1976, pp. 135 ff.): this is the formation of rough and approximate norms in order to characterize a phenomenon which is not fully understood or which is only vaguely differentiated for us. Every time (and it is a common experience) we are able to account for a new dramatic or theatrical experience only in very imprecise terms ('bizarre', 'experimental', 'avant-garde', etc.), either through ignorance of the specific generic rules in force or because they scarcely exist, we are applying a loose subcode produced by undercoding.

Every performance of interest will involve a complex dialectic of code-observing, code-making and code-breaking. Conventional factors will be modified by innovations which appear less rule-bound but which may in turn help to establish new norms. This already fluid situation is further complicated by what are best described as 'idiolectal' factors: any dramatist, director, actor or designer of note will impose, over and above the constitutive and regulative rules, his own subcode or *idiolect*, the ensemble of personal, psychological, ideological and stylistic traits which makes a written text recognizably 'Strind-bergian' (even in imitation), an acting method 'Gielgudian' or an overall performance text 'Brechtian'. This further level of overcoding is essential to the unity and distinctiveness of both written and performance texts, which are otherwise liable to be suffocated by the network of over-determining rules and become merely banal.

In the diagram below (pages 51–6) the interaction of cultural codes with theatrical and dramatic subcodes is sketchily indicated, so as to suggest the strict interdependence of the three classes of rule (but without any pretence to formality or exhaustiveness). It will be noted that the respective rules in the three columns are grouped horizontally according to the type of principle involved: systemic (regulating the various systems of signs available to performance) logical, aesthetic, ethical, epistemic (regulating cognition) etc. What results is a preliminary 'map' of the different levels of cultural competence that an ideal spectator exercises in decoding the performance text and in understanding its dramatic characteristics (the assumption throughout being, as is suggested by the arrows, that theatrical and dramatic rules are founded on more general cultural codes).

Certain of the major correlation rules assigning meaning to stage events are considered in the sections that follow. Research into these codified, overcoded and undercoded norms is at a preliminary stage, so that the indications given here are designed simply to mark out, as it were, the more inviting zones of an uncertain and unstable territory.

The meanings of space: proxemic relations

However significant the temporal structure of the performance, there is good reason for arguing that the theatrical text is defined and perceived above all in spatial terms. The stage is, in the first instance, an 'empty space', to use Peter Brook's phrase (Brook 1968), distinguished from its surroundings by visible markers (a raised platform, a curtain, or simply a conventional distance signalling the boundary between acting area and auditorium) and potentially 'fillable' visually and acoustically. The first factor that strikes us when we enter a theatre is the physical organization of the playhouse itself: its dimensions, the stage–audience distance, the structure of the auditorium (and thus the spectator's own position in relation to his fellows and to the performers) and the size and form of the awaiting stage. The performance itself begins with the information-rich registering of stage space and its use in the creation of the opening image. (It is not unknown for audiences to gasp or even applaud at this initial sensation of witnessing a well-arranged scenic pattern.) Even with the unfolding of the time-bound theatrical discourse, these constraints remain the primary influences on perception and reception.

Analysis of performance systems and codes might well turn first, therefore, to the organization of architectural, scenic and interpersonal space – those factors which the American anthropologist Edward T. Hall has termed *proxemic* relations. Hall and others have elaborated a science specifically devoted to spatial codes, namely *proxemics*, defined by Hall himself as 'the interrelated observations and theories of man's use of space as a specialized elaboration of culture' (1966, p. 1). This science is founded on the well-tested hypothesis that man's use of space in his architectural, domestic, urban, workplace and aesthetic

Theatrical subcodes	Cultural codes	Dramatic subcodes
Conventions governing gesture, movement, expression	↔ General kinesic codes	↔ Rules for interpretation of movement in terms of character, etc.
Spatial conventions (regarding playhouse, set, configurations of bodies, etc.)	↔ Proxemic codes	↔ Constraints on reading of spatial arrangements in terms of inter-relationships, dramatic space, etc.
Rules for theatrical costume and its connotations	↔ Vestimentary codes	↔ Rules for interpreting costume in terms of status, character, etc.
Make-up conventions	↔ Cosmetic codes	↔ Conventions relating make-up to dramatic types, etc.
Scenic subcodes	↔ Pictorial codes	↔ Constraints on the construction of the dramatic scene
Restrictions on musical accompaniment, interludes, etc.	↔ Musical codes	↔ Norms regulating the inference of dramatic information from 'significant' music, etc.
Stage and playhouse norms, etc.	↔ Architectural codes etc.	↔ Stage and playhouse as sources of dramatic information, etc.

(Vertical label at left margin: S Y S T E M I C)

Theatrical subcodes	Cultural codes	Dramatic subcodes
⎡Decoding of per- formance on basis ⎣of constitutive rules⎤ ↔	Syntactic/ semantic/ phonological constitutive rules	↔ ⎡Interpretation of drama on basis of constitutive rules⎤
Conventions govern- ing modes of performer–audience address (in theatrical context)	Pragmatic rules (conversation and ↔ contextual rules, etc.)	Conventions relating to the ↔ interpretation of interpersonal com- munication (in dramatic context)
Rules of *pronuntiatio* (delivery)	Rhetorical ↔	Dramatic rhetorical ↔ and stylistic con- ventions (decorum, figural modes, etc.)
Overcoding of voice projection, articulation, intonation, etc.	↔ Paralinguistic	↔ Paralinguistic con- straints on character interpre- tation, etc.
Influence of 'local' or 'regional' factors on performance	↔ Dialectal	↔ Geographical and class constraints on characterization
Actors' imposition of personal traits in delivery, etc.	Idiolectal ↔ etc.	Syntactic, rhetorical ↔ and personal idiosyncrasies of characters

L
I
N
G
U
I
S
T
I
C

	Theatrical subcodes	Cultural codes	Dramatic subcodes
GENERIC — **INTERTEXTUAL**	Expectations deriving from knowledge of other performances	↔ Influence of experience of other aesthetic texts	↔ Expectations deriving from experience of other dramatic texts
	Conventional performance types ('farce', 'Expressionism', etc.)	↔ Cultural typologies	↔ Conventional dramatic genre rules
TEXTUAL — **STRUCTURAL**	Textual rules governing the semantic integration of different messages and the global syntactic order of the performance	↔ General textual competence: recognition of texts as semantically and syntactically coherent structures	↔ Textual rules regulating the referential coherence of the dramatic text and its overall semantic, syntactic and rhetorical structure
FORMAL — **PRESENTATIONAL**	Illusionistic mimetic principles 'authenticating' the representation	↔ Standards of realism, verisimilitude, conception of the real	↔ 'Authenticating' conventions constraining dramatic action as 'real'
	Conventions of direct address, metatheatrical reference, etc., breaking the mimetic illusion	↔ 'Bracketing-off' rules: ability to accept the factitious in aesthetic texts	↔ 'Rhetorical' conventions regarding the formal presentation of drama (prologues, epilogues, asides and other 'artificial' forms)

	Theatrical subcodes	Cultural codes	Dramatic subcodes
E P I S T E M I C	Theatrical frame (definition of the theatrical situation as such)	↔ Episteme (conceptual organization of world) ↔	Dramatic frame (construction of the 'possible world' of the drama as such)
	Definition of performance elements as such	↔ Encyclopedia (ensemble of points of reference, items of knowledge)	Construction of dramatic 'universe of discourse' (ensemble of referents)
A E S T H E T I C	Preferences for and conventions regarding signal-information	↘ Aesthetic principles ↗	Expectations concerning kinds and ordering of dramatic information
	Preferences regarding performance structure, acting modes, etc.	↗ ↖	Preferences regarding dramatic structure, necessity, etc., in dramatic worlds
L O G I C A L	Constraints on the logic of representation, temporal ordering of performance, etc.	↔ General principles of cause and effect, necessity and possibility, etc. ↔	Conventions regarding causation, action structure, necessity, etc., in dramatic worlds

	Theatrical subcodes	Cultural codes	Dramatic subcodes
B E H A V I O U R A L / **E T H I C A L**	Ethical norms on the performer–spectator relationships, on the 'permissive', etc.	↔ General ethical standards	↔ Ethical constraints on the judgement of character, expectations regarding 'hero' and 'villain', etc., and on reading of play's standpoint
L	Histrionic over-coding (characteristic 'theatrical' modes of comportment)	↔ Behavioural codes	↔ Stereotypes, 'comic' and 'tragic' behavioural rules, etc.
I D E O L O G I C A L	Social and economic influences on the theatrical transaction (prices, condition and location of theatre, prestige of actors and company, etc.)	↔ Socio-economic order	↔ Rules governing social hierarchy of characters and their relations (e.g. in Elizabethan tragedy)
	Ideological preferences for certain kinds of performance, theatre, etc.	↔ Political principles	↔ Constraints on interpretation of power relations, on overall decoding of textual meanings, etc.
P S Y C H O - / **L O G I C A L**	Attribution of psychological motivation to director, actors, etc.	↔ Psychological and psychoanalytic decoding principles	↔ Hermeneutics of the 'psychology' of dramatis persona (and author)

	Theatrical subcodes	Cultural codes	Dramatic subcodes
H	Awareness of	Knowledge of	Allowance for
I	traditional perform-	historical events,	historical differ-
S	ance modes, heritage	notions regarding	ences in worlds,
T	of ('quotable')	↔ period character- ↔	events, customs,
O	theatrical history	istics, received	language, character,
R		'portraits' of	contemporary
I		historical figures,	references, etc.
C		etc.	
A			
L			

activities is neither casual nor merely functional but represents a semi-otically loaded choice subject to powerful rules which generate a range of (connotative) cultural units. What makes this relatively recent science of special interest is the claim by Hall and his colleagues that they have rendered the code rules explicit, with the result that it is possible to determine the semantic content assigned to a set of distance units.

Three principal proxemic 'syntactic' systems are distinguished by Hall, according to the flexibility or otherwise of the boundaries between units. These he terms the *fixed-feature*, the *semi-fixed-feature* and the *informal* respectively. Fixed-feature space involves, broadly, static architectural configurations. In the theatre it will relate chiefly to the playhouse itself and, in formal theatres (opera houses, proscenium-arch theatres, etc.), to the shapes and dimensions of stage and auditorium. Semi-fixed-feature space concerns such movable but non-dynamic objects as furniture, and so in theatrical terms involves the set, auxiliary factors like the lighting and, in informal theatrical spaces, stage and auditorium arrangements. The third proxemic mode, informal space, has as its units the ever-shifting relations of proximity and distance between individuals, thus applying, in the theatre, to actor–actor, actor–spectator and spectator–spectator interplay.

While all three proxemic modalities are usually simultaneously operative in performance, the history of the theatre has been marked by shifts in dominance by one or other of the classes. We are still conditioned by the nineteenth-century ideal of spatial organization in the playhouse, that is to say, a maximum of grandiosity and fixity, resulting in a maximum of formality. Every theatrical element, from the usually static set to the 'imprisoned' spectator, has a more or less immutable place in the nineteenth-century theatre, allowing little scope for variation or violation of the strictly demarcated divisions. As a result, the performance text is presented as an already produced and bounded object which the spectator observes, rather than constructs, from his permanent lookout point. In the typical Western bourgeois theatre, then, the informal and semi-fixed-feature systems exist under the dominion of the fixed-feature.

Much modern theatre has tended – from Strindberg's 'intimate theatre' onwards – to transform architectural fixity as far as possible into dynamic proxemic informality. The centre of the theatrical transaction has become, during this century and particularly in recent decades, less an absolute stage-auditorium divide than a flexible and, occasionally, unpredictable manipulation of body-to-body space (for example in the theatres of Beck and Schechner). This movement towards the opening up and loosening of proxemic relations in performance, in order to escape from the tyranny of architectonic grandeur and its aesthetic and ideological implications, looks back to earlier and non-institutional forms of performance, where fixed-feature space was either nonexistent, as in the medieval mystery cycles, or secondary to semi-fixed and informal space, as in the medieval theatre-in-the-round, where actors descended into the platea to form an acting area cleared, for the nonce, of spectators: 'Here', as Elizabeth Burns remarks, 'the spectators must have become accustomed to constant forming and reforming of the boundaries of illusion through conventions shared with the actors' (Burns 1972, p. 73). Petr Bogatyrev describes, entertainingly, similar spatial conventions at work in the Russian peasant theatre, where again the acting area is defined ad hoc in terms of semi-fixed and interpersonal distance: 'The participants in the performance approach the house in which, for example, a feast is taking place. They open the door and first the Horse enters the izba (acting area) and lashes those present; everybody present gets up onto the benches and so the izba is cleared for dramatic action (Bogatyrev 1973, p. 8).

In informal performances theatre provides an exemplary instance of what the American psychiatrist Humphry Osmond has called *sociopetal* space: an area in which people are brought together (other examples being French cafés and Italian piazzas), as distinguished from *sociofugal* spaces, like waiting rooms and the offices of company chairmen, whose characteristic function is to keep people apart (see Osmond 1957; Hall 1966, pp. 108 ff.). Sociopetality applies particularly to the audience in informal theatre. In medieval and Renaissance theatre, in folk theatre and recent 'poor' theatres where lack of space necessitates cohesion, the audience is by definition a unit, responding *en masse* to the spectacle. More formal modern theatres tend instead towards sociofugality: even though necessarily contained within the architectural unit of the auditorium, and thus in theory surrendering his individual function, the spectator has his own well-marked private space, individual seat, and relative immunity from physical contact with his fellows (and even from seeing them). The result is to emphasize personal rather than social perception and response, to introduce a form of 'privacy' within an experience which is collective in origin.

Informal space is the proxemic modality which is not only of greatest interest to the theatrical semiotician – since it best characterizes the dynamic spatial relations of the performance – but also most accessible to analysis, thanks to the body of work carried out in measuring interpersonal distance and determining the semantic units attached thereto. Hall suggests a four-phase segmentation of the informal proxemic continuum, ranging from 'intimate' distance (physical contact and near-touching positions) to 'personal' distance ($1\frac{1}{2}$–4 feet), 'social' (4–12 feet) and, finally, 'public' distance (12–25 feet). This gradation is further divided into 'near' and 'far' stages, thus giving an eight-point scale for the measurement of the body-to-body dialectic.

'Intimacy', 'personality', 'sociality' and 'publicness' are, then, according to proxemic research, the four major cultural units assigned to segments of the spatial continuum by the relevant contemporary (American) cultural code. To the extent that he is concerned to reflect the prevailing patterns of social intercourse, the director will adopt similar divisions of stage space in order to portray the unspoken factors in the dramatic relationships depicted (although a marked degree of theatrical overcoding of the general cultural code will occur, especially in large playhouses, in order to emphasize the significance of the distances and to compensate for the effect of stage–audience distance: interpersonal space on stage is often deliberately exaggerated). *Interstitial* aspects of the performance – the spaces *between* stage vehicles – are quite as important semantically as the vehicles themselves. This is an important general rule of textual structure in the theatre. Most directors, at least of representational displays, are critically and even primarily concerned with 'blocking' the performance before and during rehearsal, i.e. with predetermining the configurations of bodies on stage both to create visual patterns and to emblemize relationships.

In addition to these general cultural influences on informal stage configurations, secondary theatrical rules are often strongly determining factors: the spatial conventions governing the decorative *tableau vivant* or the arabesques of the masque, for instance, had little enough to do with the general informal proxemic code. In the contemporary theatre a subcode has arisen, dictating the division of the stage into definite zones – down centre, up centre, down left, up left, etc. – which are frequently afforded great respect by actors and directors on account of their supposed impact on audience decoding, so that what Kenneth Cameron and Theodore Hoffman have called 'the vocabulary of stage placement' is crucial to the blocking of the performance (1974, p. 291). In order to ensure dominance by a given figure in the proscenium-arch stage, for example, downstage positions are usually adopted. Similar rules regulate the use of levels as indicators of status (raised = important against lowered = subordinate) and the relations established between bodies and set (a figure 'framed' by the set or associated with a 'scenic mass', e.g. a table, will receive audience attention and be perceived as 'dominant' (see Cameron and Hoffman 1974, p. 328).

Distance – particularly performer–spectator distance – will have a significant effect on other systems and channels. Where the stage–auditorium space is public and formal, corresponding inflation of paralinguistic features (especially enunciation and volume) and gestural stress will usually occur: the hyperbolic character of Victorian acting, for instance, was a question not only of taste but of informational necessity, due to the dimensions of public space involved. Post-Strindbergian 'intimate' performances tend to observe far more closely social communicational levels, while recent 'contact' modes – where

Hall's 'near' intimate phase operates not only between actors but between actor and spectator – have instituted new informational channels for performance, such as the olfactory and the tactile.

It is interesting to note that proxemic research has directly influenced the work of such American directors as Richard Schechner and Scott Burton, who, instead of relying on their directorial instinct for spatial meanings, have applied certain scientific data to their representations. Burton's *Behaviour Tableaux* (1970–2) presented eighty interpersonal situations portrayed almost exclusively in proxemic terms – that is, through the uses made of personal and social space and the adoption of certain stereotyped body postures (other informational factors having been more or less neutralized: the set minimal, costume simple and uniform, make-up very pale, etc.) – and succeeded in distinguishing unambiguously the social roles, attitudes, leader–follower behavioural patterns, etc., obtaining among the five male participants (see Argelander 1973).

Performance spatiality is not limited, however, to the *actual* interstitial areas marked out by fixed, semi-fixed and dynamic theatrical components. Any representation, if it is successfully to evoke a fictional dramatic scene, will also create what Suzanne Langer defines as *virtual* space – that is, an illusionistic 'intangible image' resulting from the formal relationships established within a given defined area (be it the framed canvas of a painting, the mass of an architectural structure or a stage). Illusionistic 'virtuality' has always been one of the dominant characteristics of the spectacle. Conventionally, the stage depicts or otherwise suggests a domain which does not coincide with its actual physical limits, a mental construct on the part of the spectator from the visual clues that he receives.

In the evocation of virtual space, theatre has traditionally drawn – at least since the Renaissance – neither on the general proxemic codes of society at large nor on specific theatrical or dramatic subcodes but on borrowed (and adapted) *pictorial* codes at work in the visual arts. In terms of the English playhouse, this importation of 'alien' modes of spatial organization began in the early seventeenth century, the period which saw the definitive enclosing of the theatre together with the use, for the first time, of proscenium-arch 'frames' around the action. In particular, the collaboration between Ben Jonson and Inigo Jones in the production of spectacularly 'plastic' and illusionistic masques, together with the increasing influence of Italian single-focus perspective sets, established an essentially painterly mode of visual representation, entrusted to a professional designer, which dominated theatrical display until modern times (see Kernodle 1944).

The decisive, and at times overwhelming, impact of pictorial conceptions of space on the stage represents a form of code-switching, well observed by the Soviet semiotician Yuri Lotman in his account of early nineteenth-century Russian theatre and its debts to painting:

> The analogy between painting and theatre was manifested above all in the organization of the spectacle through conspicuously pictorial means of artistic modelling, in that the stage text tended to unfold not as a continuous flux (non-'discrete') imitating the passage of time in the extra-artistic world, but as a whole clearly broken up into single 'stills' organized synchronically, each of which is set within the decor like a picture in a frame. (Lotman 1973, p. 278)

In its more extreme manifestations, the ut pictura spectaculum conceit reduced the actual three dimensions of the stage to something closely resembling the two-dimensionality of a canvas. Ironically, perspective painting was employed (from the seventeenth to the nineteenth centuries) in order to restore, illusionistically, the lost spatial depth, thus setting up a bizarre meta-mimetic game whereby a three-dimensional space was disguised as a two-dimensional space disguised as a three-dimensional space. The first designer to protest against the kind of scenic straitjacket that resulted was Adolphe Appia, who rejected painterly sets in his planned Wagnerian designs, complaining that 'no movement on the actor's part can be brought into vital relation with objects painted on a piece of canvas' (Bentley 1968, p. 31). Most modern designers have followed Appia in using, rather than disguising, the actual physical characteristics of the stage in the creation of virtual space.

Only in the 1960s was the dominant 'virtuality' of the performance and its spatiality radically questioned. The democratizing 'environmental' experiments of that period attempted to replace the illusionistic character of the stage as a 'special place' with a purely informal

'found space', consisting of an impromptu performance area, presented as such rather than as an 'intangible image' (see Schechner
1969).

Body-motion communication: kinesic factors

If 'fixed' and 'semi-fixed' space have traditionally borne close relations
with pictorial codes, 'informal' space relates directly to the most
dynamic aspect of theatrical discourse, the movement of the body on
stage. The kinesic components of performance – movements, gestures,
facial expressions, postures, etc. – have been the object of much
polemic but little research. Gesture, in particular, is regularly promoted
to the status of the peculiarly 'theatrical' performance constituent
(usually at the expense of language). Antonin Artaud dreamed of a
'pure theatrical language' freed from the tyranny of verbal discourse –
'a language of signs, gestures and attitudes having an ideographic value
as they exist in certain unperverted pantomimes' (Artaud 1938, p. 39).
Brechtian theatre, from quite different premises, also instituted the
priority of the geste in creating a new theatrical (and non-literary) mode
of representation: 'Epic theatre is gestural,' remarks Walter Benjamin,
'Strictly speaking, the gesture is the material and epic theatre its
practical utilization' (Benjamin 1963, p. 22).

Artaud and other director-theorists looked, in their search for a
plastic stage language, to Eastern theatrical traditions where explicit
kinesic conventions allow a sustained and autonomous gestural discourse of considerable syntactic and semantic richness: the Indian
Kathakali dance theatre, for example, with its repertory of 800 mudras or
syntactic units (64 limb movements, 9 head movements, 11 kinds of
glance, etc.) and a range of fixed meanings correlated to them (in
terms of character, emotions, etc.) (see Ikegami 1971). The absence of
such powerful subcodes in the Western theatre (with the possible historical exception of an Elizabethan repertory of 'manual' signs; see
Joseph 1951), much lamented by Artaudians, makes the kinesic continuum produced on our stages far more difficult to segment and
decode with any degree of precision.

Body motion as a communicative medium is the object of a (principally American) science more or less contemporary with proxemics,

namely *kinesics*. Its most distinguished practitioner is the anthropologist Ray L. Birdwhistell. The founding discovery of kinesics is that each culture selects from an immense stock of potential material a strictly limited number of pertinent units of movement. Of some 20,000 possible facial expressions, for example, only thirty-two movements, it is claimed, are actually employed in American kinesic behaviour. Birdwhistell terms these distinctive units – which are roughly comparable with phonemes – *kinemes*. Between fifty and sixty of them have been identified in the American system, including, in addition to the facial movements, three head nods, two lateral head sweeps, one head cock, one head tilt, movements of the brow, lids, nose, mouth, chin and cheeks, etc. Kinemes combine into more complex units, *kinemorphs*, 'further analysable into *kinemorphemic* classes which behave like morphemes', and which in turn 'prove to form *complex kinemorphs* which may be analogically related to words'. This highest order of unit, finally, is governed by 'syntactic arrangements' in the formation of '*complex kinemorphic constructions*, which have many of the properties of the spoken syntactic sentence' (Birdwhistell 1971, p. 101).

Birdwhistell's syntactic scheme and the terminology he adopts (particularly since he writes of kinesic 'dialects' which are strongly marked within a given cultural community) leaves his categories open to the suspicion of 'linguisticism', i.e. that a simple analogy with language is being applied. Indeed, kinesics has been attacked on these grounds (see Kristeva 1968a). Birdwhistell insists, however, that any comparison is formal rather than substantial: there is no direct correspondence between kinesic and linguistic units, but only a more general analogousness between language and movement as overall syntactic systems. The most important difference between the two kinds of unit is that, while language, in the words of another kinesicist, Daniel N. Stern, is a 'symbolic event', kinesic units 'are not symbols' (Stern 1973, p. 117). Whereas words may be viewed primarily as signifying units, 'complex kinemorphs' have a primarily physiological and practical function (although the semiotic status of movement does become primary in the context of performance).

Kinesics throws light on what might be called the 'gestural fallacy' common to both popular handbooks on 'body talk' and most writing on theatrical movement. It is tempting to conceive of the 'gesture' as a discrete and well-marked item, especially in the case of a highly expressive actor or, say, a demonstrative Neapolitan fruit vendor, since we may note characteristic movements which appear distinct from their behavioural context. In reality, the gesture does not exist as an isolated entity and cannot, unlike the word or morpheme, be separated from the general continuum:

> Under kinesic analysis . . . it became demonstrable that so-called gestures are really *bound* morphs. That is, gestures are forms which are incapable of standing alone . . . Just as there is no 'cept' in isolation in American English, an informant may be taught how to produce it together with 'pre-' or 'con-' and '-tion'. As bound morphs, as stem forms, gestures require infixual, suffixual, prefixual, or transfixual behaviour to achieve identity. (Birdwhistell 1971, p. 119)

One cannot, therefore, tabulate a gestural 'lexicon' in which kinesic paradigms may be conveniently set out: movement, in effect, is continuous, and is open to analysis only through the overall syntactic patterns of a (preferably filmed) stretch of kinesic behaviour.

Any atomistic notion of a gestural sign-unit combining a discrete sign-vehicle with an individual signified has to give way, in the perspective of kinesics, to a more generous conception of kinesic 'discourse' governed by global syntactic relations and a range of possible communicative functions. Of these functions, perhaps the most notable and – from a theatrical point of view – interesting is the so-called 'para-kinesic' signal, which makes 'statements about the *context* of the message situation' (Birdwhistell 1971, p. 117). Such signals serve, in the first instance, to *draw attention to* and so designate the protagonist in an interaction sequence, placing him *in relation* to others present and to the communicative situation: 'they help to define the context of the interaction by identifying the actor or his audience, and, furthermore, they usually convey information about the larger context in which the interaction takes place' (p. 117).

Here movement is seen to have a broadly indexical function, serving to tie the actor to context, addressee and the objects of discourse. Julia Kristeva has argued, in trying to establish a non-linguistic model of gesture, that the relationship in which the subject, object and 'practice' itself of the gesture are bound is, precisely, 'of an indicative but non-signifying kind' (Kristeva 1968b, p. 95). In this view, indication is prior to signification in the 'work' of the gesture.

This indicative character of the kinesic or parakinesic signal may legitimately be defined as *deictic* (Kristeva prefers the term *anaphoric*), since deixis (which is etymologically a gestural concept, i.e. 'pointing', adapted by Greek grammarians to the classification of verbal indices) has exactly the role in linguistic discourse of defining the protagonist ('I'), the addressee ('you') and the context ('here') and thus of setting up a communicative situation. Deictic gesture, indicating the actor and his relations to the stage, is of decisive importance to theatrical performance, being the primary means whereby the presence and the spatial orientations of the body are established. In the theatre, observes Patrice Pavis,

> ... the essential modality (and at the same time the function) of the gesture is its capacity to sketch out the situation-of-utterance, to become deictic, a sign which indicates the presence of the stage and of the actor ... Just as the gesture cannot be dissociated from the actor who produces it, it is always geared to the stage through innumerable corporal deixes, beginning with attitude, glance or simple physical presence. (1981)

Gesture, in brief, constitutes the essential mode of *ostending* body, stage and onstage action in (actual) space.

It is through the deixis, furthermore, that an important 'bridge' is set up between gesture and speech. Despite Artaud's insistence on an absolute semiotic polarity between language and gesture in the theatre, the fact remains that, except in extreme cases of gestural autonomy (mime), the two are bound to cooperate in the production of theatrical discourse. If language is to register within the physical context of the stage and come into contact with bodies and objects thereon, it must participate in the deictic ostension of which gesture is the prime vehicle.

One of the characteristics of the parakinesic signal is that it 'cross-references, in a variety of ways, the ... linguistic messages emitted or received' in a given communicational context (Birdwhistell 1971,

p. 117). Language-related signals include the kinesic *marker*, a movement which systematically accompanies a particular grammatical category (the relationship being reciprocal rather than one of priority either of language or of movement). Of these, the most distinct are what Birdwhistell names *pronominal* markers, but which perhaps may more properly be termed *deictic* markers, given that they accompany, in addition to personal and demonstrative pronouns ('I', 'we', 'you', 'this', 'that', etc.), deictic adverbials such as 'here', 'now', 'then' and 'there'.

Pronominal, or deictic, markers indicate gesturally the objects of the simultaneous verbal discourse. The point of definition is the speaker-actor's body, so that the proximity of the referent to the subject is the crucial factor. Two broad classes of movement, the 'proximal' (a movement *towards* the speaker's body) and the 'distal' (a movement *away*), are distinguished (again underlining the closeness of kinesic and informal proxemic factors). The speaker himself and his immediate context (the 'I' or 'we' in the 'here' and 'now', including the present tense of verbs) are distinguished kinesically from all elements extraneous to it ('he', 'they', etc., in the 'there' and 'then', together with past and future tenses of the verb). Birdwhistell (1971, p. 123) gives the following diagrammatic representation of the two pronominal marker classes (see opposite).

Recent research has suggested (Serpieri *et al.* 1978; see pp. 126 ff. below) that those deictic elements of language appertaining to the I-here-now are among the most characteristic components of dramatic discourse, so that the relations between verbal and gestural deixis are of first importance to theatrical semiotics. The 'I' of the dramatis persona and the 'here and now' of the *dramatic* communicative context are related to the actor's body and the *stage* context through the indicative gesture accompanying the utterance. Gesture, in this sense, *materializes* the dramatic subject and his world by asserting their identity with an actual body and an actual space. Without simultaneous kinesic markers, language would remain merely 'ideal' in the theatre, a series of unoriented – and thus unmotivated – 'virtual' propositions, just as without the movements whereby he 'orchestrates' his utterances (Stern 1973, p. 120) the actor cannot physically possess or control his own speech, but is rather determined by it (as a simple mouthpiece).

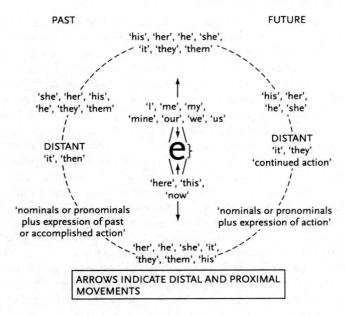

PAST   FUTURE

'his', 'her', 'he', 'she',
'it', 'they', 'them'

'she', 'her', 'his',   'his', 'her',
'he', 'they', 'them'   'I', 'me', 'my',   'he', 'she'
                           'mine', 'our', 'we', 'us'

DISTANT   **e**   DISTANT
'it', 'then'   'it', 'they'
                                                         'continued action'
                           'here', 'this',
                               'now'

'nominals or pronominals   'nominals or pronominals
plus expression of past   plus expression of action'
or accomplished action'

                           'her', 'he', 'she', 'it',
                           'they', 'them', 'his'

ARROWS INDICATE DISTAL AND PROXIMAL
MOVEMENTS

The category of the pronominal marker, then, provides a promising criterion for research into interrelated messages making up the global discourse of performance. But not all language-gesture interaction is located at the level of specific syntactic or grammatical classes. Certain modes of kinesic stress apply to broader functions of phrase, clause or utterance. A major role of gesture – particularly on stage – is to indicate the *intentionality* of a given utterance. Simultaneous movement will serve to emphasize, or even define, the kind of speech act being performed by the speaker (and thus the character) in uttering a given sequence of words, be it a question, a command, a demand, an affirmation, etc. Such signals might best be termed *illocutionary* markers, related as they are to the *illocutionary force* of language (i.e. the intentional status of the utterance; see pp. 154 ff. below). They serve, say, to distinguish a serious from an ironical command, to emphasize the intensity of a demand or the degree of obligation being imposed on the addressee, to render a question actual rather than rhetorical, and so on.

So strongly conventionalized is the participation of gesture in the illocutionary act (the act performed in saying something to someone), that it is possible, in some circumstances, to perform such an act by kinesic means alone. As J. L. Austin (from whom the theory of speech acts originally derives) points out, 'we can for example warn or order or appoint or give or protest or apologize by non-verbal means and these are illocutionary acts' (Austin 1962, p. 119). In appropriate contexts, a pointing finger is equivalent to the command 'leave the room' or 'pick up that object' or 'close that door', just as a shoulder shrug may be interpreted as a 'statement' of the kind 'I have no idea', 'it doesn't interest me', etc. These are clear cases of 'complex kinemorphic constructions' constituting a form of discourse independently of, but through a conventional association with, speech. They are among the commonest kinds of 'expressive' gesture on stage.

Related indices of speaker-gesturer intention include what can be named *attitudinal* markers, indicative not of the act intended but of the attitude adopted (towards the world, the addressee, the propositional content of the utterance) in speaking. Head nods, finger wags, eyebrow movements, and so on, come close in function, in determined communicative situations, to the linguistic modalities usually expressed by means of 'modal operators' such as 'want', 'must', 'can', 'may', 'impossible', indicating the speaker's propositional attitudes. A typology of the attitudinal functions of gesture might be founded on the kinds of modality involved: epistemic (knowledge), doxastic (belief), deontic (permission/obligation), boulomaeic (want), etc. (on these concepts, see pp. 103 ff. and 171 f. below).

The particular importance of attitudinal markers to performance is that they permit a given interpersonal relationship within the drama (e.g. Polonius's 'deontic' manipulation of Ophelia) to be kinesically embodied by the actors. Brecht attached the highest importance to the attitudinal role of movement. For epic theatre, gesture (*geste*) was the chief means of expressing the *gestus*, defined by Brecht as 'the attitudes which people adopt towards one another, wherever they are sociohistorically significant (typical)' (Brecht 1964, p. 86). Such 'mimetic and gestural expression of the social relationship prevailing between people of a given period' (p. 139) formed the basis of the social criticism effected by Brechtian theatre, since the 'social *gestus*' was 'alienated' by various means, making the audience aware of the ideo-logical structure of the represented relationship. One of Brecht's models for gestural alienation was the Chinese theatre, where the actor 'achieves the A-effect by being seen to observe his own movements' (Brecht 1964, p. 139; on the *gestus*, see Pavis 1980a). The alienation of movement for purposes of social criticism or analysis has characterized much post-Brechtian theatre (as, for example, in the use of slow motion, freezes and repetitive movements by Richard Foreman, so as to break down stereotyped actions into 'framed' sequences).

Deictic, intentional and attitudinal markers may be generally classi-fied as indexical gestures relating to the speaking-moving subject. In traditional dramatic representation, onstage gesture is for the most part interpreted by the spectator as an index (effect for cause) of some motivating physiological, psychological or social motivation on the part of the dramatic persona, so much so that Jonathan Miller is led to complain of the naïveté whereby 'both critics and audience are led to over-interpret gestures and expressions and read meanings into movements that had no significance whatever' (1972, p. 365). This over-interpretation is an aspect, of course, of the general 'semiotiza-tion' principle of performance (in which, as has been said, nothing has 'no significance whatever'). At the same time, kinesic messages have their own material and formal autonomy even in the most mimetic of performances: the establishment of patterns of recurrent movements, rhythmical variations, changes in tempo and constellations of positions has been an essential part of the aesthetic information of the spectacle throughout its history and has, indeed, been the very *raison d'être* of highly 'visual' displays, from the arabesques of masque to the hypnotic kinetic patterns of Meredith Monk.

What, in summary, is peculiar to theatrical movement, distinguish-ing it from the kinesic system at large? It is clear that many of the syntactic and indexical functions of gesture in our theatre are founded on those prevailing in society, whereby they become recognizable and thus 'expressive'. Individual actors and directors will, of course, estab-lish personal kinesic styles or idiolects (Olivier and Eduardo de Filippo or Meyerhold and Grotowski, for example), just as certain generic constraints will influence such factors as timing or the mode of across-stage movement (e.g. the rules for performing farce). But it is difficult to identify general and stable kinesic subcodes in our theatre. Perhaps the closest one can come to formulating a general 'overcoding' rule with respect to the basic kinesic system is to say that in performance selected characteristic features of social movement are heightened or exaggerated, so as to increase their very 'sociality'. As Daniel N. Stern puts it, 'a good actor will probably exaggerate just that part of the entire pattern that has the highest communicative value' (1973, p. 120). The subject-defining, attention-drawing and intention-stressing functions of kinesic markers are emphasized in order to maximize their ostensive potential. Indeed, the pejorative adjective 'theatrical' is applied to anyone (e.g. an ostentatious partygoer) who demands attention by excessive gestural stress.

One of the more prominent roles of theatrical gesture, finally – and one which distinguishes it from the simple kinesic 'accompaniment' of discourse common to everyday conversation – is that of directly *contradicting* simultaneous linguistic utterances. Tension between linguistic reference and kinesic signals is, in particular, a common source of comic effect (as in *Waiting for Godot*: ' "Let's go." (They do not move.)'). Cooperation between the two modes of 'discourse', as between performance codes in general, is a complex dialectic rather than a matter of automatic reciprocal confirmation.

Research into kinesic factors in the performance is at a preliminary stage, and it is to be hoped that far more theoretical and empirical attention will be paid to the matter in future. As with proxemics, kinesics and its findings have had certain direct influences on theatrical productions. Directors such as Robert Wilson (in *Deafman Glance*), Richard Schechner, Yvonne Rainier and Steve Paxton have applied to their work insights and methods borrowed from kinesicists (see Stern 1973). More important, however, is the establishment of effective criteria for *analysing* so important and unexplored an aspect of theatrical discourse.

Paralinguistic features

A linguistic utterance is not simply a product of the phonological, syntactic and semantic rules of the language. As we have seen, contextual constraints and the kinds of language-related behaviour accompanying the utterance are essential to its correct interpretation by the addressee. Intimately related to the speaker's parakinesic 'orchestrating' of his discourse are those vocalic characteristics with which he endows it over and above its phonemic and syntactic structure – e.g. such factors as pitch, loudness, tempo, timbre and nonverbal sounds – and which have come to be known as *paralinguistic* (or suprasegmental) features. Such features supply essential information regarding the speaker's state, intentions and attitudes, serving further (in conjunction with kinesic factors) to disambiguate the speech act: 'the conversational use of spoken language cannot be properly understood', as D. Abercrombie has suggested, 'unless paralinguistic elements are taken into account' (1968, p. 55).

Kowzan's 'tone' comprises in reality a wide range of nonvocalic qualities which may be more analytically classified and measured. George L. Trager, in a paper which virtually founded paralinguistic studies (1958), was able to identify three main classes of vocalic feature, 'voice set' (the 'background' vocal characteristics deriving from physiological factors, gender, age, build, etc.), 'voice qualities' (pitch range, lip control, glottis control, rhythm control, articulation control, tempo, resonance, etc.) and 'vocalizations' (the actual sounds emitted), which are further analysed into 'vocal characterizers' (laughing, crying, giggling, shouting, whispering, moaning, groaning, yawning, etc.), 'vocal qualifiers' (intensity, pitch height and extent) and 'vocal segregates' (distinct but extra-phonemic sounds such as clicks, 'uh-huh', 'sh', etc.). Different divisions of the paralinguistic repertory have been offered since, but, whatever the variations in descriptive classes, what emerge strikingly are the large number and the distinctiveness of elements once thought incidental and unanalysable.

Research in the past two decades has suggested that paralinguistic – like linguistic and kinesic – behaviour is learned and is thus culture-specific, so that it is possible to explicate, to some extent, not only the range but also the semiotic functions of the speaker's vocalic activity. In the first instance, vocal qualities such as tempo, articulation control and rhythm control, together with vocal qualities such as extent and the introduction of pauses, have the critical role of 'punctuating' speech, i.e. 'the marking of boundaries at the beginning and end of an utterance and at various points within the utterance to emphasize particular expressions, to segment the utterance to manageable information units', etc. (Lyons 1977, p. 65). As with kinesic markers and stress forms, the paralinguistic handling by the speaker of his own utterances assists the listener in following and absorbing his discourse by marking syntactic, illocutionary or propositional units, regulating the flow of semantic information, varying the presentation of content according to the degree and kind of attention required, and so on.

Much of the research into the functions of vocal features has concerned their so-called 'expressive', 'emotive' or 'modulating' capacities. Qualifiers like pitch height and intensity, as well as vocalizations such as laughing, crying, shouting and whispering, are taken to be indices of the speaker's emotional or psychological state and of the 'attitudinal colouring' (Lyons 1977, p. 65) that he lends to his language. J. L. Davitz's psychological tests regarding the emotional connotations attached to voice characteristics are of interest here: eight emotions were found to be associated by subjects with particular combinations of voice features – loudness, high pitch, 'moderately blaring' timbre, moderately fast tempo and regular rhythm combine to connote 'joy', etc. (see diagram opposite). Research of this kind emphasizes the fact that the descriptive terms 'expressive' or 'emotional' are not equivalent to 'arbitrary' or 'purely personal', since the expression of attitudes and feelings appears to be strongly rule-bound (codified) where the choice of vocal indicators is concerned.

Paralinguistic features constitute one of the most ancient objects of the actor's art. The rules of 'declamation' or effective delivery are in effect controls on vocal 'punctuation' (regulating articulation, pitch, tempo, loudness, resonance, rhythm control, etc.). The ability to control the flow of information and segment discourse in such a way as to maximize the attention and comprehension levels of the auditor is one of the actor's cardinal functions. The training that actors receive in articulation, breathing (and thus tempo and rhythm control) and 'projection', i.e. the achievement of audibility without the concomitant vocalization 'shouting', comprises, as it were, a set of more or less obligatory secondary paralinguistic rules specific to the art.

At the same time, methods of 'characterization' through vocal idiosyncrasies, of the kind instituted by Stanislavsky, are founded on the 'expressive' functions of non-prosodic sounds, and are designed to

Feeling	Loudness	Pitch	Timbre	Rate	Inflection	Rhythm	Enunciation
Affection	Soft	Low	Resonant	Slow	Steady and slight upward	Regular	Slurred
Anger	Loud	High	Blaring	Fast	Irregular up and down	Irregular	Clipped
Boredom	Moderate to low	Moderate to low	Moderately resonant	Moderately slow	Monotone or gradually falling	–	Somewhat slurred
Cheerfulness	Moderately high	Moderately high	Moderately blaring	Moderately fast	Up and down; overall upward	Regular	–
Impatience	Normal	Normal to moderately high	Moderately blaring	Moderately fast	Slight upward	–	Somewhat clipped
Joy	Loud	High	Moderately blaring	Fast	Upward	Regular	–
Sadness	Soft	Low	Resonant	Slow	Downward	Irregular pauses	Slurred
Satisfaction	Normal	Normal	Somewhat resonant	Normal	Slight upward	Regular	Somewhat slurred

Emotions associated with paralinguistic features (from Davitz 1964) increase the degree of dramatic information derived from the utterance as an index of motivating attitudes or emotions on the part of the dramatis persona. Roman Jakobson, in a celebrated essay on the functions of language, describes the expressive versatility of a Stanislavsky-trained Moscow Arts Theatre actor, able to evoke an immense range of emotional connotations through paralinguistic variation alone, irrespective of the explicit semantic content of the utterance:

> [he] told me how at his audition he was asked by the famous director to make forty different messages from the phrase *Segodnja večerom* 'This evening', by diversifying its expressive tint. He made a list of some forty emotional situations, then emitted the given phrase in accordance with each of these situations, which the audience had to recognize only from the changes in the sound shape of the same two words. (Jakobson 1960, p. 354)

Here the *hermeneutic* (or interpretative) importance of vocal variations is evident. The actor's enunciation of a given line or speech will greatly influence the audience's interpretation of its semantic/dramatic import: 'it is possible', notes Jonathan Miller, 'to perform the lines assigned to Hamlet in a hundred different ways, all at least *compatible* with the basic semantic references of the script' (1972, p. 362). As in the case of kinesic behaviour on stage, the peculiar 'expressivity' of theatrical enunciation derives from the selection and exaggeration of those features rendered communicationally pertinent by the paralinguistic code at large. A competent actor will be able to draw on a repertory of vocal indicators ranging from crude stereotyped indices of the Peircean kind – slurred articulation as an index (effect for cause) of 'drunkenness' (N.B. the stereotype 'stage drunk') or 'effeminate' voice set and voice qualities as indicators of homosexuality, etc. – to the subtlest shades of attitudinal colouring, by means of a trained 'ear' which allows him to distinguish and then emphasize the relevant traits.

The actor's optional vocal activities, not predicted by the phonological system of the language, carry as well as dramatic information (relating to character) a high degree of aesthetic signal-information. Consider, for example, the importance of well-controlled resonant timbre to the performances of actors like John Gielgud or Charles

Laughton and to the pleasure derived from them. Such signal-information has the effect, moreover, of drawing attention to the material tissue of speech – to the substance of the expression – and so of ostending it as a phonic event. The pitch variations and changes in tempo, smooth or rasping vocalizations, clicks and trills, jerky or modulated rhythms, have the role, quite apart from punctuation or modulation, of varying the presentation of the linguistic object itself to the auditor's attention. It is the paralinguistic elaboration of the message which enables it to fill acoustic space.

Other systems, transcodification and the actor's codes

It is not possible here to consider in detail the syntactic and semiotic functions of each contributory system in turn. Such components as make-up and costume have distinct heightening and indexical (often stereotyped) roles (see Bogatyrev 1938b) and are subject to powerful generic and other rules (consider, for example, the strict selection and combination restrictions on costume in the *commedia dell'arte* or Restoration comedy modes).

Among the 'technical' systems, perhaps the most promising object of investigation is offered by stage lighting, which has, among other things, constituted a major means of creating virtual space from stage space ever since Adolphe Appia 'created an ultimate convention. For the transparent trickery of painted forms he substituted the illusion of space built up by the transfiguration that light, directed and controlled, can give to the transient structures of the stage-carpenter' (Simonson, 1932, p. 34). For Appia the cardinal function of lighting was the defin-ition (and thus the ostension) of forms in space. In more recent times the lighting designer Richard Pilbrow (1970, pp. 14 ff.) has elaborated a preliminary code correlating four functions ('selective visibility', 'revelation of form' – Appia's 'definition' – 'composition' and 'mood') with four combinable and controllable lighting properties ('intensity', 'colour', 'distribution' and 'movement').

In accounting for the cooperation *between* the diverse codes and sys-tems in the production of the text, two major transsystemic consider-ations arise: the *sharing* of semantic content by different kinds of signal; and the semantic and stylistic *coherence* of theatrical discourse in its temporal unfolding. The unity of the text across its proxemic, kinesic, scenic, linguistic, costumic and other discourse levels depends in large measure on the phenomenon of *transcodification*, whereby a given bit of semantic information can be translated from one system to another or supplied simultaneously by different kinds of signal (see pp. 10–14, 'The transformability of the sign'). The temporal coherence of the performance, similarly, will derive both from the consistency of successive bits of semantic information (and thus from the logic of the drama; see Chapter 4) and from the organization of heterogeneous signal-information into cohesive patterns in space and time (on the textual coherence of the performance, see de Marinis 1978).

In the contemporary theatre, ultimate responsibility for the overall semantic and stylistic coherence of the performance rests with the director. At the same time, it is clear that the unifying of non-uniform messages of the kind discussed above – kinesic, 'informal' proxemic, linguistic, paralinguistic, etc. – is very much dependent on the *actor* in his role as multichannelled transmitter-in-chief. Over and above the mastery of specific codes and subcodes attached to each system, the actor imposes the *histrionic* subcodes regulating his performance as a whole and so his combining of messages into discourse. The actor, from this point of view, is the main agent of transcodification on stage.

Histrionic subcodes may be classed generically (regulating the performance of farce, romantic comedy, melodrama, the West End thriller, etc.), nationally (compare acting modes for tragedy in France and the United States, for instance (Birdwhistell 1971, pp. 54 ff., gives an interesting comparison of French and American actors regarding their relative emphasis on movement and speech)), historically (acting styles bear 'period' markers which make early films of great actors – Bernhardt *et al.* – appear unnatural or hyperbolic), or idiolectally (relating to a particular school – e.g. the Comédie Française, the Actors' Studio or Grotowski's Theatre Laboratory – or an individual actor, as with the combined mannerisms of voice, posture and movement which constitute a distinctively 'Olivieresque' or 'Dusean' style).

The relationship between these classes of rule is fluid. It is not uncommon, for instance, for an idiolect to become the style of a whole generation of actors when established by a major performer. Stanislavsky illustrates this process in a celebrated anecdote:

A certain teacher in a dramatic school went behind the scenes after the performance of an excerpt from a student production and got quite hot under the collar: 'You people never nod your heads at all. A person speaking definitely nods his head.' That nodding of the head is a small story of its own. An excellent actor, who enjoyed great success and had many imitators, unfortunately possessed one unpleasant flaw, namely, the habit of nodding his head. And all of his followers, . . . instead of acquiring from him his good qualities, which are indeed hard to acquire from another, only copied his flaws – that nodding of the head – which are things easily acquired. (Quoted in Bogatyrev 1938b, pp. 45–6)

This is not to suggest that the actor is slave to established canons: on the contrary, a good performer will constantly marry code-observing with code-breaking and code-making, so as to establish a personal style and a personal 'reading' of a play; the precise kinds and degrees of codification involved in acting remain quite unexplored, however. Whether largely determined or highly innovative, the resulting performance constitutes a *self-reflexive* discourse carrying the constant information – even in the most 'mimetic' modes where the actor attempts fully to identify with the represented character, as in the Stanislavskyan tradition – 'this is acting'. The performer is always to some degree *opaque*, putting his very histrionic strategies on show as an index of his own virtuosity. In Brechtian theatre, where the actor 'does not allow himself to become completely transformed on the stage into the character he is playing' (Brecht 1964, p. 137) and the spectator is made constantly aware of role-technique distance, the self-reflexivity of acting is paramount.

There often exists a further source of opacity or 'impurity' in the actor's performance, especially in a theatre, like our own, which is dominated by 'names'. The individual actor as recognized figure or 'personality' will bring to the performance extratextual connotations which play no small part in the audience's decoding of the text (the mere presence of, say, Olivier in *The Merchant of Venice* will influence very substantially the aesthetic information which his admirers derive from the performance, since the prestigious connotation 'great actor' is established *a priori*). A well-known actor will bring to his performance, moreover, an 'intertextual' history which invites the spectator to compare it with past performances, thus drawing attention to the performer's idiolectal traits (common to all his performances). It would be vain to exclude these extra-textual factors as incidental or non-semiotic considerations: not infrequently the primary 'meaning' of a given representation for its audience is the very presence of a favourite performer (i.e. the performance text becomes the 'vehicle' for the actor rather than vice versa).

THEATRICAL COMPETENCE: FRAME, CONVENTION AND THE ROLE OF THE AUDIENCE

The theatrical frame: transactional and interactional conventions

Performances can be properly understood only on the basis of a theatrical competence, more or less shared by performers and audiences, comprising familiarity with the kinds of code and subcode we have been discussing. But there is a more fundamental form of competence required before the spectator can begin to decode the text appropriately: the ability to recognize the performance *as such*. Theatrical events are distinguished from other events according to certain organizational and cognitive principles which, like all cultural rules, have to be learned.

How do the participants in the theatrical transaction *define* their situation in such a way that, without resort to explicit explanations, there is general agreement about the terms in which it is set up? The definition of theatrical or any other activity depends, in the terminology of such social scientists as Gregory Bateson and Erving Goffman, on the *frame* which the participants place around the event (Bateson 1972; Goffman 1974). Frames are conceptual or cognitive structures to the extent that they are applied by participants and observers to make sense of a given 'strip' of behaviour, but derive from the conventional principles through which behaviour itself is organized: 'Given their understanding of what it is that is going on, individuals fit their actions to this understanding and ordinarily find that the ongoing world supports this fitting. These organizational premises – sustained both in the mind and in activity – I call the frame of the activity' (Goffman 1974, p. 247).

The theatrical frame is in effect the product of a set of transactional conventions governing the participants' expectations and their understanding of the kinds of reality involved in the performance. The theatregoer will accept that, at least in dramatic representations, an alternative and fictional reality is to be presented by individuals designated as the performers, and that his own role with respect to that represented reality is to be that of a privileged 'onlooker' – 'The central understanding is that the audience has neither the right nor the obligation to participate directly in the dramatic action occurring on the stage' (Goffman 1974, p. 125). This definitional constraint, whereby the actors' and spectators' roles are distinguished and the levels of reality (dramatic versus theatrical) are conventionally established, is the crucial axiom in the theatrical frame.

It is on the basis of this understanding that the performers are able to interact on stage apparently oblivious to the audience and its doings, just as the spectators themselves find no difficulty in identifying which elements belong to the representation and which to the excluded theatrical context, and so do not expect to impinge directly on the interaction. This firm cognitive division is usually reinforced by symbolic spatial or temporal boundary markers or 'brackets' – the stage, the dimming of the lights, the curtain, the banging of wooden clappers (as in Chinese theatre), etc. – which allow a more precise definition of what is included in and what is excluded from the frame in space and time.

Given the conventional basis of the frame, great importance attaches to the audience's willingness to 'disattend' those events agreed to be excluded from it: what Goffman (1974, pp. 201 ff.) calls 'out-of-frame activity'. During the performance, not only may various kinds of extra-textual 'noise' arise, having to be ignored or tolerated (late arrivals, malfunctioning of equipment and, within limits, the forgetting of lines by the actors), but certain licensed activities not contributory to the representation proper may take place on stage and will be duly discounted by the spectator (the entry and exit of stagehands, for example, in set changes). It is not that the excluded events – such as audience activity – have no semiotic value (it *does* make a difference if one is allowed to see the stage hands or if the entire audience is noisily eating popcorn), but that they are understood as belonging to a different level of action. The 'disattendance' factor is weakest in naturalistic performances, where mimetic 'authenticity' is aspired to, and strongest in explicitly symbolic forms of theatre, like the Chinese:

> European spectators at Chinese plays always find it surprising and offensive that attendants in ordinary dress come and go on the stage; but to the initiated audience the stagehand's untheatrical dress seems to be enough to make his presence as irrelevant as to us the intrusion of an usher who leads people to a seat in our line of vision. (Langer 1953, p. 324)

There are, naturally, limits to the flexibility of the disattendance convention. It is unlikely today that either performers or spectators of a dramatic representation would be prepared patiently to discount the invasions of the stage, vocal participation by wits and actual outbreaks of violence known to the Restoration stage (events such as these today characterize other kinds of performance, such as soccer matches and rock concerts, where they are, indeed, more or less disattended). Similarly, the audience's tolerance of such performance 'noise' as actors' errors is liable to be stretched by a display of real, as opposed to imitated, drunken inarticulateness by the performer, since occurrences of this kind usually break the frame definitively.

Transactional conventions are sufficiently powerful to ensure that there is no genuine ambiguity concerning the frame (i.e. everyone in the theatre knows more or less what is going on). Gross errors in framing – mistaking a performance for a piece of spontaneous real-life activity – are less common in the theatre than with popular mass-media drama (e.g. the flowers and clothing sent to the studio after a television or radio soap opera 'birth'), since the conventionalized markers are much clearer. The legend of the cowboy spectator who shoots the stage villain is fairly apocryphal (although Goffman (1974, p. 363) reports an actual case of a drunken Virginian spectator shooting a 'devil' represented by a mere puppet).

Generally speaking, therefore, the function of 'defining the situation' of the performance is fulfilled by established and unspoken conventions which serve as 'ways of arriving at coordination of social behaviour without going through the procedure of explicit or tacit

agreement' (Burns 1972, p. 40). The symbolic or representational status of the performance is ordinarily assumed rather than stipulated.
There exists, nevertheless, a class of transactional (performer–
spectator) conventions concerned with explicit definition of what is
going on. Such conventions, which Elizabeth Burns (1972) terms
'rhetorical' but which might more happily be called 'presentational',
act as 'means by which the audience is persuaded to accept characters
and situations whose validity is ephemeral and bound to the theatre'
(Burns 1972, p. 31).

Conventionalized presentational devices include the apologetic prologue and epilogue, the induction (much used by Ben Jonson and by
Shakespeare in The Taming of the Shrew), the play-within-the-play, the
aside directed to the audience, and other modes of direct address.
These premeditated and 'composed' forms of actor–audience persuasion are in effect metadramatic and metatheatrical functions (see Abel 1963;
Calderwood 1969), since they bring attention to bear on the theatrical
and dramatic realities in play, on the fictional status of the characters,
on the very theatrical transaction (in soliciting the audience's indul-
gence, for instance), and so on. They appear to be cases of 'breaking
frame', since the actor is required to step out of his role and acknowledge the presence of the public, but in practice they are licensed
means of confirming the frame by pointing out the pure facticity of the
representation.

On the Renaissance stage, where presentational conventions reached
an unequalled level of richness and elaboration, the function of prologues, inductions and direct address is ceremonial and structural
rather than strictly explanatory, since the laws of the playhouse were
well enough established to permit the tacit application of the theatrical
frame. This was not the case, however, with medieval street performances of morality plays and interludes, where the distinction between
represented and ongoing reality had to be laboriously stipulated in
order to identify the performance unambiguously: 'Thus at the very
beginning one finds dramatists having to deal with the problem of
defining the play as a play, of separating it from the current of ordinary
living from what amounts to proclamation' (Burns 1972, p. 41).

If presentational conventions depend on the audience's willing disattendance of the apparently frame-breaking effects of direct address, a

similar degree of flexibility is called for in reading performer–
performer interaction onstage as a model of face-to-face social intercourse. Here a set of what may be termed *interactional* conventions arise,
applying not so much to the actor–audience transaction as to the actor–
actor exchange on stage. What passes for the representation of interpersonal communication on stage, in practice, 'departs radically and
systematically from an imaginable original' (Goffman 1974, p. 145),
and it is only on the basis of a considerable compensation or 'correc-
tion' by the spectator that it is seen as an acceptably 'iconic' portrayal of
social encounter.

Dialogic exchange in the drama, in the first place, is organized in
an ordered and well-disciplined fashion quite alien to the uneven
give-and-take of social intercourse. The exchange proceeds, usually,
in neat turn-taking fashion, with a relative lack of interruption and
the focus firmly centred on one speaker at a time. Sentences are
syntactically complete and always fluently enunciated, larger units
being marked, as a rule, by a semantic coherence unknown in impro-
vised conversation. The writtenness or composedness of the dialogue
is assumed, so much so that absolute departures from the rules of
everyday discourse such as the unheard 'blind' aside (directed at
nobody in particular and heard only by the audience) or the
contemplative or oratorical soliloquy, do not raise problems of
'fidelity', except in naturalistic theatre. (On dramatic versus 'everyday'
discourse, see pp. 162 ff. below.)

What is more, onstage interaction is hardly ever genuinely 'face-to-
face', since it is imperative that the spectator have a full view – as
privileged onlooker – of facial reactions: 'spoken interaction is opened
up ecologically; the participants do not face each other directly or
(when more than two) through the best available circle, but rather
stand at an open angle to the front so that the audience can literally see
into the encounter' (Goffman 1974, p. 140). Again the spectator is
bound to 'correct' the actors' actual positions in order to interpret their
relationship as a direct eye-contact and front-to-front encounter. Here
the actors' specific 'vocabulary of stage placement' provides secondary
aids: the device known as 'cheating', whereby the actor's body is
turned away from the audience but his head angled towards it, allows
facial reactions to be seen while conserving the canonical body

position for a verbal exchange (see Cameron and Hoffman 1974, pp. 330 ff.).

Given the crucial importance of conventional rules at the levels of transaction and of interaction, it is clear that the verisimilitude or authenticity of the representation is not determined by 'iconic' fidelity alone but by what is sanctioned by the established performance canons. In general terms, verisimilitude may be defined as that which is rendered 'natural' by the theatrical frame (but which to any observer uninitiated in the code rules is liable to appear merely baffling: the authenticity of a Kabuki representation is more or less inaccessible to the average Western spectator). Verisimilitude, as Tzvetan Todorov has said, 'is the mask which conceals the text's own laws and which we are supposed to take for a relation with reality' (1968, p. 3, quoted in Culler 1975, p. 139).

Intertextual relations and decodification

Mastery of the 'rules of the game' by the theatregoer is in large part a matter of experience. In the absence of any explicit contract stipulating the respective roles of actor and audience or the various ontological distinctions in play ('actual' versus 'imaginary', etc.), the spectator is bound to master the organizational principles of the performance inductively, that is, by experiencing different texts and inferring the common rules. In reality, initiation into the mysteries of the dramatic representation – the differences between play-acting and other behaviour and between performing and looking on – occurs in infancy, through games, children's shows, and so on, so that even a five-year-old will usually have acquired sufficient theatrical competence to be able to follow, say, a Nativity play without experiencing framing difficulties.

Such considerations underscore the *intertextual* basis of the theatrical frame. Appropriate decodification of a given text derives above all from the spectator's familiarity with *other* texts (and thus with learned textual rules). By the same token, the genesis of the performance itself is necessarily intertextual: it cannot but bear the traces of other performances at every level, whether that of the written text (bearing generic, structural and linguistic relations with other plays), the scenery (which

will 'quote' its pictorial or proxemic influences), the actor (whose
performance refers back, for the cognoscenti, to other displays), directorial style, and so on. 'The text', remarks Julia Kristeva, 'is a permu-
tation of texts, an intertextuality. In the space of a single text several
énoncés from other texts cross and neutralize each other' (1970, p. 12).
An 'ideal' spectator, in this sense, is one endowed with a sufficiently
detailed, and judiciously employed, textual background to enable
him to identify all relevant relations and use them as a grid for a
correspondingly rich decodification.

Needless to say, intertextual relations are not confined to other plays
and performances. The theatrical frame is never, in this regard, 'pure',
since the performance is liable to draw upon any number of cultural,
topical and popular references assuming various kinds of extra-
theatrical competence on the part of the spectator. Consider the 'quotation' of music-hall conventions in the original (and any) performance
of *Waiting for Godot*, or of circus techniques in Peter Brook's *A Midsummer
Night's Dream* and in any performance by Le Grand Magic Circus. Certain
extra-theatrical and non-dramatic intertextual influences on decodification constitute canonical cultural references and are thus virtually
inescapable. It is all but impossible for any reasonably literate contemporary spectator to witness a production of *Oedipus Rex* or *Hamlet*
without applying in some form, however unwillingly, Freudian principles of interpretation, since these have become not only part of our
common understanding of behaviour but, still more, part of the plays'
own history.

Among inter- and extra-textual constraints on the spectator's
understanding of the performance, a privileged and occasionally
decisive influence is exerted by the critic, especially in the case of
Broadway and West End productions, where 'Not only is the audience
behaviour well regulated, but newspaper critics help write the scripts:
after reading a review, an audience member knows what he is going
to see and how he should respond. His role in the total event is made
clear beforehand' (Schechner 1969, p. 162). The review sets up,
before the event, a secondary and explicit frame of a 'metalinguistic'
kind (i.e. parasitic on the object 'language', the performance; see p.
140 below) which will determine the decodification to a greater or
lesser extent, depending on the credence given by the spectator to the

critic's judgement. Academic criticism represents a less immediate but often more diffuse intertextual influence: A. C. Bradley's literary readings of Shakespearian tragedy set up the canonical terms in which the plays were both encoded and decoded in the English theatre for decades.

The spectator's cognitive hold on the theatrical frame, his knowledge of texts, textual laws and conventions, together with his general cultural preparation and the influence of critics, friends, and so forth, make up what is known in the aesthetics of reception as the *horizon of expectations* (*Erwartungshorizont*; see Jauss 1970; Segers 1978, pp. 40 ff.), whereby the 'aesthetic distance' created by the performance – through its innovations, modifying future expectations – is measured. An aesthetics of *theatrical* reception, a genuine phenomenology of audience competence founded on empirical research – of the kind being conducted on readers (see Segers 1978) – is an indispensable, though so far neglected, component of any proposed theatrical poetics. (Such a project is outlined by Pavis 1980b.)

However expert the spectator, however familiar with the frames of reference employed by dramatist and director he may be, there is never a perfect coincidence between the producers' codes and the audience's codes, especially where the text is in any degree innovative. For the spectator, the condition of 'undercoding' – of an incomplete or evolving apprehension of the producers' codes – will be more or less constant throughout the performance, and indeed much of the audience's pleasure derives from the continual effort to discover the principles at work. With the innovative text, 'the receiver', as Jurij Lotman says, 'attempts to decipher the text, making use of a code different from that of its producer. . . . The receiver tries to perceive the text according to canons known to him, but through the method of trial and error he is convinced of the necessity of creating a new code, as yet unknown to him' (1972, p. 33).

Every spectator's interpretation of the text is in effect a new *construction* of it according to the cultural and ideological disposition of the subject: 'the text [in being decodified] is subjected to a new codification' (Lotman 1972, p. 33). It is the spectator who must make sense of the performance for himself, a fact that is disguised by the apparent passivity of the audience. However judicious or aberrant the spectator's decodification, the final responsibility for the meaning and coherence of what he constructs is his.

Audience signals

The spectator's semiotic initiative is not limited to his role in de- or re-codifying the text. In an important sense it is the spectator who *initiates* the theatrical communication process through a series of actions at once practical and symbolic, of which the first is the simple act of buying a ticket. The economic basis of the transaction has the symbolic value of a 'commission'. In sponsoring the performance, the audience issues, as it were, a collective 'directive' to the performers, instructing them to provide in return a bona fide product (or production) of a certain kind – hence the outrage of certain spectators whose expectations are openly flouted, as with various 1960s 'experiments'. The audience's relative passivity as 'receiver' is in fact an *active* choice which imposes certain obligations on the elected 'senders'. The audience, as William Dodd notes, 'delegates, so to speak, the communicative initiative to the actors onstage, making a contract whereby the actors are conceded a superior degree of articulation' (1979a, p. 135). If the delegated initiative appears to be abused, the audience is entitled to withdraw from the contract.

Of all successive audience signals, the most significant is its simple presence, which constitutes the one invariable condition of the performance. The scope of spectator–performer signals is restricted, although they may be transmitted along both visual and acoustic channels and appertain to different systems (kinesic, linguistic, para-linguistic). Such functions are subject not only to a more or less stable subcode regulating their connotations ('pleasure', 'attention', 'disapproval') but to generic rules regarding their decorum: what is accepted as an appropriate response (a 'good audience') in the case of tragedy, i.e. quiet attention, is considered anathema to farcical comedy.

Conventionally excluded (in our own day) from impinging on stage events – that is, not openly acknowledged by the performers, except during curtain calls – audience reaction nevertheless exerts a double influence, on the performance itself and on its reception. Spectator–performer communication will affect, if nothing else, the degree of the actor's commitment to his work. Spectator–spectator communication, meanwhile, usually ignored as a semiotic factor, has three main effects, important to an overall homogeneity of response: *stimulation* (laughter in one part of the auditorium provokes a similar reaction elsewhere), *confirmation* (spectators find their own responses reinforced by others) and *integration* (the single audience member is encouraged, in consequence, to surrender his individual function in favour of the larger unit of which he is part).

It is with the spectator, in brief, that theatrical communication begins and ends.

4

DRAMATIC LOGIC

THE CONSTRUCTION OF THE DRAMATIC WORLD

Dramatic information

Traditionally, the purpose of the elaborate codes and conventions on which the theatrical frame is founded is to permit the spectator to 'read' the performance appropriately as a dramatic representation. He derives from the conventionalized onstage happenings a range of dramatic information which enables him to translate what he sees and hears into something quite different: a fictional dramatic world characterized by a set of physical properties, a set of agents and a course of time-bound events. There are, of course, theatrical performances – especially contemporary offerings – which more or less refuse this representational status. In this chapter, however, we shall be concerned only with the drama proper (the specific mode of fiction represented in performance) and its peculiar logic.

The drama is usually considered as a 'given', offered to the spectator as a ready-structured whole through the mediation of the performance. The reality of the process is altogether different. The spectator is called upon not only to employ a specific *dramatic* competence (supplementing his theatrical competence and involving knowledge of the generic and structural principles of the drama) but also to work hard and continuously at piecing together into a coherent structure the partial and scattered bits of dramatic information that he receives from different sources. The effective construction of the dramatic world and its events is the result of the spectator's ability to impose order upon a dramatic content whose expression is in fact discontinuous and incomplete.

It should not be thought that a reader of dramatic texts constructs the dramatic world in the same way as a spectator: not only does the latter have to deal with more varied and specific kinds of information (through the stage vehicles), but the perceptual and temporal conditions in which he operates are quite different. The reader is able to imagine the dramatic context in a leisurely and pseudo-narrative fashion, while the spectator is bound to process simultaneous and successive acoustic and visual signals within strictly defined time limits. Nevertheless, the basic action-structure and logical cohesion of the drama is accessible through analysis of the written text, which is of unquestionable value as long as it is not confused with performance analysis (on the dangers of such confusion, see de Marinis 1975, 1978; the dramatic text/performance text relationship is discussed in Chapter 6).

The 'possible worlds' of the drama

What kind of world is it that, within the conventional bounds of the representation, is constructed in the course of the performance? Clearly, with respect to the 'real' world of performers and spectators, and in particular the immediate theatrical context, it is a spatio-temporal *elsewhere* represented as though actually present for the audience. Innumerable attempts have been made by critics to explore and describe individual dramatic worlds and their inhabitants (say, the world of *Macbeth* or of *Ghosts*), at least as they appear in written texts, but relatively little attention has been paid to their peculiar logical and ontological status. One of the tasks of a poetics of the drama is to explicate the general 'world-creating' principles of dramatic representation.

In dealing with fictional constructs, semioticians have made use in recent years of a conceptual framework borrowed from logical semantics, namely the so-called 'theory of possible worlds' (for applications to literature and drama, see Van Dijk 1975; Petöfi 1975, 1977; Pavel 1975; Versus 1977, 1978a; Eco 1979). For logical semanticists, the notion of possible worlds is useful in solving certain problems of referentiality, and in particular the matter of the 'extensional' (referential) status of 'intensional' (conceptual or 'possible') objects. Possible – as opposed to actual – states of affairs may be set up through hypothesis, through the expression of wishes, through orders (which project a situation different from that currently existing), or through counterfactual conditionals (i.e. hypothetical propositions that run counter to the actual state of affairs: 'If I were rich I would buy a summer house'), etc. Very loosely defined, possible worlds are 'ways things could have been' (Lewis 1973, p. 84; see also Plantinga 1974, p. 44).

The possible worlds of logic are formal constructs stipulated by *state descriptions* or '*books*', i.e. maximal (complete) sets of propositions which specify the make-up of the world, the number of its individuals and the properties ascribed to them (see Jeffrey 1965, pp. 196–7; Hintikka 1967, p. 41; Plantinga 1974, p. 46). Such a world is restricted to the individuals and properties stipulated: it may be limited, for example, to a set of four individuals, *a, b, c* and *d*, to whom are ascribed – in varying combinations – four properties, E, F, G and H. This purely formal 'world' may be represented as follows:

	E	F	G	H
a	+	+	+	+
b	+	+	+	−
c	+	+	−	−
d	+	−	−	−

(The + sign indicates that the property is ascribed to the individual in question and the − sign that it is not.) Here, if E = the property 'male', F = 'blond', G = 'bearded' and H = 'bespectacled', we have a state of affairs comprising four males, three of them blonds, two bearded, one bespectacled, etc. (see Rescher 1975).

Such formal devices would appear to have little to do with complex fictional domains. While the possible worlds of logic are abstract and empty constructs, those of fiction are, on the contrary, full, or, in the jargon, 'furnished' (see Eco 1979, p. 123). The 'books' of logical worlds are necessarily complete − the propositions they contain are descriptively exhaustive − while fictional worlds are only partially and fragmentarily described. Nevertheless, even the logicians' worlds are fictions of a kind (sometimes explicitly so, as in Saul Kripke's famous example of Sherlock Holmes who 'does not exist, but in other states of affairs, he would have existed' (1971, p. 63)) and have similar ontological status to those of the narrative or drama.

A *semiotic* − as opposed to logical − theory of possible worlds is concerned with the 'world-creating' operations of *texts* and the conceptual labours they call for from their decoders (readers, spectators, etc.). The textual worlds of concern to the semiotician are determined by *cultural* rather than logical models, and must be investigated according to the interpretative processes required for their construction rather than according to formal calculi.

The need for a notion of *dramatic* 'possible worlds' arises on the following grounds:

1   The ability of the spectator to read the performance consistently in terms of an alternative context (often incompletely and unevenly specified) on the basis of conventional clues.

2   The necessary *projection* by the spectator of possible future developments in the action, his inferring of probable causes and effects, his filling of gaps in information, etc. The spectator, in other words, is called upon to create his own 'worlds' in the course of the representation which may or may not correspond to the course of events revealed (he may be surprised: see pp. 104−5 below).

3   The drama is structured on the clashing of different and often opposing possibilities, i.e. conflicting possible states of affairs, and cannot be understood unless some notion of hypothetical worlds − realized or abandoned in the course of the drama − is applied.

Dramatic worlds are hypothetical ('as if') constructs, that is, they are recognized by the audience as counterfactual (i.e. non-real) states of affairs but are embodied *as if* in progress in the actual here and now.

The spectator will conventionally interpret all stage doings in the light of this general 'as if' rule:

> The auditors who are acquainted with the conventions of drama will expect the playwright to provide them with a hypothetical, counter-factual background. . . . The story of the play is this counter-factual interpretation. Any member of the audience who does not realize that the interpretation is counter-factual will be mistaking drama for actuality. (Urmson 1972, p. 338)

'Counterfactual backgrounds' to onstage doings will be more or less detailed depending on the degree of realism involved. We learn a good deal about the properties of the world – the period, the locations, the histories of the individuals, their social status, etc. – in Chekhov's *The Cherry Orchard* and practically nothing in Beckett's *Happy Days*. The specifications of the world are given gradually (it is not fully 'known' until the end of the drama) and are subject to continual change, since the dramatic state of affairs is dynamic rather than static.

Unlike the restricted formal constructs of logical semantics, dramatic worlds are never completely stipulated. It is assumed by the spectator that the counterfactual background to a representation of *Henry VI, Part 3*, will include a series of battles not explicitly described or represented, a number of minor figures barely individuated (soldiers, lesser nobles, etc.) and the general 'world' of the Wars of the Roses, mere glimpses of which are offered to the audience (see pp. 25–6 above on synecdoche). While logical worlds are assumed to be exhausted by their *state descriptions* (as defined above: they comprise only the individuals and properties stipulated), the possible worlds of the drama have to be 'supplemented' by the spectator on the basis of his knowledge and hypothesizing before they are fully constituted.

This raises the important question of the *accessibility* of the constructed world in relation to the real world: 'The key question for us', in Nicholas Rescher's words, 'is always: How does one get there *from here?*' (1975, p. 93). Accessibility is usually defined as a relationship R between two worlds (W_1, W_2) such that one world may be conceived of in, or generated by, the other through certain simple changes (having, for example, the same set of individuals but with changed properties). Thus $W_1 R W_2$ represents the accessibility of W_2 from W_1: if W_1 is a world comprising four individuals, three of them married, two of them fat and one long-haired, then a world W_2 in which all four individuals are married, only one fat and none of them long-haired is accessible to W_1. Similarly, the state of affairs in W_1 is conceivable in W_2, making it accessible in turn: in this case, the worlds are said to be *symmetrical*.

It may be, however, that one world is accessible to another but not vice versa. Imagine a world W_x accessible to the actual world, W_o, from which it differs in a single respect: the property 'married' does not exist in it. $W_o R W_x$ obtains, since W_x is conceivable in W_o on the basis of the removal of the qualification 'married' from the individuals affected; $W_x R W_o$, however, does not obtain since, the property 'married' not existing in W_x, a world W_o some of whose members are married cannot be generated. In this case, the worlds are said to be *asymmetrical* (the relationship of accessibility being one-way).

Dramatic worlds, to the extent that they are representable in W_o (that is, in the actual world of the spectators), are always accessible to that world: indeed, the world W_D of the drama is necessarily *based on* the spectators' actual world. A state of affairs where, for example, a character Caesar Julius is murdered by means of his own act of stabbing another character Brutus Marcus is *unrepresentable* in full, since it involves the reversal of the laws of physical cause and effect and thus the invention of a new physics (including, for instance, the inversion of the law of gravity) for the performance. The spectator assumes that the represented world, unless otherwise indicated, will obey the logical and physical laws of his own world, i.e. W_D 'takes for granted a background W_o with all its logical truths' (Eco 1978, p. 45).

If the background W_o were not assumed, it would be necessary for the drama to specify *all* the essential properties of W_D. No reference could be made, for example, to a 'woman' or a 'battle' without defining the referents in full. No drama in history has undertaken to set up an alternative world in such an encyclopedic fashion. Instead, it is assumed that the semantic and cultural rules operative in W_D will be those exercised in the spectator's social context: the dramatic world 'picks up a pre-existing set of properties (and therefore individuals) from the "real" world, that is, from the world to which the (spectator) is invited to refer as the world of reference' (Eco 1978, p. 31).

There is, then, a considerable degree of *overlap* between every W_D and the spectator's W_O. It is important to insist on this point, since it is tempting to think of fictional constructs as complete in themselves, each work being seen to explore 'its own autonomous world' and to contain 'its own ontological perspective' (Pavel 1975, pp. 172, 175). This position appears to be supported by dadaist, surrealist or absurdist works where the logical principles and even, at times, the physical laws governing W_O are seen to be violated according to the 'world-creating' principles of the fantastic (the growing corpse in Ionesco's *Amédée* being a vivid case in point). But it is precisely as deviations from actual-world laws whose very violation underlines their indispensability that the devices of absurdist drama are perceived. 'Avant-garde' suspension of the cultural and ontological principles of W_O may cause us to reflect on our understanding of our own world but do not break with it entirely.

One can illustrate this point with reference to a basic rule in our understanding of our own or any possible world: namely, the *co-referential* rule. If, in referring to W_O, one names a certain individual or object – say, John Smith or a red car – it is understood that successive references to John Smith or the red car will denote *the same* individual or object and not a homonymous individual or an identical car in this or some other world. Absurdist drama makes considerable play with this 'world-creating' rule, as in the havoc wreaked with names (which should be 'rigid designators', indicating a single individual) in Ionesco's *The Bald Soprano*:

MRS SMITH.   You know very well that they have a boy and a girl. What are their names?

MR SMITH.   Bobby and Bobby like their parents. Bobby Watson's uncle, old Bobby Watson, is a rich man and very fond of the boy. He might very well pay for Bobby's education.

MRS SMITH.   That would be proper. And Bobby Watson's aunt, old Bobby Watson, might very well, in her turn, pay for the education of Bobby Watson, Bobby Watson's daughter. That way, Bobby, Bobby Watson's mother, could remarry . . .

Ionesco's over-Watsoned world is comic, rather than genuinely logic-breaking, precisely because, as the Soviet semioticians O. G. Revzina and I. I. Revzin have shown, it *demonstrates* the 'principle of identity' in the flamboyant act itself of torturing it (Revzina and Revzin 1975, pp. 251–2). (On coreference, see also pp. 137 ff. and 165 ff. below.)

There is often another and more direct sense in which W_D picks up the properties and individuals of W_O. In Peter Weiss's play *Marat/Sade*, the title figures are taken to refer not to some purely fictional individuals in a hypothetical world imagined by the dramatist but to two historical characters in the W_O, however inventive the elaboration of the dramatis personae. The German playwright Rolf Hochhuth ran up against this 'referential' rule in the 1960s when his play *Soldiers* was banned in England because the central figure, 'Churchill', was seen at once to refer to and to defame (through inventive elaboration) the W_O original. Arguments in favour of the autonomy of the dramatic world in this case were not persuasive.

The problem here is not whether the actual-world individuals are really transferred to the W_D, since the 'as if' status of the latter rules out such naïve realism. It is rather a question of what in possible-worlds semantics is known as the *trans-world identity* of individuals. To what extent can an individual in one world, say the actual world, be considered the 'selfsame' individual if imagined in an alternative state of affairs? This matter has led to considerable flights of metaphysical speculation, but for our purposes the crucial consideration is not the real ontological standing of historical figures in the dramatic world – this is not an issue – but the referentiality of the drama. Here the only criterion that can be adopted is to consider the culturally determined *essential properties* of the figure in question and to judge whether they are preserved in the world of the drama.

'Cleopatra' as a historical figure has certain more or less agreed essential properties in our culture: let us define them as her having been a woman, Queen of Egypt and contemporary of Julius Caesar; other properties, such as her having been the lover of Mark Antony, might be deemed (perhaps arbitrarily) 'accidental'. Any play – such as Shakespeare's *Antony and Cleopatra* or Shaw's *Caesar and Cleopatra* – which portrays the heroine in these essential terms will be taken to refer to the historical figure, however much 'non-historical' information is added.

A conceivable play in which Cleopatra is Mark Antony's distant cousin, rather than his lover, in which she is blonde rather than swarthy, etc., will still be understood to make reference to the W_O individual (only accidental properties have been changed), while a comedy in which a nineteenth-century Italian washerwoman is given the name Cleopatra will not have the same referential force: the dramatis persona here is a namesake or pun.

What this suggests is that dramatic texts and dramatic performances can use considerable licence in imaginatively incorporating individuals 'picked up' from the W_O into the counterfactual states of affairs (which may or may not reflect historical texts) without destroying the assumed 'trans-world' identity of the figures in question. The fact that 'Florence Nightingale' in Edward Bond's *Early Morning* succeeds in growing a beard and acquires a Scottish accent (so as to resemble another Victorian figure, John Brown) does not alter her original identity for the audience, since she retains the culturally determined essential properties of nurse, popular heroine, favourite of Queen Victoria, etc. Her physical peculiarities are judged mere 'accidental' variants.

It should not be thought that the 'accessibility' of dramatic worlds renders them always and necessarily realistically mimetic. On the contrary, it is precisely the constant assumption that W_D is defined in relation to W_O as a hypothetical variation which allows any number of invented and even fantastic elements to be introduced into the drama without destroying the audience's ability to recognize what is going on. 'Fantastic' drama is interpreted according to the 'world' laws of the genre. The contemporary spectator is perfectly able to countenance a $W_{Oresteia}$ where mortals commune with the gods or a $W_{Don\ Juan}$ where a statue moves and speaks, despite the fact that these elements have no place in his conception of W_O. It is not that these plays establish their own autonomous ontological perspective but that, being in any case a merely hypothetical construct projected from the actual world and governed by particular textual (and intertextual) laws, the W_D is allowed to introduce non-actual phenomena without raising the question of their truthfulness (the question of their verisimilitude is another matter, and will depend on the conventions at work; see p. 83 above).

Because of the mixing of the referential and the merely possible, the actual and the hypothetical, the literally conceivable and the fantastic, dramatic worlds must be considered *remotely* possible worlds, as opposed to the *proximately* possible variety comprising the same individuals as W_O in somewhat different from (e.g. a world in which Jimmy Carter is a poor peanut farmer). Even the most rigorously 'faithful' historical dramas will usually introduce supernumerary (i.e. invented) individuals, if only among the minor characters. The degree of remoteness, of course, is variable: *Twelfth Night* presents an imaginary 'Illyria' peopled by individuals who are supernumerary with respect to the actual world, but still has to make continual reference to W_O in order to be accessible (e.g. to puritanism, courtship rites, duelling customs).

In view of the flexibility of the 'as if' basis of the dramatic world, allowing the 'actual' to conjoin with the purely hypothetical in an imaginary state of affairs, it is not necessary to accept the Coleridgean notion of the audience's 'suspension of disbelief' in the presented world. On the contrary, disbelief – i.e. the spectator's awareness of the *counterfactual* standing of the drama – is a necessary constant, since it permits him to judge and enjoy what is represented according to less literal standards than he might apply to his own social experiences: 'the attitude of the theatregoer is a very sophisticated one which one has to learn from long experience ... The spectator who can distinguish drama from reality is constantly aware that his interpretation is counterfactual' (Urmson 1972, p. 339). A spectator familiar with dramatic worlds can become engrossed in the representation without ever losing a detached consciousness that what he is witnessing is simply the way 'things could have been'.

There is another important factor in the W_O–W_D relationship conditioning the accessibility of the latter: this is that W_O, defined as 'actual' by the spectator, is nevertheless a possible world in itself – that is, construct deriving from the conceptual and textual constraints on the spectator's understanding. It is only because our notion of the world and its individuals and properties is founded on a certain epistemological (and thus ideological) order – rather than on absolute and fixed universal laws – that it is possible to have access to other conceptual organizations or worlds. The individual, for example, is not a simple given but a cultural construct: the essential properties ascribed to 'man' are subject to radical changes from culture to culture and from period to period, as, indeed, are the worlds defined as real and possible (to the Greeks, for example, the $W_{Oresteia}$ was far more proximately possible than to us, since the legendary figures, together with gods who intervene directly in the world of men, were not merely elements of 'licence' but essential constituents of W_o).

Here again intertextual factors are significant. Our understanding of W_o and its history is very much text-based: 'Cleopatra' belongs to the actual world only to the extent that historical and fictional texts have established her place in it and the properties by which she is defined. The appearance of a Cleopatra in another text-based world thus presents the spectator with few problems of epistemological orientation.

Nevertheless, if W_o R W_D is a constant, the reverse does not hold: the two worlds are *asymmetrical*. Being conventional projections from W_o, with no ontological autonomy, the individuals of W_D are clearly not in a position to conceive of our world (that of the audience) as a hypothetical alternative to their own. One of the basic tenets governing the theatrical frame is that the spectator is allowed to 'see into' the dramatic world, but that his own (theatrical) context is not in turn seen into – or even conceived of – by the characters on stage.

This would be a superfluous consideration – nobody thinks that 'Richard III' has access to our world or is capable independently of the drama of projecting *anything* – were it not for the attempts by some modern dramatists to 'bend' the asymmetry rule and present dramatis personae who interact directly with the public and its context. Notable cases in point are Peter Handke's *Offending the Audience* (where the spectators are harangued), *Waiting for Godot* (the tramps comment unfavourably on the public) and, still more, Pirandello's *Six Characters in Search of an Author*, which shows the 'lost' dramatis personae in question supposedly entering from W_o and explicitly requesting to be given a home in a suitable W_D. Here, clearly, the supposed W_o depicted is an illusion, part of W_D so disguised as to trick the audience into believing that it is really his own world: Pirandello's experiment 'represents a case of trompe l'œil: even the author takes part in Pirandello's [world]' (Eco 1978, p. 53).

The dramatic world can be extended to include the 'author',

the 'audience' and even the 'theatre' but these remain 'possible' surrogates, not the 'actual' referents as such (even the public insulted by Handke's characters is a virtual rather than real entity, however genuinely taken aback the audience may be).

The 'actualization' of the dramatic world

Access to all possible worlds – including the dramatic – is, naturally, conceptual and not physical, since 'one must "begin from where one is", and WE are placed within this actual world of ours' (Rescher 1975, p. 92). Possible worlds are *realized* only when our actual world changes so as to become them. Early in 1939 it was only too easy to hypothesize a state of affairs in which half the actual world was at war, and this, indeed, ceased rapidly to be merely possible. Counterfactual worlds are actual only for their supposed inhabitants, and we can never genuinely experience their condition, since this involves the transformation of the 'here' (our physical context) into a remote and hypothetical 'there'. Perhaps the only exceptions to this 'here'-bound condition which limits the full conceivability of other worlds are oneiric ('dream world'), hallucinogenic (other-worldly 'trips') and psychotic (e.g. schizophrenic) experiences, which allow the individual's context to be alienated and an alternative state of affairs to be perceived as more immediately real.

There is, none the less, an important distinction to be drawn – important especially to the semiotician of the drama – between imaginary worlds which remain explicitly remote and others which are presented as *hypothetically actual* constructs. The states of affairs stipulated by state descriptions (see p. 90 above) or, equally, described in novels are at an evident remove from the stipulater's or reader's immediate context, so much so that classical narrative is always oriented towards an explicit *there and then*, towards an imaginary 'elsewhere' set in the past and which has to be evoked for the reader through predication and description.

Dramatic worlds, on the other hand, are presented to the spectator as 'hypothetically actual' constructs, since they are 'seen' in progress 'here and now' without narratorial mediation. Dramatic performance metaphorically translates conceptual access to possible worlds into 'physical' access, since the constructed world is apparently *shown* to the audience – that is, ostended – rather than being stipulated or described. 'A fictional story', notes the philosopher of language John Searle, 'is a pretended representation of a state of affairs; but a play, that is, a play as performed, is not a pretended *representation* of a state of affairs but the pretended state of affairs itself' (Searle 1975, p. 328).

This is not merely a technical distinction but constitutes, rather, one of the cardinal principles of a poetics of the drama as opposed to one of narrative fiction. The distinction is, indeed, implicit in Aristotle's differentiation of representational modes, namely *diegesis* (narrative description) versus *mimesis* (direct imitation). It has, as we shall see, important consequences for both the logic and the language of the drama.

Unlike other possible worlds, which come into (conceptual) being only when they have been fully specified or at least (as in the case of the novel) partially described and located, the dramatic world is assumed by the spectator to exist before he knows anything about it. The W_D is conventionally 'discovered' in *medias res*, prior to the specification of its properties, and only in the course of the representation do its peculiar characteristics, the identity of its individuals, its chronological and geographical properties, its 'history', etc., emerge. To the extent that the spectator is supposedly shown a set of individuals and their spatio-temporal context, taken to be already in existence (the dramatis personae and their environment have a pre-textual 'past'), the construction of the W_D is allowed to contravene the norm whereby hypothetical worlds are not 'reached' or 'visited' but simply specified:

> Generally speaking, another possible world is too far away. Even if we travel faster than light, we won't get to it. A possible world is given by the descriptive conditions we associate with it. . . . Possible worlds are *stipulated*, not discovered by powerful telescopes. (Kripke 1972, pp. 266–7)

In the absence of narratorial guides, providing external description and 'world-creating' propositions, the dramatic world has to be specified *from within* by means of references made to it by the very individuals who constitute it. Although inevitably our knowledge of, say, $W_{Tamburlaine}$ will in part derive from explicit predications made concerning it (giving information about the protagonist's humble origins, his charismatic public presence, his success as a general, etc.), these, by a conventional shortcut, are attributed to the individuals whose properties they reveal. It is, above all, 'Tamburlaine' who characterizes himself as a constituent of $W_{Tamburlaine}$.

Dramatic worlds, then, are revealed through the persons, actions and statements which make them up, and not through external commentary. This principle might be called that of the *reflexivity* of the W_D, since its individuals, their properties and doings supposedly constitute their own description. The spectator infers the make-up of the world by apparently witnessing it, thus allowing the W_D to define itself rather than be set up from without by a third party.

It is because the dramatic world is conventionally discovered ready-constituted (at least in its initial state in the drama) and because it is specified reflexively that it is possible for it to be 'embodied' onstage by actors and set. All onstage vehicles not excluded from the drama proper (stagehands, etc.) are taken as ostensive definitions of the properties of the world. If, instead, the W_D had to be laboriously described, the happenings within it narrated and the dramatis personae characterized by literary 'sketches', actors and set would be wholly redundant: one would require simply a narrator onstage. *Mimesis* is thus equivalent to *definition through ostension* of the represented world (literally, of course, it is the actor and stage, very much part of this world, that are ostended and only metaphorically the hypothetical world as such).

Once set up as a hypothetically actual – and thus physically concrete – context, the environment of the dramatis personae can be referred and 'pointed' to directly. The actor will indicate the stage, the set and his fellow actors *as if* they were the dramatic referents themselves, so as to strengthen the illusion of direct presentation of the constructed world. In this way the gestural and proxemic relations obtaining on stage – given their accepted conventionality – provide an indexical definition of the identity and location of referents in the dramatic context: 'Thus individuation within antecedently specified worlds can also proceed ostensively – knowing where its constituents are located and whither members of its populace are (*ex hypothesi*) pointing, one can also identify objects in nonexistent worlds in a quasi-ostensive way' (Rescher 1975, pp. 92–3).

Crucial importance attaches to the role of verbal indices in 'actualizing' the dramatic world. For its inhabitants, a possible world is 'actual' to the extent that it can be referred to as the spatio-temporal *here and now*. Deictic definition is the crucial marker of the present context as opposed to the remote 'theres' that one can imagine or describe: 'Actual', observes David K. Lewis, 'is indexical, like "I" or "here", or "now": it depends for its reference on the circumstances of utterance, to wit the world where the utterance is located' (1973, p. 86). Thus in order to set up the W_D from within as an 'actual' world, supposedly in progress in the present (even if explicitly set in the chronological past), the dramatis personae must be 'seen' (and 'heard') to establish, in the words of Alessandro Serpieri, 'relationships between each other or with the objects or space of the stage, *through deictic, ostensive, spatial* relations. From this derives the involving, engrossing force of the theatrical event . . . because the theatre is mimesis of the lived, not the detachment of the narrated' (1978b, p. 20). (On the role of deixis in dramatic discourse, see pp. 126 ff. below.)

The founding principle of dramatic representation, then, is the fiction of the *presence* of a world known to be hypothetical: the spectator allows the dramatis personae, through the actors, to designate as the 'here and now' a counterfactual construct, on the understanding that 'The inhabitants of other worlds may truly call their own worlds actual, if they mean by "actual" what we do [i.e. that they live in it]' (Lewis 1973, pp. 85–6). The spectator does not 'enter' the here and now of W_D – his own indexically defined context remains theatrical and not dramatic – but agrees to be engrossed in it and to accept that part of W_O (stage, set and actors) may be indicated as if located in the fictional world.

Worlds-within-the-world: characters' and spectators' subworlds

Our perception of our own world is inevitably conditioned by the beliefs, fantasies, fears and wishes that we project onto it – that is, all the possible states of affairs that we imagine and propose. The 'actual' world of the drama is similarly subject to the speculations and

projections not only of the characters within it but also of the spectators who observe it. Since the course of events represented is not fully
'known' until the end of the drama, the hypotheses, predictions and
projections made by dramatis personae and audience members alike
about the W_D and its possible development are of major importance to
the progressive construction of the world in question. When characters
or spectators hypothesize a state of affairs in W_D, whether it proves true
or false, one can talk of the *subworlds* projected on to it. The construction
of subworlds is often responsible for the continued interest of the
spectator (the desire to discover whether a predictable outcome 'really'
occurs), dramatic surprise and *peripeteia* (when the spectator's or character's expectations are proved wrong), the creation of tension and
'suspense' (which of two projected possibilities will be realized?) and
so on.

Being tied entirely to the drama, of course, the dramatis personae do
not actually construct possible worlds of their own. Rather, the utterances attributed to them *propose* in various ways possible states of affairs
which do not correspond to the 'actual' state of affairs in the W_D as
constituted at that point, or which are only later proved 'true' or 'false'.
At the beginning of *Hamlet*, when the spectator (i.e. the ideal spectator –
presumably a Martian – who knows nothing about the play) is in a state
of 'pure' ignorance about W_{Hamlet}, two conflicting possibilities are
predicated: a world haunted by the ghost of the old king (the guards'
proposition) or a world untroubled by such mysteries (Horatio's
proposition – 'Horatio says 'tis but our fantasy', i.e. he considers the
ghost not part of the actual W_{Hamlet} but part of an imaginary world
projected by Marcellus and Barnardo). In the event, it is the guards'
subworld which is realized, with the appearance of the ghost, and
Horatio is forced to abandon his proposed spectre-less world and
accept the reality of the W_D as shown.

The 'world-creating' propositions expressed by different dramatis
personae are qualified by what Bertrand Russell termed *propositional attitudes*: that is, each subworld is founded on a particular modality,
expressible through verbs such as 'believe', 'wish', 'know', 'hope',
'fear', 'command', indicating the speaker's attitude to the proposition
uttered. There is a marked difference between the modalities of such
utterances as 'I have won £10,000', (i.e. I *know*), 'I think I have won

£10,000', 'I hope I have won £10,000' and 'I wish I had won
£10,000'. It is thus possible to talk of the world of a speaker's knowledge (or epistemic world), the world of his beliefs (or doxastic
world), the worlds of his hopes, wishes or fears (boulomaeic worlds),
the worlds of his dreams, day-dreams and fantasies (oneiric worlds)
and the worlds of his commands (deontic worlds, i.e. the states of
affairs that he orders to be brought about).

The drama is structured on the conflict between such subworlds.
Returning to W_{Hamlet} we can see not only how different doxastic or belief
worlds clash – Horatio's beliefs versus the guards', Hamlet's versus
Claudius's or Gertrude's (as in the bedroom scene, III. iv, where for
Hamlet the ghost is 'actual' but for his mother it remains a product of
Hamlet's lunacy) – but how much of the drama is structured on the
conflicting deontic worlds projected by the ghost's and Claudius's
commands respectively. Old Hamlet orders his son to bring about the
death of Claudius, while Claudius commands the death of Hamlet
himself, first on the voyage to England and then through the duel with
Laertes. It appears that the subworlds proposed are mutually exclusive
(in logical jargon, 'incompossible'), since each involves the elimin-
ation of the protagonist of the other (Hamlet and Claudius respectively). But one of the ironies of the play is that both orders are carried
out almost simultaneously in the final scene.

Spectators' subworlds are not expressed through propositions but
are nevertheless characterized by such attitudes as belief, hope, fear,
wish, etc., depending on the spectator's 'involvement' in the drama
and the basis of his projections. It is quite common for the audience to
be led to construct a 'false' doxastic or belief world – which for them
may appear an epistemic world to the extent that they have no doubts
about it – whereby they think a certain state of affairs exists in the
drama but later discover, often with a sense of delighted shock, that it is
not the case.

In Edward Albee's Who's Afraid of Virginia Woolf, the two principal
characters, George and Martha, propose jointly a world which includes
an individual referred to very often, namely their son. Admittedly, the
properties ascribed to the absent son – regarding his age, his 'history',
the colour of his eyes and hair, etc. – vary from account to account,
causing some perplexity to both the theatrical public and the dramatic

'audience', George and Martha's guests, but both are encouraged to accept the existence of the boy, who, indeed, appears to be the main point of reference in the couple's lives. The play's two main *coups de théâtre* derive from the 'destruction' of the son, first through the announcement of his death and then through the revelation that he is an invention. In this case, the spectators' belief world coincides with that of two of the characters and with the fantasy worlds (though they are slightly differentiated) of the other two. The play's dénouement comprises the abandonment of these non-actual worlds by all concerned.

DRAMATIC ACTION AND TIME

The dynamism of the dramatic world: temporal levels

It is evident that the possible worlds of the drama are never simple and static states of affairs but, rather, complex *successions* of states. The dramatic world of *Macbeth* is not merely a set of individuals (Malcolm, Macduff, Macbeth . . .) and their properties (Scottish, noble, warlike . . .) located in a particular chronological and geographical setting (medieval Scotland) but a series of connected events involving these individuals within a changing context. 'Instead of possible situations or states of affairs', as Teun A. Van Dijk suggests, 'we may therefore also take possible worlds as COURSES OF EVENTS' (1977, p. 30). Thus the fictional world $W_{Macbeth}$ is not constituted by the initial or final state of affairs represented but by the entire sequence of actions, events and situations dramatized.

One has to include in any account of the dramatic world, therefore, a temporal structure which indicates this passage from an initial state (W_D at time t_1) to a final state (W_D at t_x) through a series of intermediary states (W_D at t_n . . .). The problem is at what level of the drama to locate this structure.

There are, in effect, four temporal levels in the drama, excluding actual performance time, which has to do only with W_O. Most immediately, there is the fictional *now* proposed by the dramatis personae – the temporal deixis which 'actualizes' the dramatic world. This remains a constant: the action, notes Thornton Wilder, 'takes place in a perpetual present time. . . . On the stage it is always now' (quoted in Langer 1953, p. 307). This can be termed *discourse time*. Though 'perpetual', it is dynamic, since the moment referred to deictically as the present is, clearly, unrepeatable. The German critic Peter Szondi puts the matter well:

> . . . dramatic action always occurs in the present. This does not imply any staticness; it simply indicates the particular type of passage of time in the drama – the present passes and is transformed into the past, but as such ceases to be the present. The present passes effecting a change, and from its antitheses there arises a new and different present. The passage of time in the drama is an absolute succession of 'presents'. (Szondi 1956, p. 15)

At the same time, the changing situations and events presented in the 'now' of discourse (together with those referred to retrospectively as 'then') appear in a certain temporal order in the play which does not always correspond to their logical order. In *Macbeth* the first event represented (the initial appearance of the witches) is a form of 'prelude' to the main action, and is followed by a battle scene where reference is made to background events logically and chronologically prior to it, etc. This purely strategic temporal sequence, the order in which events are shown or reported (including incidental business, comic interludes, and so on) constitutes what can be called *plot time*. It is in effect the structure of dramatic information within the performance time proper.

From the information derived from the plot, the spectator is able to abstract the actual temporal ordering of events, including those merely reported, and so mentally constructs the *chronological time* of the W_D, that is, the period of time supposedly passed between t_1 and t_x, with its internal structure, irrespective of the order in which events are shown or reported. Chronological time belongs to the *fabula* of the drama (see next section).

Very often, especially where events and individuals 'picked up' from the W_O are involved, the events of the drama are taken to be set in a particular historical period – a more or less definite *then* transformed into a fictional *now*. This fourth temporal level, *historical time*, identifies more closely the precise counterfactual background to the dramatic representation. It is, of course, related to chronological time in that the historical time assumed to be referred to at t_x is clearly different from that at t_1 (one day, a year, ten years further on, for instance).

In his conceptual construction of the dramatic world from the information given (scenically, gesturally or verbally) in the course of plot time, the spectator infers *chronological* time as the temporal structure of the W_D proper. This, against the particular 'historical' background of the play (and actualized deictically), constitutes the dynamism of the W_D *as an abstraction*, while the dynamics of the play as a formal structure are entrusted to the plot.

Plot and *fabula*

The distinction between the dynamic structure of the W_D as a mental construct and the structure of the strategic ordering of information corresponds to the Russian formalists' differentiation between *fabula* ('story') and *sjuzet* ('plot') in narrative analysis. The *fabula*, the basic story-line of the narrative, comprises the narrated events themselves in their logical order, abstracted by reader or critic from the *sjuzet* or plot, which is the organization in practice of the narration itself (including omissions, changes in sequence, flashbacks and all the incidental comments, descriptions, etc., that do not contribute directly to the dynamic chain of events).

Being mimetic rather than strictly diegetic – acted rather than narrated – the drama does not lend itself to a distinction between *narrative* order and the structure of events. None the less, the *sjuzet*/*fabula* distinction holds good for the drama (see Pagnini 1970) to the extent that the actions and events supposedly occurring in W_D have to be inferred from a representation which is non-linear, heterogeneous (some events are 'seen', others not), discontinuous (the plot passes from one line of action to another, e.g. from the witches to the battlefield and then back to the witches) and incomplete (not everything assumed to make up the W_D and its temporal structure will be explicitly shown or described: years may pass, large 'gaps' may appear between incidents and have to be filled by the spectator).

Thus the world $W_{Macbeth}$ constructed by the spectator as *fabula* or story will be quite a different matter from the *sjuzet* or plot of *Macbeth* itself. In the former, the predictions of the witches, the murder of Duncan, the death of Lady Macbeth, the encounter between Macbeth and Macduff, etc., occur on the same level and form a logical and chronological chain. In the latter, these happenings are strongly differentiated in the mode of their representation. Some (the witches' forecasts and the Macbeth-Macduff encounter) are shown directly, the others reported *a posteriori*. The *sjuzet*/plot, similarly, includes happenings which, though part of the immediate 'actual' dramatic world – such as the exchange between Macduff and the Porter in II. iii – will not be included by the spectator in the structure of the *fabula*/story proper (since they contribute nothing to the progress of events: in narratological terms, they are not propulsive 'cardinal' functions but indices or static 'catalysers' (see Barthes 1966, pp. 79 ff.; see also the application of Barthes's categories to the drama in Pagnini 1970)).

It is clear that the *fabula*, being an abstraction from the *sjuzet*/plot as such, is a *paraphrase* of a pseudo-narrative kind, made, for example, by a spectator or critic in recounting the 'story' of the drama. It is usually the prime object of the spectator's hypothesizing in witnessing the representation: he anticipates events, attempts to 'bridge' incidents whose connection is not immediately clear and generally endeavours to infer the overall frame of action from the bits of information he is fed. In trying to project the possible world of the drama, the spectator is principally concerned with piecing together the underlying logic of the action.

Action

If the *fabula* that constitutes the global structure of the drama is a dynamic chain of events and actions, considerable importance attaches to the way in which these two terms are defined. The notion of *event* implies, as Van Dijk notes, the concept of *change* within a given state of affairs:

> This change may be viewed as a relation between, or operation on, possible worlds or states of affairs. More particularly, a change implies

a DIFFERENCE between world-states or situations and hence requires a TEMPORAL ORDERING of worlds. (Van Dijk 1977, p. 168).

A dramatic event is thus a change within the existing state of affairs (at a given point in time t_n) in W_D.

Among the kinds of event possible within the drama (which include, for example, natural disasters, *deus ex machina* interventions, death by natural causes – happenings strictly beyond human volition), absolute privilege has always been accorded to *action*. Aristotle's definition of tragedy as an 'imitation of action' has invariably been echoed by commentators on drama of all genres. But what precisely is meant by 'action' and how does it figure in the dramatic world?

That branch of philosophy known as the theory of action has specified certain necessary conditions for the performance of an action (see Rescher 1966; Von Wright 1968; Danto 1973; Van Dijk 1975, 1977): there is a being, conscious of his doings, who intentionally brings about a change of some kind, to some end, in a given context. Six constitutive elements of action are thus identifiable: an *agent*, his *intention* in acting, the *act* or *act-type* produced, the *modality* of the action (manner and means), the *setting* (temporal, spatial and circumstantial) and the *purpose*.

Such a scheme is sufficiently broad to include all possible acts, from the lighting of a cigarette to the blowing-up of parliament, while excluding casual or unconscious *doings*, such as doodling, scratching one's head or moving in one's sleep. Further categories are usually introduced to distinguish between types of act and the degrees of complexity involved. Thus *basic* actions, those which 'contain no further actions as components' (Danto 1973, p. 28) (raising an arm, turning a door handle), make up *compound* or *higher-order* actions (the complete act of opening a door, for instance). These more complex acts may be further combined into *sequences* (where there is an overall purpose linking the distinct acts involved, as in the driving of a car, where several component actions are necessary) or into *series* (where distinct but unconnected actions occur in succession, as with the various acts one might perform in taking an afternoon stroll – looking in shop windows, talking to passers-by, buying an ice-cream, etc.).

One can add to these 'positive' or productive acts – acts which change the state of affairs in which they are performed – two classes of *negative* action: the *prevention* of changes and thus the maintenance of the status quo (one stops a child running across the road) and the *forbearance* from performing a productive act, especially where it is expected (omitting to pay one's rent is usually interpreted as an intentional act by one's landlord).

Actions may involve a single agent or more than one individual: in the latter case, that of *interaction*, various other considerations arise. The action can be performed by two agents together, two *collaborators*, or by one principal agent (the *protagonist*) and an auxiliary or auxiliaries (*helpers*). One or more of the individuals involved, on the other hand, may be the object or victim of the interaction, rather than an active participant, in which case he is properly the *patient* rather than the agent of the action (punishments, murders and the receiving of orders are examples). Interactions, finally, will sometimes take the form of an opposition between agents, *antagonists*, whose purposes are contradictory.

With all kinds and combinations of actions – basic, higher-order, interactions, sequences – the crucial structuring principles (those that distinguish them from mere doings) are the *intention* and *purpose* of the agent or agents in acting. The difference between these two mental constraints on action may be illustrated by the following example: a family decides to spend a Sunday afternoon at the zoo, and so sets out in the family car only to find, on arrival, that the zoo is closed. In this case the intended action sequence (driving to the zoo) is duly performed, but its purpose (to allow the family to spend the afternoon looking at animals) is not fulfilled: Van Dijk (1977, pp. 174 ff.) distinguishes, on such a basis, between *intention–success* (the intended action is performed) and *purpose–success* (the desired end, in the example, is not achieved).

The conceptual constraints on action – the fact that it cannot be defined only in terms of external doings but must be given an intentional and teleological (purpose-bound) structure – have particular weight when one is dealing with the observation and interpretation of behaviour. Actions are not only intentional but also *intensional* objects: that is, their definition depends on the interpretation given to the objective doings involved. Different interpretative 'frames' may be placed around identical doings: in banging his hand on a table, the agent might be understood (by himself or by observers) to be killing a fly, protesting, calling for silence, exercising his karate, etc. Actions are not ready-defined but ascribed.

All of this is of some consequence with regard to our interpretation of the drama, to which all the factors considered here are directly pertinent. At the level of the plot or *sjuzet*, one is presented with a *series* of higher-order actions, more often than not interactions, which are recognizable as intentional acts of a certain type but whose connection and ultimate purpose is not always immediately apparent and still less fulfilled: in Act I of *Macbeth* the collaborative interaction between the witches (fixing an appointment), the (reported) heroic deeds of Macbeth in battle, the (reported) acts of treachery by the Thane of Cawdor, the witches' predictions to Macbeth and Banquo, and so on, constitute a series of distinct actions whose intentionality is clear enough (we have little trouble in identifying *what* is going on) but whose relationship remains to be established.

It is only at the level of the *fabula* or story that the series of distinct actions and interactions of the plot are understood to form coherent *sequences* governed by the overall purposes of their agents. Macbeth's plan to seize the throne provides the chief interpretative frame for the play, involving the protagonist and his helper (Lady Macbeth) in a sequence of interactions with both patients (Banquo, Duncan) and antagonists (Macduff, Malcolm, etc.). The spectator's chief role in following the plot is to convert the series (discrete acts) into a sequence (connected acts) by projecting the appropriate teleological structure and thus the possible results of the entire interaction (in this case, the possible purpose-success of Macbeth is pitched against the possible purpose-success of Macduff, Malcolm and their allies).

Whether individual or collective, productive or negative (consider, for example, Hamlet's forbearance from killing the praying Claudius, one of the central acts of that play), the higher-order actions of the drama are, then, subject to two interpretative operations: that regarding their intentional structure (the recognition of them *as* acts) and that regarding what might be termed their macro-purpose and thus their long-term results. The dynamism of the drama derives from the *suspension* − and thus the projection into the future − of the purpose-success/purpose-failure of the sequence, so that every distinct act is replete with the possible global result: '[The drama's] basic abstraction is the act, which springs from the past, but is directed towards the future, and is always great with things to come' (Langer 1953, p. 306). In *Macbeth*, to return to our example, it is the 'virtual' future marking the series of murders, battles and debates – the eventful success or otherwise of the protagonist's strategy – which serves as the structural principle of the play.

When it is said, as it so often is, that the drama is both etymologically and 'in essence' founded on action, there is as a rule an accompanying confusion not only between the different 'proairetic' or action levels of *sjuzet* and *fabula* respectively but, still more, between represented action and its stage representation. It is commonly assumed that the constitutive events of the drama are directly 'acted out' by the performers, so that, for instance, the action paraphrasable as 'Macbeth and Macduff engage in a swordfight' is embodied on stage by an actual swordfight between James Smith and John Brown, the actors concerned.

What is really happening on stage in a more or less 'realistic' production of *Macbeth* at the moment when, in V. viii, Macbeth and Macduff supposedly encounter each other? The two actors approach each other and, in the words of J. O. Urmson, 'engage in certain physical movements that I shall crudely call "banging swords together"' (1972, p. 338). That is to say, the actors as such do not perform the higher-order action (or interaction) 'swordfighting' but simply the *basic* action 'sword-banging'. In other words, the intentional status of the act (and, of course, its purpose) is not the same for the actors as for the dramatis personae they represent. The more complex action (swordfighting proper) is ascribed by the spectator to the characters on the basis of the 'as if' rule of the representation: 'the historical truth is that certain relatively basic actions . . . are performed on stage by actors. The auditors . . . will then interpret the more basic actions on the stage as more complex actions in the light of the counter-factual hypothesis' (Urmson 1972, p. 338).

Thus a three- (rather than two-) tiered interpretation is called for in the audience's mental construction of dramatic action. At the lowest level, we have the external doings of the actors, which constitute recognizable (basic) acts in themselves but whose intention and purpose are limited to their physical execution alone (an actor and actress may literally kiss on stage, but are not themselves engaging in courtship, lovemaking, seduction, etc., or, if they are, it is quite irrelevant to the performance). On to these objective doings the spectator projects a fictional intention − that of the character in performing his act ('seduction', for example) − so identifying the discrete actions of the plot; from these actions, finally, are derived the 'underlying' global sequences (in *Richard III* Gloucester's seduction of Lady Anne is seen as part of a larger plan: the protagonist's scheme for the conquest of power).

This interpretative scheme is valid for those actions which are more or less 'iconically' figured onstage. But the actions making up *sjuzet* and *fabula* will often be equally well understood by the spectator without the actual performance of basic acts at all. Instead of banging swords or kissing, the actors might engage in stylized movement, such as dance, in order to evoke the event in question, or produce purely symbolic gestures, interpreted conventionally in terms of particular dramatic happenings (see p. 24 above).

Much of the drama, finally, is taken up with what Pirandello aptly termed 'spoken action', both in the form of direct 'speech acts' (acts performed in or by saying something, see pp. 142 ff. below), and in the form of verbal reportage. Action *description* of the latter kind comprises a set of so-called *action sentences*: sentences 'with at least one action predicate and at least one name (term for an agent) as an argument' (Van Dijk 1975, p. 299). Thus 'For brave Macbeth . . . with his brandish'd steel . . . carv'd out his passage'; 'Sweno, the Norways' King, craves composition'; 'The tyrant's people on both sides do fight', etc. Action sentences make-up what is known as *action discourse* (see Van Dijk, pp. 299 ff.; Vaina 1977, p. 5) − but, in the case of the drama, the entire performance to the extent that it represents different levels of interaction, may properly be considered as a multi-message action discourse, at once verbal, scenic and gestural.

ACTANT, DRAMATIS PERSONA AND THE DRAMATIC MODEL

Dramatic 'calculus': the actantial model

One of the characteristic features of structuralist approaches to both narrative and drama has been the attempt to reduce the structure of narrated events to an underlying 'grammar', comprising certain binary oppositional categories and the modes of their combination. Narratology of the kind influenced by Vladimir Propp's analyses of folk tales and A. J. Greimas's extension of structural semantics to literature supposes the presence within any given narrative of a 'deep structure' responsible for generating the surface structure of events. In particular, the individual agents or characters involved are found to cover a very limited number of what Greimas calls *actantial* roles, that is, universal (oppositional) functions analogous to (and, indeed, supposedly derived from) the syntactic functions of language. A single actantial model accounts, it is claimed, for the varieties of structural configurations discovered in different narratives and plays, for, however many the individual characters (or *acteurs*) and whatever the form of their relationships, the underlying actants remain the same. (See Greimas 1966, 1970; Culler 1975, pp. 233 ff.; Hawkes 1977a, pp. 87 ff.)

Greimas's notion of the actant is inspired not only by Propp, who identifies seven actantial roles (or dramatis personae as he terms them, namely the villain, donor, helper, sought-for person and her father, dispatcher, hero and false hero) fulfilled by the characters of the Russian folk tale, but equally – and perhaps more directly – by the dramatic theorist Étienne Souriau, whose somewhat alarmingly titled *The 200,000 Dramatic Situations* appeared in 1950. Like Propp, but apparently independently, Souriau proposes a 'morphology' or 'calculus' of roles to which the analysed texts are reducible. He identifies six rather than seven actants (his term is 'functions') which, he insists, are valid for drama of all periods and genres. To these he gives colourful 'astrological' names and conventional symbols for purposes of formally transcribing the dramatic 'calculus':

1   ♌ *The Lion*, or incarnated 'thematic force' of the drama, residing

in its principal character (the protagonist – Propp's 'hero'). This character 'represents and puts into play the force which generates all the dramatic tension present' (p. 85). The embodied force in question might be love, ambition, honour, jealousy, etc.

2 ☉ *The Sun*, or representative of the Good or Value sought by ♌. The Good or Value is, for example, the crown, liberty, the holy grail, etc. It may be embodied in a particular individual (Propp's sought-for person) or remain an ideal end.

3 ♁ *The Earth*, or receiver of the ☉ sought by ♌: the protagonist desires the Good not necessarily on his own behalf but often for another individual or even a community (liberty is sought for the protagonist's country).

4 ♂ *Mars*, or the opponent. The protagonist has to deal with a rival or antagonist who offers an obstacle to the fulfilment of his goal.

5 ♎ *The Scale*, or arbitrator of the situation, whose role is to attribute the Good to, for example ♌ or ♂. This role might be covered by God or the gods in *deus ex machina* fashion, by the ruler of the community, or by the representative of the Good itself, as when the object of love chooses between the protagonist and his rival.

6 ☾ *The Moon*, or helper, whose function is to reinforce any one of the other five (by assisting the protagonist, so giving ☾ (♌), the opponent – ☾ (♂) – the representative of the Good – ☾ (☉) – etc.).

Any one of Souriau's six functions may be fulfilled by more than one character simultaneously, just as important figures may cover more than one of the listed roles. Nor is the configuration of roles necessarily stable within a given drama – it is possible, say, for the representative of the Good to change and subsequently become the opponent (the protagonist's love is redirected towards another object, and the original loved one blocks his way). In the case of *Macbeth*, the initial arrangement of roles would appear to be as follows:

♌   Macbeth himself embodies the thematic force 'ambition'.
☉   The Good sought is the crown of Scotland.
♁   The potential receiver of the Good is Macbeth himself.
♂   The protagonist's path is blocked by Duncan, the king.

♎   The desired Good is attributed to Macbeth by destiny, represented by the witches' prophecies.

☾   Macbeth is assisted in his quest by Lady Macbeth.

This situation is transcribable in terms of Souriau's calculus thus (the dashes stand for the divisions between characters; Lion and Earth are both covered by Macbeth):

$$\text{♌ ♂} - \text{☉} - \text{☾ (♌)} - \text{♂} - \text{♎}$$

Once Macbeth's ambition is fulfilled, however, the disposition of roles changes sharply. A new thematic force arises, 'justice', embodied by Macduff. The desired end becomes liberty from tyranny and its potential receiver Scotland. The new protagonist acquires a legion of helpers, while Macbeth – now the opponent – loses his helper with the death of his wife. It is again destiny, still represented by the witches, which decides the issue. The resulting 'horoscope' (Souriau's term) changes but slightly, while the roles have been radically redistributed:

$$\text{♌} - \text{☉} - \text{♂} - \text{☾ (♌)} - \text{♂} - \text{♎}$$

On the basis of the *ars combinatoria* – the divisions, doublings, treblings, etc. – made possible by the model, Souriau claims (if with an eye to dramatic effect himself) that precisely and no less than 210,141 different dramatic 'situations' (arrangements of functions) are generated, accounting for every conceivable dramatic structure. Clearly, however, the system works best for those dramas founded on clearly marked and stereotyped formulae, such as the romantic 'triangle' where the six roles are distributed among three characters, producing thirty-six possible combinations transcribable thus (in no. 1 the enamoured protagonist seeks happiness with the beloved for his own benefit, while the loved one herself is at once object, arbitrator and helper in his quest. In no. 2, on the contrary, she helps the rival, and so on):

1 $\text{♌ ♂} - \text{☉} \, \text{♎} \, \text{☾ (♌)} - \text{♂}$

2 $\text{♌ ♂} - \text{☉} \, \text{♎} \, \text{☾ (♂)} - \text{♂}$

3 ♌ ♁ – ☉ ♎ – ♂ ☾ (♌)
4 ♌ ♁ – ☉ ☾ (♌) – ♂ ♎
5 ♌ ♁ – ☉ ☾ (♂) – ♂ ♎
6 ♌ ♁ – ☉ – ♂ ♎ ☾ (♌)
7 ♌ ♁ ☾ (♂) – ☉ – ♂ ♎
8 ♌ ♁ ☾ (♂) – ☉ ♎ – ♂
9 ♌ ♁ ♎ – ☉ – ♂ ☾ (♌)
10 ♌ ♁ ♎ – ☉ ☾ (♌) – ♂
11 ♌ ♁ ♎ – ☉ ☾ (♂) – ♂
12 ♌ ♁ ♎ ☾ (♂) – ☉ – ♂
13 ♌ ♎ – ☉ – ♂ ♁ ☾ (♌)
14 ♌ ♎ – ☉ ☾ (♌) – ♂ ♁
15 ♌ ♎ – ☉ ☾ (♂) – ♂ ♁
16 ♌ ♎ – ☉ ♁ – ♂ ☾ (♌)
17 ♌ ♎ – ☉ ♁ ☾ (♌) – ♂
18 ♌ ♎ – ☉ ♁ ☾ (♂) – ♂
19 ♌ ♎ ☾ (♂) – ☉ – ♂ ♁
20 ♌ ♎ ☾ (♂) – ☉ ♁ – ♂
21 ♌ ☾ (♂) – ☉ – ♂ ♁ ♎
22 ♌ ☾ (♂) – ☉ ♁ – ♂ ♎
23 ♌ ☾ (♂) – ☉ ♎ – ♂ ♁
24 ♌ ☾ (♂) – ☉ ♁ ♎ – ♂
25 ♌ – ☉ – ♂ ♁ ♎ ☾ (♌)
26 ♌ – ☉ ♁ – ♂ ♎ ☾ (♌)
27 ♌ – ☉ ☾ (♌) – ♂ ♁ ♎
28 ♌ – ☉ ☾ (♂) – ♂ ♁ ♎
29 ♌ – ☉ ♎ – ♂ ♁ ☾ (♌)
30 ♌ – ☉ ♁ ☾ (♌) – ♂ ♎
31 ♌ – ☉ ♁ ☾ (♂) – ♂ ♎
32 ♌ – ☉ ♁ ♎ – ♂ ☾ (♌)
33 ♌ – ☉ ♎ ☾ (♌) – ♂ ♁
34 ♌ – ☉ ♎ ☾ (♂) – ♂ ♁
35 ♌ – ☉ ♁ ♎ ☾ (♌) – ♂
36 ♌ – ☉ ♁ ♎ ☾ (♂) – ♂

Souriau's model is inviting in its supposed exhaustiveness (it is presented as an extremely powerful code capable of producing all dramatic 'messages'), and does seem to deal successfully with structurally simple dramas whose characters are largely determined by their function in the action. Applied to complex plays, where the disposition of roles is less significant than the unfolding of plot and discourse, the usefulness of the model as an analytic tool diminishes (identifying the actants of *Macbeth* does little to explain its distinctive structure). Like Propp in his studies of fairy tales, Souriau takes as the exemplary pattern of the drama the *quest*. But while it is unquestionable that much classical, popular and folk drama adopts such a form (*Oedipus* and *Everyman* being notable examples), it is by no means clear that this is the appropriate framework in which to consider, say, *Miss Julie* or *Travesties*.

Greimas's adaptation of Souriau – or Souriau married with Propp – is in part terminological and in part theoretical. Greimas wishes to derive his six actantial roles from the structure of language which, he says, is in itself 'dramatic', since the sentence 'is in reality nothing but a play which *homo loquens* presents to himself . . . the content of the actions changes continually, the actors vary, but the utterance-play remains always the same' (1966, p. 173). Thus Greimas prefers the terms 'subject' and 'object' for the central actantial opposition or 'category' (equivalent to Souriau's Lion and Sun), to which he adds the quasi-linguistic categories sender/receiver (Souriau's Scale and Earth) and helper/opponent (Moon and Mars).

Greimas insists that his modifications represent an improvement on Souriau's model both because of their linguistic basis and because the actants are set in oppositional relations (like phonemes) rather than simply listed (although this hardly does justice to the relational nature of Souriau's 'horoscopes'). Souriau, like Propp, has the merit, on the other hand, of arriving at his categories inductively from a corpus of plays, rather than deductively from supposedly 'universal' features of language. His calculus has an immediate, if limited, applicability to the drama which Greimas's model is not designed to have. Souriau is concerned with the play as a kind of code-generated 'utterance', while Greimas's interest is primarily with the utterance as a kind of 'play'.

Whatever its precise form, the actantial model has a certain utility in accounting for the basic structure of the *fabula* in those plays founded on the protagonist's obstacle-laden quest. As a universal code of dramatic structure, its claims are far more questionable. Those of its elements which appear to have widest applicability (protagonist, opponent, helper, end or purpose) can be assimilated into a more general and more flexible theory of action of the kind outlined in the previous section. The advantage of this less rigid 'model' of dramatic action is that it does not claim to predetermine the dominant proairetic (action) mode of the drama (the search is but one possible action type).

The status of the dramatis persona

An actantial account of the drama is concerned with the individual character only in so far as he embodies one or more action functions. Such an approach, quite evidently, is at the opposite pole from the post-Romantic 'psychologistic' view of character, still current in literary criticism, which sees the dramatis persona as a more or less complex and unified network of psychological and social traits; that is, as a distinct 'personality' rather than as a functive of dramatic structure. The question arises as to whether a choice between these two extremes – one reductively mechanistic and the other naïvely idealistic – is inescapable in dealing with the individuals of dramatic worlds.

Philippe Hamon has suggested that a semiotic approach to character (whether in the drama, novel, film, etc.) should begin, not by deciding the status of the object *a priori*, but by considering it in the first instance as an empty 'sign', or 'as a sort of articulated morpheme, a migratory morpheme manifested by a *discontinuous signifier* (a certain number of distinctive features) which points to a *discontinuous signified* (the "meaning" and "value" of the character)' (Hamon 1972, pp. 124–5). It might be well, at this point, to consider the various factors that may be grouped under the mobile 'sign' of the dramatis persona:

1   His global action (or actantial) role, where relevant: the character fulfils a predominant overall function in the *fabula* (as protagonist, opponent, helper, etc.).

2   His role as agent or patient of the distinct actions of the *sjuzet*/plot (thus the protagonist of the *fabula*, for instance, will be actively or passively involved in different micro-acts).

3   His possible classification as stock type (romantic hero, villain,

fool, victim, braggart, etc.). This does not necessarily coincide with his actantial role (a villain or fool may appear as protagonist). Here Northrop Frye's typology according to generic modes (*eiron, alazon,* fop, pedant, etc.) is useful (see Frye 1957).

4   His standing as supposed individual in the dramatic world, in which capacity he is ascribed a name and certain personal and social properties (as male, married, father, king, etc.).

5   His relationship with the actual world – if the name ascribed to him is 'picked up' from the real world, thereby automatically bestowing on him certain assumed qualities.

6   His intertextual status, i.e. the properties and roles inherited from other plays and texts (the characters in *Rosencrantz and Guildenstern are Dead* are directly 'taken over' from *Hamlet* and so, to some degree, pre-defined).

7   The qualities attributed to him by virtue of the physical, vocal, gestural characteristics of the actor, together with costume, make-up, etc.

8   His *pronominal* status: he assumes the role of speaking 'I', becomes a receiving 'you' or a referential 'he', etc. Here it is the grammatical sense of 'person' – derivative from the dramatic persona (see next section) – which defines him.

9   As a speaker, the character (a) posits possible worlds and reveals propositional attitudes; (b) enters into dialectic relations with his interlocutors; (c) manifests himself as a particular rhetorical force, with his own idiolect or style.

This list is not necessarily exhaustive, but it is sufficient to suggest the diversity of factors – signifying and signified – gathered to form the 'migratory morpheme' of the dramatic character. Clearly, not all these categories will be equally predominant in all forms of drama – in folk drama the action and type factors will usually prevail, in modern drama the plot and discourse factors. But at all levels the individual status of the dramatis persona emerges and is defined dialectically, i.e. through the relationships – proairetic, pragmatic, linguistic, proxemic – established between the figures involved. It is in this sense that Hamon's 'morpheme' metaphor is apt, since the character, like the units of language, is defined only 'through opposition' (Hamon 1972, p. 128).

The dramatic model

To the extent that it provides a framework for the construction of 'worlds', the drama can be understood as what Yuri Lotman terms a 'secondary modelling system' (others being literature, painting and man's cultural activities in general), founded on the primary system whereby man organizes and 'models' his world, namely language (see Lotman 1973; Shukman 1977).

This does not mean, however, that the drama simply models or reflects an existing reality, or that it is merely parasitic on language. On the contrary, the dramatic 'model' is essential to our understanding of our own world, not only in the sense that we continually apply dramatic metaphors to all spheres of activity (situations are perceived as 'tragic', 'comic', 'farcical' or just 'dramatic', etc.) and to the analysis thereof (such concepts as 'role', 'performance' and 'mask' are indispensable to the study of social interaction – (see, for example, Goffman 1959; Burns 1972)), but also because the way in which we make sense of our lives and their component acts is very considerably influenced by our experience of dramatic worlds, where actions are seen in their intentional and teleological purity. In this sense, the elements of a general theory of human action (protagonist, antagonist, etc.) are not only directly applicable to but directly derivative from the drama. (On the dramatic model, see Burke 1945; Sacksteder 1975.)

What is more, our understanding of the *primary* 'modelling system', language, is dependent in important ways on the dramatic model. Thus the grammatical category of 'person' – in addition to the general concept of the person as individual – derives from a dramatic conception of syntax, as John Lyons notes:

> The Latin word 'persona' (meaning 'mask') was used to translate the Greek word for 'dramatic character' or 'role', and the use of this term by grammarians derives from their metaphorical conception of the language-event as a drama in which the principal role is played by the first person, the role subsidiary to his by the second person, and all other roles by the third person. (1977, p. 638)

In this light, Greimas's equation of the sentence with an elementary drama in which the subject, 'someone who performs the action', enters into relationship with the object, 'someone who suffers the action' (i.e. a patient), appears, perhaps, less fanciful (Greimas 1966, p. 173).

5

DRAMATIC DISCOURSE

DRAMATIC COMMUNICATION

Language in the drama

In the theatrical communication model sketched above (p. 35), a basic distinction was drawn between the context of the performer-spectator transaction and the (fictional) dramatic context of character-to-character communication. In this chapter we shall be primarily concerned with this second communicational level – the supposed semiotic exchange occurring within the dramatic world – and with the functions of language at large in the drama.

While it is no doubt impossible to identify a set of intrinsic properties 'specific' to dramatic discourse – as distinct, for example, from literary or 'everyday' uses of language – it is nevertheless one of the more pressing tasks of a semiotics of the drama to investigate those linguistic functions most characteristically 'dramatic'. The semantic, rhetorical and, above all, pragmatic principles of dramatic dialogue remain substantially unexplored to date.

Speakers and listeners

Whatever the properties ascribed to dramatis personae as individuals in a fictional world, and whatever personal, actantial, social and other rules they are seen to fulfil as functions of dramatic structure, it is in the first instance as *participants in speech events* that they are usually perceived. It is the *discourse* level of the drama – the dialogic exchange of information-bearing utterances which constitutes, at the same time, a form of interaction in itself – that is most immediately present to the spectator or auditor. Aristotle relegates language – *lexis* – to a subordinate position in the hierarchy of dramatic elements and insists on its subjugation, in particular, to action. It is part of the aim of this chapter to suggest the rigidity of such a distinction and to indicate the crucial constitutive role of speech events, at least in Western drama.

To identify dramatic characters as participants in communicative events is to do more than simply state the obvious – that the more important figures are seen (or heard) to speak throughout the drama. It is, rather, to assign the specific and far from empty roles of *speaker* and *listener* to them, entailing a set of projected qualities and capacities:

1   A supposed *linguistic competence*, i.e. mastery of the rules (phonological, morphological, syntactic, lexical, etc.) of the language in question.

2   A broader communicative or semiotic competence incorporating 'the psychological, cultural and social rules which discipline the use of speech in social settings' (Dell Hymes, quoted in Giglioli 1972, p. 15). This includes such factors as knowledge of the pragmatic rules of linguistic interaction (so-called conversation rules, see pp. 155 ff. below), the ability to use language for given communicative ends, the capacity for producing appropriate utterances adapted to their context, awareness of social and deictic roles, and mastery of the non-linguistic semiotic systems necessarily involved in the communicative exchange (gestural, proxemic, etc.).

3   A 'background' knowledge of the persons, objects and events referred to and an ability to locate them in the dramatic world.

4   An explicit or implicit social status giving the speaker authority to

make certain utterances ('Off with his head!') in an appropriate way, and determining the listener's duty or right to receive such utterances.

5   A set of intentions and purposes, as speaker, in making the utterances.

6   The ability on the part of the speaker to assume the role of listener and vice versa.

7   The capacity to 'create' non-actual worlds referred to in the course of the dialogue, expressing a set of supposed desires, wishes, hypotheses, beliefs, fantasies, etc.

8   A location in an 'actual' spatio-temporal context.

In granting dramatic figures the status of agents (and patients) of speech events, in other words, we necessarily attribute to them the qualities and the various forms of competence which allow us to participate in communicative exchanges. As we shall see, this has important consequences for our understanding of the 'interpersonal' dynamics of the drama.

CONTEXT AND DEIXIS

Types of context

What, precisely, is the 'dramatic context', marked off from the per-formance proper, in which character-to-character communication is taken to occur? Apart from the macro-context of the dramatic 'world' at large, there are two distinct components of interest here: the *situation* in which a given exchange takes place, that is, the set of persons and objects present, their physical circumstances, the supposed time and place of their encounter, etc.; and the communicative context proper, usually known as the *context-of-utterance*, comprising the relationship set up between speaker, listener and discourse in the immediate here-and-now.

The context-of-utterance can be represented as speaker, listener, time of utterance *now*, location of utterance *here* and utterance. It is constant in that dramatic discourse is always tied to speaker, listener and its immediate spatio-temporal coordinates, but is at the same time dynamic to the extent that the participants and the time and location of utterance indicated undergo continual change. In effect, the relationship is, in Van Dijk's words, a 'course of events' (1977, p. 192). The primary allegiance of language in the drama, over and above its larger 'referential' functions, is precisely to this course of events, the dynamic pragmatic context in which it is produced. But how is this crucial function manifested, and with what consequences for a semiotics of the drama?

Deixis

In the opening exchange of Shaw's *Heartbreak House*, the cardinal role of dramatic discourse in setting up the very communicative context in which it is supposedly produced is illustrated emblematically. An immediate relationship is established between two speaker-listeners and the here-and-now of their utterances before any detailed information is given regarding the participants and their world (my italics):

> THE WOMANSERVANT. God bless us! [*The young lady picks up the book and places it on the table.*] Sorry to wake *you* miss, *I'm* sure; but *you* are a stranger to *me*. What might *you* be waiting *here* for *now?*
>
> THE YOUNG LADY. Waiting for somebody to show some signs of knowing that *I* have been invited *here*.
>
> THE WOMANSERVANT. Oh, *you're* invited, are *you?* And has nobody come? Dear! dear!

It will be noted that what allows the dialogue to create an interpersonal dialectic here within the time and location of discourse is the *deixis* (as the italics indicate). What we have is not a set of propositions or descriptions but references by the speakers to themselves as speakers, to their interlocutors as listener-addresses and to the spatio-temporal coordinates (the here-and-now) of the utterance itself by means of such deictic elements as demonstrative pronouns and spatial and temporal adverbs (see pp. 23–4 and pp. 64–6). It is important now to note that the drama consists first and foremost precisely in this, an I addressing a *you here* and *now*.

The primarily deictic articulation of language in the drama was first noted by Jindřich Honzl, who attributes its centrality to 'the supremacy of dialogue over recitation' in the development of Greek tragedy, entailing 'the supremacy of action over narrative' (1943, p. 118). In replacing the pure choric dithyramb by verbal interaction, and thus a descriptive by a pragmatic mode of discourse, Aeschylean tragedy introduced 'an epic deictic reference within the drama' which 'serves as a semantic filter that enables the dramatist to create an image of the world . . . the words acquire dramatic justification through verbal deictic reference to action on stage, which deixis was for Euripides, Sophocles, and Aeschylus a basic compositional device' (1943, pp. 121–2). Deixis, therefore, is what allows language an 'active' and dialogic function rather than a descriptive and choric role: it is instituted at the origins of the drama as the necessary condition of a non-narrative form of world-creating discourse.

More recently Alessandro Serpieri, in an important contribution to dramatic and theatrical theory, has argued that all linguistic and semiotic functions in the drama derive from the deictic orientation of the utterance towards its context, so that what Jakobson (1971a, p. 26) terms the 'shifter' (empty verbal index) becomes the founding semiotic unit of dramatic representation at large:

> In the theatre . . . meaning is entrusted *in primis* to the deixis, which regulates the articulation of the speech acts. Even rhetoric, like syntax, grammar, etc., are dependent, in the theatre, on the deixis, which subsumes and unites the meaning borne by the images, by the various genres of language (prose, poetry), by the various linguistic modes of the characters, by intonation, by rhythm, by proxemic relations, by the kinesics of the movements, etc. (Serpieri 1978b, p. 20)

As Serpieri observes, the high degree of indexicality which characterizes the drama is verifiable in statistical as well as functional terms: in even so 'conceptual' a play as Hamlet, where, the allegiance of language to the pragmatic context might appear relatively slight, more than 5000 of a total of 29,000 words are explicitly deictic – that is, they are either personal or possessive pronouns ('I', 'you', 'he', 'mine', 'yours', 'his', etc.) or adjectives ('my', 'your', 'his'), or demonstrative

pronouns and adjectives ('this', 'that') or adverbs ('here', 'now').
Poetic and, still more, narrative texts are normally far less dense in
'shifters'.

Deixis, as was noted on pp. 101–2 above, allows the dramatic context
to be referred to as an 'actual' and dynamic world already in progress.
Indeed, deictic reference presupposes the existence of a speaker
referred to as 'I', a listener addressed as 'you', a physically present
object indicated as 'this'. It resides in 'shifters' ('empty' signs) in so far
as it does not, in itself, specify its object but simply points, ostensively,
to the already-constituted contextual elements. An indexical expression
such as 'Will you give me that, please' remains ambiguous unless
uttered in a context where the 'shifters' *you*, *me* and *that* have evident
referents. A mode of discourse, like the dramatic, which is dense in
such indexical expressions, is disambiguated – acquires clear sense –
only when it is appropriately contextualized, therefore. It is, in other
words, *incomplete* until the appropriate contextual elements (speaker,
addressee, time, location) are duly provided.

The 'incompleteness' marking dramatic reference is apparent in the
following passage from Arthur Miller's *All My Sons* (my italics):

JIM.   Where's *your* tobacco?
KELLER.   *I* think *I* left it on the table. *Jim goes slowly to table on the arbor,*
          finds a pouch, and sits there on the bench, filling his pipe. Gonna
          rain tonight.
JIM.   Paper says *so*?
KELLER.   Yeah, right *here*.
JIM.   Then it can't rain.
          Frank Lubey enters . . .
FRANK.   Hya.
KELLER.   Hello, Frank. What's doin'?
FRANK.   Nothin'. Walking off *my* breakfast. *Looks up at the sky.* *That*
          beautiful? Not a cloud.
KELLER,   *looking up.* Yeah, nice.
FRANK.   Every Sunday ought to be like *this*.
KELLER,   *indicating the sections beside him.* Want the paper?
FRANK.   What's the difference, it's all bad news. What's today's
          calamity?

KELLER. *I* don't know, *I* don't read the news part any more. It's more interesting in the want ads.

FRANK. Why, *you* trying to buy something?

KELLER. No, *I'm* just interested. To see what people want, y'*know*?

Not only the explicitly deictic pointers here (again italicized) to the participants and their immediate situation but also such references as 'today', 'tonight', 'the table', 'the paper', 'not a cloud', etc., acquire specific values only if they are at once related to corresponding objects. It is this factor that makes the drama so eminently 'representable' through visual and other means: stage performance provides precisely the kind of contextualization – by representing the appropriate elements of communicative context and situation – which the otherwise ambiguous references call for.

In this respect the role of gesture is often crucial (see pp. 65 ff. above). Disambiguation of indexical expressions, especially demonstratives, frequently depends upon an accompanying and specifying kinesic indicator allowing the object of the deixis to be ostended: as Émile Benveniste says, the demonstrative 'this' is identifiable with 'the object designated by simultaneous ostension in the present situation of discourse' (1966, p. 253). This is particularly the case with pronominal forms, for while an utterance such as 'Look at that beautiful blonde' may be referentially self-sufficient, the same is not usually true of the more abrupt 'Look at that!', which will normally be supported by a nod or sweep of the head, an eye or hand movement. Thus when Polonius issues his famous triple-decker index 'Take this from these if this be otherwise', the accompanying gestures – absolutely indispensable to the sense of the utterance – are inscribed in the language itself, rendering quite redundant the stage directions added by such modern editors as John Dover Wilson ('he points to his head and shoulders').

In its 'incompleteness', its need for physical contextualization, dramatic discourse is invariably marked by a performability, and above all by a potential gesturality, which the language of narrative does not normally possess since its context is described rather than 'pragmatically' pointed to. Deixis, as Francesco Antinucci puts it, creates 'the possibility of exchanging information operating on the sensori-motor rather than the symbolic level' (1974, p. 243); that is, it involves the speaker's body directly in the speech act. The language of the drama calls for the intervention of the actor's body in the completion of its meanings. Its corporality is essential rather than an optional extra: in the words of J. L. Styan, 'the words as spoken are inseparable from the movements of the actors who speak them' (1971, p. 2).

Not all indices have the same status in the drama, however. A central position is occupied by those deictics relating to the context-of-utterance (I-you-here-now), which serve as an indexical 'zero-point' from which the dramatic world is defined. In particular, it is on the 'pronominal drama' between the I-speaker and the you-listener/addressee that the dramatic dialectic is constructed. 'I' and 'you' are the only genuinely active roles in the dramatic exchange: 'It is important to note', as Lyons puts it, 'that only the speaker and addressee are actually participating in the drama' (1977, p. 638). Others are defined negatively by means of the unmarked third person, which, as Benveniste notes (1966, pp. 228 ff.), is not strictly personal at all, indicating, as it does, an excluded and non-participant other presented merely as object of discourse. The central I-you dialectic is defined by the principle of interchangeability, whereby 'he who "I" defined as "you" considers himself, and can in turn assume, "I", and "I" becomes a "you"' (Benveniste 1966, p. 230). The primary exchange in the drama, from which its tension and dynamic derive, is thus representable as

$$I \longrightarrow You$$
$$You \longleftarrow I$$

(See Serpieri 1978b, p. 30.)

But it is clear that within this relationship it is the first person that is dominant. Dramatic discourse is egocentric: the speaking subject defines everything (including the you-addressee) in terms of his own place in the dramatic world. The here-and-now simply marks his position as speaker. It is for this reason that the semantically marked 'proximal' deictics relating to the speaker's present context and situation of utterance ('here', 'this', 'these', 'now', the present tense, etc.) have a far more important function in the drama than the unmarked 'distal' variety regarding distant or excluded objects, times and places ('there', 'that', 'those', 'then', the past tense, etc.), which, instead, are typical of narrative language.

Spatial deixis, finally, takes priority over the temporal. It is above all to the physical *here* represented by the stage and its vehicles that the utterance must be anchored. The general semantic process which Lyons terms the 'spatialization of time' (1977, p. 718) is especially powerful in a mode of discourse which must relate the several temporal levels at work to the immediate presence of the speaker within a strictly defined space. The 'now' of discourse registers the instant of this spatial presence. The dramatic speaker presents himself in the first instance as I-here: 'Here I am Antony', in Mark Antony's words, 'Here is my space'.

Deictic strategies and the segmentation of the dramatic text

What are the implications of the deictic density of dramatic language for the purposes of semiotic analysis? It might be helpful here to recall Émile Benveniste's classic distinction (1966, pp. 237 ff.) between two levels or modes of utterance: between *histoire*, the 'objective' mode dedicated to the narration of events in the past, which eliminates the speaking subject and his addressee, together with all deictic references, from the narration; and *discours*, the 'subjective' mode geared to the present, which indicates the interlocutors and their speaking situation. *Histoire* abstracts the *énoncé* – the utterance produced – from its context, while *discours* gives prominence to the *énonciation*, the act of producing the utterance within a given context.

Benveniste's distinction has notable methodological consequences for the analysis of the drama. For while narrative texts – or at least classical narratives – are cast predominantly in the form of *histoire* (they refer to past events and are relatively lacking in indications of a concrete situation of utterance), the drama is invariably presented in the form of *discours*, a network of 'pragmatic' utterances or *énonciations* rather than a series of abstracted *énoncés*. What this suggests is that the adaptation of literary-critical and, above all, narratological models to the drama, whereby it is reduced to a set of *énoncés* and becomes just 'another narrative art, one of several modes in which mankind has learned to present a story' (Alternberd and Lewis 1966, p. 1), will inevitably sacrifice the very level – that of pragmatic discourse – at which it characteristically unfolds.

The question that arises, then, is whether, in place of a method dedicated to *sjuzet* and *fabula* alone (see Chapter 4), it is not possible to devise what might be called a *dramatological* approach which respects, and indeed is grounded in, the dialectical play of utterances within the dramatic here-and-now. Is there, in other words, a way of segmenting the dramatic text – for it is clearly at this level rather than that of the performance that such an analysis must be conducted – in such a way as to come to terms with its characteristic articulation by means of utterances geared to specific (concrete) contexts.

A segmentation of the dramatic text based on the analysis of *discours* has been proposed by Alessandro Serpieri (1978b, pp. 28 ff.). It takes as its basic unit the individual 'deictic orientation' adopted by the speaker: each time the speaker changes indexical direction, addresses a new 'you', indicates a different object, enters into a different relationship with his situation or his fellows, a new semiotic unit is set up. The speaking 'I', for example, can address a single interlocutor, a crowd or himself, can apostrophize the gods or some absent figure (through what Honzl terms the 'phantasma-oriented deixis' (1943, p. 124)), can turn to the audience, and so on. He can indicate deictically his own body, the scene, the present moment, his addressee or a distant object. Within a given dramatic macro-sequence – say, an exchange between two characters – a number of micro-sequences will be distinguishable according to the deictic strategies manifested by the participants. These minimal units will not always correspond with the individual lines or speeches of the interlocutors but rather with their changes of semiotic axis within the exchange. A typically errant encounter between the two main characters in Beckett's *Endgame* illustrates the importance of these shifts in indexical directions (my italics).

1 HAMM. Come back! (*Clov returns to his place beside the chair.*)
2   *Where* are *you?*
3 CLOV. *Here.*
4 HAMM. Why don't *you* kill *me?*
5 CLOV. *I* don't know the combination of the larder. *Pause.*
6 HAMM. Go and get two bicycle-wheels.

7 CLOV.   There are no more bicycle-wheels.
8 HAMM.   What have *you* done with *your* bicycle?
9 CLOV.   *I* never had a bicycle.
10 HAMM.   The thing is impossible.
11 CLOV.   When there were still bicycles *I* wept to have one.
12   *I* crawled at *your* feet. *You* told *me* to get out to hell.
13   Now there are none.
14 HAMM.   And *your* rounds? When *you* inspected *my* paupers. Always
           on foot?
15 CLOV.   Sometimes on horse.
           (*The lid of one of the bins lifts and the hands of Nagg appear,*
           gripping the rim. Then his head emerges. Nightcap. Very white
           face. Nagg yawns, then listens.)
16   I'll leave *you*, *I* have things to do.
17 HAMM.   In your kitchen?
18 CLOV.   Yes.
19 HAMM.   Outside of *here* it's death.
20   (*Pause*). All right, be off. (*Exit Clov. Pause.*)
21   *We're* getting on.

Each of the numbered units here represents a micro-sequence marked out according to a change (explicit or implicit) in orientation. Every such change brings about a particular development in the dramatic relationship, so that it is possible to chart its movement quite precisely.

Unit 1 sets up the communicative situation as such and establishes the (apparent) dominance-subordination terms of the relationship, with Hamm assuming the semiotic initiative. This leads into an immediate minor deictic drama in 2–3 regarding Clov's spatial location: throughout the play Hamm's blindness allows a dramatization of spatiality, worked out as an opposition between acoustic and visual signals and as a tension between deictic location (*here*) and actual proxemic relations (Clov's position in relation to Hamm). Hamm's absolute dependence on sound makes orientation a constant struggle. Unit 4 sharply alters the relationship in proposing a possible action (in contrast with their actual futile inactivity) of which Clov is agent and Hamm patient; but Clov deflates the proposal immediately with reference to the realities of the situation in 5. This pattern is repeated in

6–7, and suggests a marked difference between the participants and their respective relationships to the dramatic context (Clov is 'pragmatic', tied to the here-and-now and aware of his sorry position as 'I' within it, while Hamm, disoriented through his physical condition, constructs alternative possible worlds). Units 8–10 develop this clash as a direct disagreement concerning the properties of the dramatic world, and in particular of Clov himself (who remains, both as speaking 'I' and as addressee 'you', the constant deictic focus of the exchange, suggesting, contrary to immediate appearances, Hamm's dependence on him).

With unit 11 the indexical axis shifts from a primarily spatial dimension to an explicit temporal opposition between an indefinite pseudo-narrative past (characterized as relatively replete with opportunity and mobility) and the wretched and impoverished *now*, an opposition carried over through 12–15. This somewhat spurious exposition of the 'historical background', in which the participants dramatize the master-servant basis of their relationship, departs from and feeds into the current context-of-utterance (that is, it remains dramatic *discours* rather than narrative *histoire*), since, in Roman Jakobson's terms (1971a, p. 133), the 'participants of the narrated event' (the *énoncé*) and the 'participants of the speech event' (the 'I' and 'you' of the *énonciation*) are the same.

Sequence 16, in which Clov presents himself as potential agent in contrast with Hamm's necessary immobility, brings the discourse back to a spatial dimension, proposing an unseen scenic 'elsewhere', the province of Clov alone. This provokes Hamm's dramatic declaration in 19 in which an absolute distinction is drawn between the known, reassuring (if miserable) proximal space (*here*) and the mysterious, threatening (indeed fatal), distal 'outside'. One notes again the way in which the establishing of context in itself is used to generate dramatic tension. Unit 20 corresponds to 1 as an order signalling the close of the macro-sequence, which ends with a reflexive (and ironical) *coda* commenting on the dynamics of the situation (21).

It is evident that an analysis of this kind can furnish no more than the rudimentary 'skeleton' of the sequence and its dialectic, and in no sense exhausts the semiotic factors at work here. Nevertheless, certain insights into the articulation of the drama emerge. It is possible, for example, to construct on this basis a preliminary 'typology of discourse' of the kind proposed by Ducrot and Todorov (1972, pp. 408 ff.). It is notable that Hamm employs a mode of discourse 'organized around the addressee', i.e. based on 'you' (see units 2, 4, 8, 14, 17), while Clov's utterances are distinctly egocentric, 'founded on the speaker' (see units 5, 11, 16, etc.). Clov's discourse is always context-bound and rich 'in indications of its *énonciation*', while Hamm is less geared to the pragmatic situation and is capable of generalized propositional *énoncés* (see unit 10, for example). Analysis extended to the entire text permits a far more exact definition of the characteristic deictic strategies employed by each figure in his discourse relations with the other. (For more extensive segmentations based on the unit of the deictic orientation, see Serpieri *et al.* 1978.)

UNIVERSE OF DISCOURSE AND CO-TEXT

Information and reference

If the most immediate function of dramatic language is the indexical creation of a dynamic context, it is clear that the utterances tied to the here-and-now must also come to fulfil a larger 'referential' role in carrying information concerning the dramatic world at large. The properties of that world, its individuals and events must emerge, in short, from the give-and-take of discourse.

How is the dramatic world characterized reflexively, from within? In other words, how do its individuals divulge the necessary dramatic information without resorting to narration and external description? In part, this is a matter of duly 'fleshing out' the speaking 'I' and the addressed 'you', making them 'iconic' as well as indexical, through more detailed specifications. Since the participants, however, are presumed to know who they are, self-characterization must be oblique or disguised in order to sustain the hypothetical 'actuality' of the world – 'the audience is given the information it needs covertly, so the fiction can be sustained that it has indeed entered into a world not its own' (Goffman 1974, p. 142). A fairly extreme example of deictic reference to the context-of-utterance carrying covert information about the 'I' concerned occurs in the opening scene of Shaw's *Saint Joan*, where the speaker disguises a veritable 'self-portrait' in the form of an aggressive interrogation of the interlocutor:

ROBERT.   Now listen to me, you.
STEWART   [humbly]. Yes, sir.
ROBERT.   What am I?
STEWART. What are you, sir?
ROBERT   [coming at him]. Yes: what am I? Am I Robert, squire of Baudricourt and captain of this castle of Vaucouleurs; or am I a cowboy?

Reference, of course, is not limited to the current situation. In the course of an exchange any number of external individuals in the dramatic 'there' and 'then' will be referred to, who may later become participants in speech events themselves and refer in turn to the present interlocutors as third-person 'others'. It is the sum of the information carried by these intersubjective references which sets up, internally, a coherent macro-context or world. We must now turn to the question of the 'world-creating' powers of dramatic language: how do merely fictional 'referents' come to be, and by what principles are they held together in a coherent whole?

Object and universe of discourse

In order for something to be referred to in the course of the dialogue, it has to be granted a certain kind of existence. But it is sufficient for the referent to exist as what is commonly called an *object of discourse* (see Bonomi 1979). Objects of discourse are those entities, real or not, which we are able to talk about. Just as it is possible for us to discuss Father Christmas without being committed thereby to a belief in his extralinguistic existence (even if we assign him certain agreed qualities), so it is possible for reference to be made in The Tempest to Caliban and for the audience to grant him a for-the-nonce existence as object of dramatic discourse, without entailing his extra-dramatic reality as 'referent'.

'Referents' which exist only as objects of discourse are said to be located in a *universe of discourse* (the term derives from Peirce 1931–58,

Vol. 2, § 519; see Eco 1979, pp. 39 ff.; Bonomi 1979; Van Dijk 1977, p. 26; Lyons 1977): that is, they are created as points of reference by the discourse in question. Dramatic referents are objects of this kind: they are created for the duration of the drama and exist for as long as they are mentioned, ostended or otherwise referred to in the dialogue (or, in performance, in the 'theatrical discourse' at large, thus including visual ostension, etc.; see pp. 39 ff. above). The speakers posit objects in the dramatic universe of discourse so that they can be referred to again.

It is clear that the universe of discourse is more extensive than the dramatic world as such, as constructed by the spectator, since it is possible for the speaker to mention individuals and events *en passant*, or refer to objects which exist only in some alternative possible world of his own creation (Hamm's bicycle-wheels, for example), and these factors will not be included by the spectator in his construction of the world of the play.

Nevertheless, the constitutive properties of the dramatic world are defined, in the first instance, as objects in the discourse-created universe. Whatever the speaker refers to or ostends, including himself and his context, *is*, unless we learn otherwise. In this way, the world of the drama is set up reflexively, through the deictic and other references made to it by the speakers who are its inhabitants.

Co-reference, anaphora, co-text

Those objects of discourse which are important components of the dramatic world (e.g. of the *fabula*) must be perceived as stable and consistent entities. Their position, that is, in the dramatic universe of discourse must be coherent rather than capricious (the Caliban referred to is always the same). What guarantees the stability and consistency of the referents is the principle of *co-reference*: subsequent references to the object, once located in the universe of discourse, are assumed to concern the same entity.

Co-referential rules are in part responsible for the semantic and pragmatic coherence of the dialogue. The Wars of the Roses emerge as a unifying 'topic' of discourse in the *Henry VI* plays to the extent that they are the recurrent point of reference for all the participants and to the extent that they are assumed to refer to the same events rather than random happenings arbitrarily united under a single name. But the flagrant contravention of such rules (see p. 94 above) is a frequent source of comic business, as when two speakers believe themselves to be referring to a single object while the audience is aware that there are distinct referents in play. A good instance occurs in Tom Stoppard's *Jumpers*, where two distinct happenings (respectively, a noisy party and a murder committed during it) come to form what is apparently a single point of reference in Inspector Bones's interrogation of the witness and possible culprit George:

> BONES. Well, your wife says you can explain everything, and you say you are wholly responsible, but–
> GEORGE. Are you still going on about that? – for goodness sake, I just lost my temper for a moment, that's all, and took matters into my own hands.
> BONES. Because of the noise?
> GEORGE. Exactly.
> BONES. Don't you think it was a bit extreme?
> GEORGE. Yes, yes, I suppose it was a bit.
> BONES. Won't wash, Wilfred. I believe you are trying to shield her.
> GEORGE. Shield who?
> BONES. It's quite understandable. Is there a man who could stand aside when this fair creature is in trouble—
> GEORGE. Aren't you getting a little carried away? The point is, surely, that I'm the householder and I must be held responsible for what happens in my house.
> BONES. I don't think the burden of being a householder extends to responsibility for any crime committed on the premises.
> GEORGE. Crime? You call that a crime?
> BONES. *(with more heat)*. Well, what would you call it?
> GEORGE. It was just a bit of *fun*! Where's your sense of humour, man?

The confusion here (Bones thinks that George is confessing to the murder while George believes that Bones is concerned with a complaining telephone call he made to the police) is aggravated by the fact – characteristic of co-reference – that the events and their agents are not specified but are indicated pronominally as 'that', 'it', 'her', etc.:

through that form of indexical reference known as *anaphora*. Anaphora differs from deixis in that, instead of pointing to the object directly, it picks up the referent of the *antecedent* word or expression, in this case merely assumed. (In the two statements 'My cousin is a sheep farmer. He lives in Tasmania', 'he' picks up the referent of the antecedent 'my cousin'.)

Anaphoric reference is important to dramatic dialogue in that it creates, through co-reference, the appearance of continuity in the universe of discourse: it maintains the stability of the object once introduced. As such it is subordinate to the deixis proper, which ostends the object directly and introduces it as dramatic referent: 'Anaphora presupposes that the referent should already have its place in the universe-of-discourse. Deixis does not; indeed, deixis is one of the principal means open to us of putting entities into the universe-of-discourse so that we can refer to them subsequently.' (Lyons 1977, p. 673; see also Serpieri 1978b, pp. 26–7.)

'Backward-looking' anaphoric reference is particularly significant as a means, at the beginning of the play or of individual acts and scenes, of creating the sense of a world in *medias res*, with its own pre-dramatic history which can be referred back to. Roderigo's complaint at the beginning of *Othello* 'that thou shouldst know of this', where the anaphoric 'this' picks up the referent of a presumed, but unheard, antecedent or, similarly, Mrs Alving's 'Kind of you to say so, Pastor' at the opening of Ibsen's *Ghosts*, have precisely the role of suggesting that the spectator is 'discovering' a world – and, indeed, a communicative event – already in progress.

Equally important is the role of anaphora in establishing *internal* relations within the body of discourse itself and thus favouring the creation of a coherent *linguistic* context or *co-text* (see Petöfi 1975, pp. 1 ff.). The dialogue has not only a 'world-creating' and outward-looking (*exophoric*) function but, equally, an interior co-textual structure essential to any play whose language is more than functionally 'transparent'. It is foregrounded, that is, as an object of interest in itself. Not only all forms of word-play and semantic patterning but also the fundamental dialogic dynamic, whereby one utterance provokes or generates another, are strictly dependent on inward-looking (*endophoric*) factors. Anaphora, and a closely related form of index, the so-called *textual deixis* (see Lyons 1977, p. 667), which points directly to the co-text itself rather than the extra-linguistic context (e.g. in *As You Like It: 'Le Beau.* I will tell you the beginning . . . / *Celia.* Well, the beginning, *that* is dead and buried'), are indispensable to the *self-generating* power of dramatic language, allowing it a *self*-ostensive autonomy as structure and event (see Elam 1978, pp. 106–8).

Metalanguage and object-language

In picking up and pointing to a word, phrase, sentence or larger unit of discourse in the linguistic co-text, the speaker may come to comment on it as a phenomenon of interest or concern in its own right: language itself, that is, may be presented as the object of discourse. In *Who's Afraid of Virginia Woolf* George, the protagonist, seizes upon his guest's innocuous query ('Sir?') and anatomizes it severely:

> I wish you wouldn't go 'Sir' like that . . . not with the question mark at the end of it. You know? Sir? I know it's meant to be a sign of respect for your (*Winces*) elders . . . but . . . uh . . . the way you do it . . . Uh . . . Sir? . . . Madam?

Here the 'backward-looking' indices ('that', 'it') serve not only to create endophoric relations between the two utterances involved but to allow the second to base itself *parasitically* on the first. The speaker is using what linguists and logicians term *metalanguage*, which is a form of language dedicated to describing or commenting on another, the *object-language* (see Hjelmslev 1943, p. 119; Carnap 1947, p. 4).

Roman Jakobson (1960, p. 356) limits the metalinguistic function to those modes of communication which allow the participants 'to check up whether they use the same code' – glosses, explanations, comments on usage, etc. Later in the exchange between Albee's George and his guest Nick, the latter corrects a term hazarded by the host (thereby invoking the linguistic code, and in particular the lexicon) –

> GEORGE. You're the one's going to make all that trouble . . . making everyone the same, rearranging the chromozones, or whatever it is. Isn't that right?

NICK. (*With that small smile*). Not exactly: chromosomes.

— just as George and his wife Martha become involved in semantic dispute, again referring to the language as code as well as to an individual message:

MARTHA. He's a biologist. Good for him. Biology's even better. It's less . . . abstruse.
GEORGE. Abstract.
MARTHA. ABSTRUSE! In the sense of recondite. (*Sticks her tongue out at George.*) Don't you tell me words.

But the object-language will not always be either the speaker's common code as system of elements and rules or a particular message generated by it. It is possible, for example, for one speaker to characterize metalinguistically another's general mode of speaking, his 'idiolect', as in Professor Higgins's ironic praising of Doolittle's unstudied eloquence in Shaw's *Pygmalion* —

. . . this chap has a certain natural gift of rhetoric. Observe the rhythm of his native woodnoted wild. 'I'm willing to tell you: I'm wanting to tell you: I'm waiting to tell you.' Sentimental rhetoric! that's the Welsh strain in him.

— or Jack Absolute's surprised remarking of Bob Acres's novel way of cursing in Sheridan's *The Rivals*: 'Spoke like a man! But pray, Bob, I observe you have got an odd kind of a new method of swearing —'. Or he may reflect philosophically, morally, psychologically, etc., on the uses and limits of language at large. Meditative metalanguage of this kind belongs characteristically to highly ideational drama, of which *Hamlet* is the classical instance and the plays of Pirandello perhaps the best modern representatives:

And those people profit from [your weakness], they make you suffer and accept their way of thinking. . . . Or at least they believe so. Because really, what do they manage to impose on you? Words! words which everyone understands and repeats in his own way. Ah, but in this way so-called current opinions arise. And woe betide anyone who is branded by one of these words that everyone repeats! For example, 'madman!' For example, 'imbecile!'

(Pirandello, *Henry IV*)

In general terms, a metalanguage is 'a semiotic whose content plane is a semiotic' (Hjelmslev 1943, p. 119). The range of object-languages, or linguistic levels, commented upon is potentially limitless. In the drama, the metalinguistic function often has the effect of foregrounding language as object or event by bringing it explicitly to the audience's attention in its pragmatic, structural, stylistic or philosophical aspects. At an extreme of linguistic self-consciousness, such commentary serves to 'frame' the very process of character-to-character or actor-to-audience verbal communication, and so becomes part of a broader meta-dramatic or metatheatrical superstructure. Peter Handke's *Offending the Audience*, in which discourse is oriented deictically towards the performance itself and its public, reflects consistently on the dramaturgical (or anti-dramaturgical) strategies of its own language:

While we are insulting you, you won't hear us, you will listen to us. The distance between us will no longer be infinite. Due to the fact that we're insulting you, your motionlessness and your rigidity will finally become overt. But we won't insult *you*, we will merely use insulting words which you yourselves use. We will contradict ourselves with insults. We will mean no one in particular. We will only create an acoustic pattern.

SPEECH ACTS

Language as action

We have seen how language is used in the I–you exchange to indicate or ostend, to refer to and, in general terms, to create the dramatic macro- and micro-contexts. But what takes place between the participants in the communicative event is constitutive of the drama in another crucial sense. The speech event is, in its own right, the chief form of interaction in the drama. The dialogic exchange, that is, does not merely, in Honzl's terms, *refer* deictically to the dramatic action but directly *constitutes* it. The proairetic (or 'action') dynamic of the play is carried, above all, by the intersubjective force of discourse.

Such a conception of the function of dialogue – quite alien to that adopted in dramatic criticism, whereby 'action' is taken to be limited to 'external' events such as murders, battles, the physical comings and goings of characters, and so on – must be justified: in what ways can discourse be said directly to 'enact' the events that make up the drama? What types of acts are performed through language?

Types of speech act in the drama

Speech-act theory, one of the major branches of contemporary philosophy of language and linguistics, is concerned with linguistic phenomena less in their formal aspects than as elements of a 'rule-governed form of behaviour' (Searle 1969, p. 12). It aims to bring speech events, in other words, under the rubric of a general theory of action. It is to this language-as-action theory that we must turn in order to understand the proairetic functions of discourse in the drama.

A theory of language as a mode of social action was first proposed by the Oxford philosopher John Austin (1962) in reaction to the traditional philosophical treatment of utterances as statements, or mere vehicles for true or false propositions. It was Austin's aim to show that in issuing utterances we are not only or always producing a certain propositional content but are, above all, *doing* such things as asking, commanding, attempting to influence or convince our interlocutors, etc. Austin brings philosophical attention to bear, therefore, on the pragmatic status of speech as an interpersonal force in the real world.

Austin's initial strategy (later modified) was to distinguish from so-called 'constative' utterances – the proposition-bearing statements traditionally dear to philosophers of language ('Paris is the capital of France') – a class of 'performative' utterances which are not subject to considerations of truth or falseness since they do not so much state as *do*. These 'executive' uses of language perform conventional social acts such as appointing, marrying, baptizing and sentencing, and are usually in the form of verb phrases comprising the first person singular pronoun and simple present indicative verbs ('I name this ship . . .', 'I declare this conference open', 'I promise to pay £10', etc.).

But this rigid distinction had to be abandoned in favour of a more radical position, namely that *all* utterances have an 'executive' or 'performative' force, including so-called 'constative' ones (indeed it is possible to make this explicit through the use of performative verbs: 'I assert that Paris is the capital of France'). The original constative/ performative polarity was replaced by a tripartite classification applicable to linguistic behaviour in general. Three types of act may be performed in the delivery of a *single* utterance. First, a *locutionary* act: the basic act of producing a meaningful utterance in accordance with the phonological, syntactic, morphological and other rules of the language. This category has been largely replaced in later speech-act theory by more analytic categories. (John Searle (1969, pp. 24–5) suggests the *two* classes, instead, of the *utterance* act, the physical production of morphemes and sentences, and the *propositional* act, that of referring and predicating.) Second, an *illocutionary* act: the act performed in saying something, such as asking a question, ordering someone to do something, promising, asserting the truth of a proposition, etc. (It is the 'illocution' which constitutes the speech act proper.) And, third, a *perlocutionary* act, performed *by means of* saying something, such as persuading someone to do something, convincing one's interlocutor, moving him to anger, and so on. (This depends upon the effect – the so-called *perlocutionary effect* – which the utterance has upon the listener.)

It must be emphasized that these classes of act are not *alternatives*, but are, as it were, *levels* of the pragmatic make-up of the utterance. In saying to one's interlocutor 'Give me ten dollars, please' one performs the utterance act of producing an acceptable English sentence, the propositional act of referring to oneself and the ten dollars, the illocutionary act of requesting the ten dollars and, perhaps – if one is in luck and the request has the desired perlocutionary effect – the perlocutionary act of persuading the listener to give one ten dollars. It is clear that the utterance and propositional acts are more basic than the other two, since one cannot make a request in English without producing an English sentence and referring to the object of one's desire. Not all illocutionary acts will have a perlocutionary effect (the greeting 'Hello, my name is Richard', for example), while it is impossible to perform a successful perlocutionary act without performing an illocution.

It is this social, interpersonal, executive power of language, the pragmatic 'doing things with words', which is dominant in the drama. Dramatic discourse is a network of complementary and conflicting illocutions and perlocutions: in a word, linguistic *interaction*, not so much descriptive as performative. Whatever its stylistic, poetic and general 'aesthetic' functions, the dialogue is in the first place a mode of *praxis* which sets in opposition the different personal, social and ethical forces of the dramatic world. 'In a play', as Richard Ohmann has said, 'the action rides on a train of illocutions . . . movement of the characters and changes in their relations to one another within the social world of the play appear most clearly in their illocutionary acts' (1973, p. 83). The emergence of relationships, and particularly of dramatic conflict, through the encounter of illocutionary and would-be perlocutionary strategies is seen clearly in the following verbal confrontation taken from Marlowe's *Edward II*:

Enter SOLDIERS *with* KENT *prisoner*.

Y. MOR.	What traitor have we there with blades and bills?	
FIRST SOLD.	Edmund the Earl of Kent.	
K. EDW. THIRD.	What hath he done?	
FIRST SOLD.	'A would have taken the king away perforce,	2420
	As we were bringing him to Killingworth.	
Y. MOR.	Did you attempt his rescue,	
	Edmund? speak.	
KENT.	Mortimer, I did; he is our king,	
	And thou compell'st this prince to wear the crown.	
Y. MOR.	Strike off his head: he shall have martial law.	2425
KENT.	Strike off my head! base traitor,	
	I defy thee!	
K. EDW. THIRD.	My lord, he is my uncle, and shall live.	
Y. MOR.	My lord, he is your enemy, and shall die.	
KENT.	Stay, villains!	
K. EDW. THIRD.	Sweet mother, if I cannot pardon him,	2430
	Entreat my Lord Protector for his life.	
Q. ISAB.	Son, be content; I dare not speak a word.	

K. EDW. THIRD.   Nor I, and yet methinks I should command;
                 But, seeing I cannot, I'll entreat for him.—
                 My lord, if you will let my uncle live,   2435
                 I will requite it when I come to age.
Y. MOR.   'Tis for your highness' good and for the realm's.—
                 How often shall I bid you bear him hence?
KENT.   Art thou king? must I die at thy command?
Y. MOR.   At our command. – Once more away with him.   2440
KENT.   Let me but stay and speak; I will not go.
                 Either my brother or his son is king, And none of both
                 them thirst for Edmund's blood:
                 And therefore, soldiers, whither will you hale me?

SOLDIERS *hale* KENT *away, and carry him to be beheaded.*

(*Complete Plays*, London: OUP, 1966)

One notes how, here, after the initial setting-up of the communicative situation through information-seeking questions and corresponding information-bearing responses (the latter serving in Austin's terminology, as natural 'illocutionary sequels' invited by the requests), the interaction develops as a series of directly conflicting semiotic moves, on the outcome of which the life of Kent is seen to depend. Mortimer's brutal command (l. 2425) – whose perlocutionary effect is delayed until the end of the sequence – is countered by Kent's explicitly performative act of defiance (articulated as a rhetorical question and an assertion). The young king attempts to intervene by means of an executive affirmation of his regal power, promptly overridden by Mortimer's counter-affirmation, indicating the latter's relative potency. Kent attempts a defensive perlocutionary move, unsuccessfully ordering the guards to ignore Mortimer's original command. The king performs, on Kent's behalf, a kind of meta-illocution, entreating his mother to entreat, in turn, the protector; this again is perlocutionarily unsuccessful, causing him to appeal directly to Mortimer, in an elaborately explicit fashion, but again without result. Mortimer's rhetorical question in l. 2438 is an effective, if indirect, reassertion of his opening move, the command to execute Kent. The latter's response, also a rhetorical question, acts as a further statement of defiance, denying

Mortimer's *right* to perform the illocution of sentencing him to death. The illocution in question, however, is impatiently and overtly repeated (l. 2440), at which Kent attempts a desperate syllogistic persuasion of the guards – the final stage direction indicates which of these two final speech acts meets with perlocutionary success.

This is an emblematic – but in no sense unusual – instance of the essential dramatic action (or interaction) being directly constituted by discourse itself. The dialogue *is* immediate 'spoken action' rather than reference to, or representation *of*, action, so that the central personal, political and moral oppositions which structure the drama are seen and heard to be *acted out* in the communicational exchange, and not described at a narrative remove: 'Thus conflict is enacted, not in an idealized clash of positions or beliefs, whatever that would be. Illocutionary acts move the play along' (Ohmann 1973, p. 89).

Among the politico-ethical conflicts carried by the speech acts in the Marlowe passage is, as we have seen, the very question of the legitimacy of Mortimer's illocutions. Kent disputes the latter's *authority* to assume the role of 'commander' of the guards. This meta-pragmatic dispute raises explicitly one of the major problems confronted by Austin and later speech-act theorists, namely that of the *felicity conditions* governing the performance of illocutionary acts and, in particular, determining whether they are successful or defective (happy or unhappy, in Austin's terminology (1962, pp. 136 ff.)). Searle (1969, pp. 60 ff.) distinguishes three principal kinds of conditions which must be met in order to fulfil a non-defective speech act.

1   *Preparatory* conditions: the speaker must be authorized to perform the act. For instance, he must be legally entitled to name the ship or, as in the Marlowe piece, to sentence to death; he must have evidence for what he says; he must be ignorant, in the case of a question, of what he inquires about, etc.

2   *Sincerity* conditions: the speaker must mean what he says, believe it to be true, etc.; he must genuinely want, for example, the requested information; he must be genuinely grateful for what he gives thanks for, must believe that his advice is of authentic benefit to the listener, and so on.

3   *Essential* conditions: he is obliged by a promise to undertake the

action indicated; he is committed by an assertion to a particular belief – the utterance, that is, *counts as* a particular kind of social commitment or undertaking.

It is evident that much of the drama is structured precisely on the *abuse* of these conditions, and thus on the production of speech acts known to be defective to the audience but accepted as 'happy' by the dramatic interlocutor. All plays based on acts of deception depend on such abuse. The most familiar instance, perhaps, is Iago's deceiving of Othello in a scene (III. iii) where the spectator is able to follow Iago's global illocutionary-perlocutionary strategy (he performs what Van Dijk (1977, pp. 238 ff.) terms a *macro*-speech act, i.e. a sequence of individual illocutions – in this case indirect – which count as a single overall act, that of accusing Desdemona) fully aware that it is defective on every ground. Iago abuses all the 'felicity conditions' in equal measure: the preparatory conditions, since he has no evidence for his insinuations; the sincerity conditions, since he knows what he is insinuating to be false; and the essential conditions, since he is plainly not committed to the fact that the advice he gives – 'Look to your wife; observe her well with Cassio' – is in any way of benefit to his interlocutor. Again, the moral and the semiotic issues are indivisible in the play.

There is a further form of 'infelicity' which is commonly manifested in the drama, in this case in comedy especially. Being an intersubjective phenomenon, the speech act cannot be successfully performed unless the speaker gets the listener to *recognize* his illocutionary intentions. The utterance 'There's a bull in that field' does not count as a successful warning if the listener takes it as a nature-lover's effusion: 'I cannot be said to have warned an audience unless it hears what I say and takes what I say in a certain sense' (Austin 1962, p. 116). Austin calls the listener's recognition of the speaker's illocutionary intentions the 'securing of uptake' (1962, p. 117): without it, the intended illocution is doomed to failure. Comedy is full of such 'infelicities' caused by the non-securing of uptake, the result usually being a form of 'talking at cross-purposes' where the interlocutors reciprocally defeat each other's attempts at conversational progress:

DOCTOR.   What can I do for you?

ALEXANDER. I have a complaint.
DOCTOR. (*Opening file*) Yes, I know – pathological development of the personality with paranoid delusions.
ALEXANDER. No, there's nothing the matter with me.
DOCTOR. (*Closing file*) There you are, you see.

(Tom Stoppard, *Every Good Boy Deserves Favour*)

A would-be complaint is taken as a confession, and a denial as an indirect confirmation. This is a risk that all speakers run, due to the awkward fact that distinct semiotic functions may be fulfilled by the same syntactic form: 'the same utterance act may be performed with a variety of different intentions . . . one and the same utterance may constitute the performance of several different illocutionary acts' (Searle 1969, p. 70). In appropriate contexts, the interrogative sentence 'Is the window open?' may act as a request for information, an assertion of surprise, as a command (to close the window), and so on. It is the listener's task to attribute to the utterance its correct *illocutionary force* – its status *as* question, assertion, command, etc. Only if the listener interprets the force accurately is the designed speech act fully carried out.

The question of 'uptake', the recognition of illocutionary force, enters directly, like other speech-act problems, into the proairetic ('action') and moral fabric of the drama. The interpretative efforts of the listener are dramatized in *Richard II*, where Exton endeavours to divine accurately the force of a rhetorical question issued by Bolingbroke, which he takes to be an indirect request addressed personally to him:

Didst thou not mark the king, what words he spake?
'Have I no friends will rid me of this living fear?'

And speaking it, he wistly looked on me,
As who should say, 'I would thou wert the man
That would divorce this terror from my heart' . . .

(v. iv. 1–2, 7–9)

Exton's initiative in reading an interrogative utterance act in terms of a designed request – that is, as an indirect speech act – is of some moment to the outcome of the drama, since his acting on his conclusions takes the form of the murder of Richard (for which 'perlocutionary' sequel Exton is not thanked). The opposite process – an all too literal reading of an interrogative utterance act, with the consequent failure to 'secure uptake' by recognizing its illocutionary force – is meditated on by Paul de Man with reference to a piece of popular television drama, where the consequences are farcical rather than tragic:

> . . . asked by his wife whether he wants to have his bowling shoes laced over or laced under, Archie Bunker answers with a question: 'What's the difference?' Being a reader of sublime simplicity, his wife replies by patiently explaining the difference between lacing over and lacing under, whatever this may be, but provokes only ire. 'What's the difference' did not ask for difference but means instead 'I don't give a damn what the difference is'.

The problem is again the distinction between form and function, since 'A perfectly clear syntactical paradigm (the question) engenders a sentence that has at least two meanings of which the one asserts and the other denies its own illocutionary mode' (de Man 1973, p. 29).

What is the speaker really 'saying' when he 'says' a particular sequence of morphemes? This interpretative problem is not limited to dramatic listeners but involves us as auditors, readers, directors or actors of the drama. The difference between 'sentence-meaning' and 'utterer's meaning' (see Grice 1968) is one of the crucial concerns in any 'reading' of a play. Does Cordelia intend her refusal to outdo her sisters in praise as a statement of defiance, as an apology (for her lack of facility), as a plea (for exemption) or as a cool assertion of a state of affairs?

Such ambiguity is what permits the actor to 'interpret' the role rather than merely recite the lines. By disambiguating (or by rendering still more ambiguous) the illocutionary mode of the utterances through such 'illocutionary force indicators' as stress, intonation, kinesic markers and facial expressions (see Austin 1962, pp. 73 ff.; Searle 1969, pp. 30 ff.), the actor is able to suggest the intentions, purposes and motivations involved. If dramatic discourse were illocutionarily self-sufficient on the page, the performance would be all but superfluous.

It is never possible, then, to determine finally and absolutely from the written text all the illocutions performed in a play, although such factors as the use of explicit performative verbs ('I beg you') and the reactions of the interlocutors will often assist the process of interpretation, allowing a speech-act analysis (which will also be hermeneutic reading) of the drama to be conducted. For such a purpose, however, one requires an adequate classification of act-types, and in particular of illocutionary acts.

Various typologies of illocutionary acts have been devised, some, like Austin's, on the basis of English verbs and others, like Searle's, on more analytic grounds. It is Searle's (1975b) taxonomy which is perhaps most directly useful for purposes of dramatic analysis. He distinguishes five broad classes of illocution, which can be illustrated by more or less familiar (and explicitly performative) Shakespearian examples:

1   *Representatives*, committing the speaker to the truth of the proposition asserted. They are close to Austin's original 'constatives' (but are none the less acts): 'I say the earth did shake when I was born' (*1 Henry IV*, III. i. 21); 'I tell thee, fellow, thy general is my lover' (*Coriolanus*, V. ii. 13); 'I swear to you, I think Helen loves him better than Paris' (*Troilus*, I. ii. 114–15).

2   *Directives*, attempts to get the listener to do something, whether it be to perform a deed, to give the speaker something, or simply to provide information (thus commands, requests, challenges, advice, questions, etc.): 'Keep close, I thee command' (*Henry V*, II. iii. 66); 'Good brother, let me request you off' (*Antony and Cleopatra*, II. vii. 126–7); 'I beg for justice which thou, prince, must give' (*Romeo*, III. i. 186).

3   *Commissives*, committing the speaker to a future course of action (thus promises, vows, contracts, undertakings, etc.): 'Here on my knees, I vow to God above, I'll never pause again' (*3 Henry VI*, II. iii. 29–30); 'By the hand of a soldier, I will undertake it' (*All's Well*, III. vi. 76); 'I warrant, an I should live a thousand years, I never should forget it' (*Romeo*, I. iii. 46–7).

4   *Expressives*, conventional acts such as thanking, greeting,

congratulating, whose sincerity conditions include a particular psychological state: 'I thank thee, most imperious Agamemnon' (*Troilus*, IV. v. 171); 'Fair princess, welcome to the court of Navarre' (*Love's Labour's Lost*, II. i. 90); 'I greet your honours from Andronicus' (*Titus Andronicus*, IV. ii. 5).

5   *Declarations*, those acts which, if performed 'happily', actually bring about the state of affairs proposed, e.g. designating someone a candidate, declaring war, marrying a couple. Such acts were included among Austin's original 'performatives'. They are of particular importance to the drama, since their successful performance usually changes the course of events in an immediate ('dramatic') fashion: 'We banish thee for ever' (*Timon of Athens*, III. v. 100); 'We here create thee the first Duke of Suffolk' (2 *Henry VI*. I. i. 65); 'We do condemn thee to the very block' (*Measure for Measure*, V. i. 415).

The immediate utility of such a taxonomy to dramatic analysis is that it allows the extension of the 'typology of discourse' founded on interpersonal deictic strategies. Certain 'stock' figures will tend to operate on a single illocutionary axis (e.g. Polonius on that of the 'directive', at least with his children), while rhetorically rich characters will exploit a range of illocutionary modes, depending on context and addressee (consider the rapid changes of axis adopted by Richard III or Volpone). Still more, the relationships between figures can be more accurately defined in terms of their reciprocal illocutionary moves within the I–you exchange (for an application of the taxonomy to a dialogic exchange, see pp. 170–1, 174 ff. below).

Richard Ohmann has suggested a further possible extension of the speech-act anatomy of the drama: that is, as a basis for a *generic* typology of dramatic discourse:

> Thus comedy, particularly as it approaches farce, is likely to establish its world through a repetitive or mechanical series of speech acts [he quotes as an example *The Importance of Being Earnest*]. . . . By contrast, tragedies are often more varied in illocutionary acts, as if to establish at the start a fuller range of human emotion and action. *Hamlet* begins with a question, a refusal, two commands, a kind of

loyalty oath ('Long live the king'), a question, a statement, a compliment, a statement, an order, thanks, and a complaint – all this, of course, between two guardsmen. (1971, p. 253)

What must be emphasized is that a breakdown of the illocutionary-perlocutionary interaction in the drama is not limited to its 'surface structure' (mere *lexis*) but, more often than not, accounts for the central events of the play. A reasonably detailed paraphrase of the plot of such a work as *Doctor Faustus* (not usually thought of as 'lacking in action') is in large measure an annotation of individual and global (macro-) illocutions: Faustus determines to abandon his academic studies in favour of magical practices (commissive); he is assailed by the good and evil angels, who advise him, respectively, to refrain from and to pursue the black arts (conflicting directives); Faustus reaffirms his pledge (commissive) and is encouraged by Valdes and Cornelius who promise him wondrous potency (complementary commissives); Faustus declares his pleasure at the prospect (expressive) and requests to see demonstrations of such powers (directive); Faustus conjures up a devil and Mephistophilis (perlocutionarily successful directives), and so on until the critical event of the play, itself a global speech act (a long-term and complex commissive), Faustus's exchanging of his soul for twenty-four years of super-mundane potency.

Speech acts on stage

Speech acts are subject to all the conditions outlined on pp. 108 ff. for the definition of action, and, in particular, of interaction. They involve agents (speakers), patients (listeners), intentions (illocutionary), purposes (perlocutionary) – and so intention-success and purpose-success (see Van Dijk 1977, pp. 198 ff.) – together with an act-type, a modality (they can be oral, written or even, on occasion, gestural) and a setting (the communicative situation). Like other acts, moreover, they are articulated at different levels of 'basicness'.

This raises the possibility of applying to dramatic discourse the distinction drawn on p. 108 between the 'basic' onstage doings of the actors and the higher-order deeds attributed, on this basis, to the dramatic agents. Who is it who actually performs the illocution: the dramatis persona or the actor who utters his words? Who, in other words, is really 'speaking'? It might seem that the 'basic', 'complex' distinction valid for the representation of other acts does not apply to the linguistic variety. In order to represent the utterance (itself a 'representative') 'Living night and day with another human being has made me predatory and suspicious', supposedly issued by John Osborne's Jimmy Porter, the actor does nothing different from the character: he actually *says*, together with a certain gestural and paralinguistic colouring, 'Living night and day. . . .' In so doing, does he not carry out the full speech act attributed to the character?

In fact, he does not, and for much the same reason that an actor playing Macbeth does not actually engage in a swordfight with Macduff (or with the actor portraying him). What the actor performs is the basic utterance act of articulating or 'saying' the lines in a comprehensible fashion. He has no illocutionary intentions in saying them – the request, say, *as* a request belongs only to the dramatic context, defined according to the interpersonal relations obtaining in it. Responsibility for the utterance as a full speech act, with all its possible moral and social consequences, is attributed to the dramatic and not the stage speaker:

> [Actors], as opposed to the fictional characters they portray, do not command, question and assert by their use of imperatival, interrogative and declarative sentences respectively. E.g. they, as opposed to the characters they portray, cannot be charged with having asserted something false, having issued an unwise command, etc., for they only pretend to assert and command these things. (Gale 1971, p. 337; see also Urmson 1972; Searle 1975c)

It is the audience's task to interpret the physical 'sayings' on stage as higher-order speech events in the dramatic world. In order to do so, it must project both a set of intentions on the part of the speaker and a semiotic competence (allowing 'uptake' to be secured) on the part of the listener. This is a major aspect of the spectator's role in 'constructing' the dramatic world.

THE SAID AND THE UNSAID: IMPLICATURES AND FIGURES

Conversational rules and implicatures

As we have seen – it is Exton's problem – not everything 'meant' by the speaker is explicitly said. If the drama can be justly said to 'ride on a train of illocutions', then it must be added that these are often oblique and call for an interpretative 'reading between the lines'. But on what principles are these unspoken meanings communicated in the drama?

Participants in speech events are engaged in a form of interaction, which means that they share not only a common language and more or less similar logical and epistemological principles but also an agreed end in view, that is, the achievement of an effective and coherent exchange. As H. P. Grice observes, the successful conduct of linguistic interaction is possible only on the basis of a joint commitment to the communicative objective:

> Our talk exchanges do not normally consist of a succession of discon-nected remarks, and would not be rational if they did. They are charac-teristically, to some degree at least, cooperative efforts; and each participant recognizes in them, to some extent, a common purpose or set of purposes, or at least a mutually accepted direction. (1967, p. 45)

Grice formulates this general requirement as a global conversational rule, which he names the *cooperative principle*: 'Make your conversational contribution such as is required, at the stage at which it occurs, by the accepted purpose or direction of the talk exchange in which you are engaged' (1967, p. 45). What he argues, then, is that the exchange is regulated by indispensable principles of decorum allowing coherence and continuity. These principles are stated as maxims implicitly governing the participants' contributions:

1   The maxims of *quantity*. (a) The contribution should be as informa-tive as is required for the purposes of the exchange. (b) The contribution should not be more informative than is required.

2   The maxims of *quality*, expressible as the supermaxim 'Try to make

the contribution one that is true'. (a) The speaker should not say what he knows to be false. (b) He should not say that for which he lacks evidence. (N.B. these correspond to Searle's 'sincerity conditions'.)

3 The maxim of *relation*, i.e. 'Be relevant'.

4 The maxims of *manner*, expressible as a supermaxim, 'Be perspicuous'. (a) The speaker should avoid obscurity. (b) He should avoid ambiguity. (c) He should avoid unnecessary prolixity. (d) He should be orderly.

Such rules are in themselves very generic and by no means always applicable to an equal degree, but it is, in effect, the *breaking* of these canons which is of interest. Grice goes on to show how the speaker may exploit the maxims in order to mean more than he says – it is on the basis of these conversational rules that 'unspoken' meanings are often understood. If, when asked by an author to give a judgement of his novel, a critic replies 'Well, I read it carefully. It has an interesting cover and an attractive layout', the novelist will normally take the statement as an oblique comment on the book's content. It is evident that the first maxim of quantity has been broken here, not because the critic cannot give the requested information (he has read the book) and not, presumably, because he is being uncooperative (he chooses to answer) but, plainly, because he has an opinion which he is reluctant to express directly. The critic, in Grice's terminology, *implicates* the unspoken meaning, which thus has the status of a *conversational implicature*.

Implicatures may be produced through the deliberate 'flouting' or 'exploiting' of any one of the maxims listed above, and are understood by the listener on the basis of his assumption that the speaker is *continuing to cooperate* in the exchange, and so, since his contribution is apparently defective or inadequate in itself, must mean more than he says. The blatant flouting of the maxim of relation, for example, generates an implicature in the following situation: A remarks to B 'I haven't seen your wife for a long time. How come?', at which C, after a pause, tells A 'What a fine tie you have'. A will conclude from C's apparently irrelevant intervention that his remark is for some reason out of place (B's wife has died, run off with the milkman, etc.). The supermaxim of manner – 'Be perspicuous' – similarly, can be exploited in order to communicate something which a third party is not to know (and to communicate the *fact* that he is not to know), as when a husband wishes to inform his wife, in front of their child, of a friend's amorous adventures, and comments, obscurely, 'Young Bill's been sowing a lot of seeds lately'.

Implicatures are produced in the drama on similar grounds, that is, the assumed observance by the participants (unless otherwise indicated) of a cooperative principle during the exchange. The conversational maxims, naturally, must be modified according to the dialogic, monologic and rhetorical conventions at work (the requirement 'avoid prolixity', for instance, is scarcely applicable in the case of Elizabethan and modern poetic drama). We do, nevertheless, expect dramatic speakers to produce utterances which are informative (indeed, this constraint is, perhaps, stronger than in the case of 'everyday' talk), 'true' with respect to the dramatic world (unless strategically insincere), comprehensible and relevant to the occasion. On such expectations the audience bases – and supposes the dramatic listener to base – the 'reading between the lines' which makes up a considerable part of its decoding.

In Trevor Griffiths's play *Occupations* the Bulgarian Communist Kabak encounters Terrini, a Commendatore from the Prefect's office, whose task it is to order him out of Italy. The exchange proceeds through indirection, however, since Terrini is reluctant to declare his mission openly:

KABAK. What can I do for you, Commendatore?
TERRINI. Your presence in Turin this past three weeks hasn't gone entirely unnoticed, Mr Kabak.

Terrini implicates the *undesirability* of Kabak's presence to the police, and does so by flouting the first maxim of quantity (his reply is not as informative as is required to explain his visit, yet the visit itself indicates his willingness to communicate: conclusion, he is obliquely requesting the *removal* of Kabak's presence). Later in the same exchange Terrini produces a further implicature by infringing the first maxim of manner, 'avoid obscurity':

KABAK. I'm supposed to have done something? Infringed a business code, perhaps? Even so, it's hardly a matter for the Prefect to concern himself with.

TERRINI. Not . . . business, Mr Kabak. Not, at least, the sort of business you are ostensibly here to pursue.

Terrini's circumlocutory mode here suggests, without specifying, that the 'business' in question is political (both speakers know of Kabak's revolutionary activities, Terrini is presumably still willing to cooperate, hence the circumlocution must be intended as a negative definition).

Exploitation in the drama of the second maxim of manner ('avoid ambiguity') is a common source of that form of double meaning which is seen to be strategic rather than inadvertent. Juliet's apparent expression of mortal hatred towards Romeo after the death of Tybalt is a celebrated instance:

JULIET. Indeed, I never shall be satisfied
With Romeo, till I behold him – dead –
Is my poor heart so for a kinsman vex'd.

(III. v. 94–6)

According to one 'reading' – that which she wants the interlocutor, Lady Capulet, to accept – Juliet is declaring a desire for revenge ('till I behold him [Romeo] dead'). Punctuated differently, however, the utterance becomes, instead, an expression of longing for the 'kinsman', i.e. Romeo ('till I behold him / Dead is my poor heart . . .'). In this case, the second meaning is communicated only to the audience, which, unlike Lady Capulet, is in possession of the knowledge necessary for such an interpretation (for an analysis of this passage, see Rutelli 1978, pp. 94–5).

Implicatures generated by the flouting of the relation rule ('be relevant') are, perhaps, most commonly found in comedies depicting 'polite society', where social gaffes or unwelcome comments meet with loaded silences, changes of subject or indirect disapproval. Lady Windermere, in Wilde's play, communicates her displeasure at a proffered compliment by producing (after a significant silence) an apparently unconnected response:

LORD DARLINGTON (*sitting down*). I wish I had known it was your birth-
day, Lady Windermere. I would have covered the
whole street in front of your house with flowers for
you to walk on. They are made for you. (*A short
pause.*)

LADY WINDERMERE. Lord Darlington, you annoyed me last night at the
Foreign Office. I am afraid you are going to annoy
me again.

The examples given are all cases of rule-infringement manifested
within the framework of a presumably continuing commitment to
communicative cooperation. It is, of course, possible for one of the
participants to refuse such cooperation either by opting out of the
exchange altogether or by violating the maxims in such a way as to
undermine the interaction (and thus the efforts of the interlocutor).
This latter strategy is that adopted, notably, by Hamlet in his relations
with such interlocutors as Claudius and Polonius: his violations of the
maxims of manner ('Not so, my lord; I am too much in the sun'; 'The
body is with the king, but the king is not with the body'), quantity
('There's ne'er a villain dwelling in all Denmark / But he's an arrant
knave'), quality ('excellent well, you are a fishmonger') and relation
('*Pol*. My lord, the queen would speak with you, and presently / *Ham*.
Do you see yonder cloud . . . ?') function not as vehicles for indirect
meanings directed (co-operatively) towards the dramatic listener but
rather as means of subverting the logic (and so the power) of his
antagonists.

Certain forms of modern drama are based on the radical suspension
of interactional 'decorum'. This is the case, for example, with dadaist
and absurdist drama and the plays of such contemporary writers as
Foreman and Handke. The 'violation of the postulates of normal communication' in Ionesco's *The Bald Soprano* has been analysed by the Soviet
semioticians Revzina and Revzin (1975). Ionesco's dialogue – in
Grice's terms – contravenes consistently the maxims of relation ('*Mr
Martin*. One doesn't polish spectacles with black wax. / *Mrs Smith*. Yes,
but with money one can buy anything.'); quantity (i.e. the second
maxim, by giving superfluous information: 'There, it's nine o'clock.
We've drunk the soup, and eaten the fish and chips, and the English

salad. The children have drunk English water . . .'); and quality ('Fire Chief. I should like to remove my helmet but I haven't time to sit down. [He sits down, without removing his helmet.]'). The Soviet analysts define Ionesco's aberrant discourse as a 'semiotic experiment', since in transgressing communicational rules it explores their character and extent:

> He implicitly introduces the concept of 'normal' communication and studies the conditions under which such communication is possible. . . . The basic principle of the experiment remains the same: by violating the customary canons we define their borders and the extent to which their operation is necessary. (Revzina and Revzin 1975, pp. 245, 266)

Rhetorical figures

This kind of rule-based analysis can be extended, according to Grice, to include those 'figures of speech' which, in making evidently non-literal reference to the context or to the world at large, are seen to contravene the first maxim of quality (the 'truthfulness' rule). Falstaff's banal antiphrasis (one-word irony) in addressing his diminutive page as 'Sirrah, you giant' (2 Henry IV, I. ii. 1) functions in this way by clearly predicating of the addressee the exact contrary of his verifiable qualities, just as his later litotes (understatement) in referring to his own legendary stature – 'with a white head and something a round belly' (I. ii. 188) – sets up a comical distance between the reference and the all-too-visible referent.

Irony and litotes are among those rhetorical figures which, according to the Belgian linguists of Groupe μ, 'imply knowledge of the referent in order to contradict its faithful description' (thereby breaking Grice's 'quality rule') (1970, V. O. 1). Such logical and referential figures (as opposed to semantic and syntactic ones) are named *metalogisms* by Groupe μ. They are context-bound devices to the extent that they depend on the audience's ability to *measure* the gap, as it were, between reference and referent ('you giant' does not work as an antiphrasis if the addressee is a basketball player). Other metalogistic figures include paradox, antithesis and – the 'positive' counterpart of litotes – hyperbole, colourfully exemplified in Volpone's effusive apostrophe to his gold:

> Hail, the world's soul, and mine! . . .
> That, lying here amongst my other hoards,
> Show'st like a flame by night, or like the day
> Struck out of chaos, when all darkness fled
> Unto the centre.

Metalogisms, being 'pragmatic' figures par excellence, appear, as Serpieri has argued, to have a central place in the rhetoric of the drama: they belong primarily 'to the ostensive, deictic situation; in a word to the énonciation. And where is this seen more radically than in the theatre?' (1979, p. 155). In the past, rhetorical analysis of plays has been principally devoted to the study of imagery, tropes, and schemes – that is, it has been limited to a largely literary approach concerned with those semantic and syntactic patterns which, typically, characterize poetic discourse in general. But while tropes and schemes unquestionably abound in much drama, it is arguable that dramatic rhetoric is carried less by imagery patterns than by figurative acts defined as such within the speaking situation and involving the speaker, the addressee and their 'world' directly.

The role of rhetorical figures in the dramatic interaction is perhaps seen most clearly in the case of the metalogistic figure of antithesis, which in poetry often has the effect of creating a logical or conceptual balance, but in the drama, typically, carries the conflicting propositional, illocutionary and ethical commitments of the speakers. It appears conspicuously in the encounter between Richard III and Anne of Gloucester (where it is compounded with a further metalogism, asteismus, the 'picking up' of a term in the linguistic co-text in order to modify its sense or reference):

> GLOUCESTER. Fairer than tongue can name thee, let me have
> Some patient leisure to excuse myself.
> ANNE. Fouler than heart can think thee, thou canst make
> No excuse current, but to hang thyself.
> GLOUCESTER. By such despair I should accuse myself.

ANNE.   And by despairing shouldst thou stand excus'd . . .

(I. ii. 81 ff.)

TEXTUALITY

Dramatic and 'everyday' discourse: some considerations

In its 'pragmatic' articulation as a mode of context-bound interaction, dramatic discourse is close to verbal exchange in society, and follows certain of the constitutive and regulative rules of extra-dramatic conversation. The equation, however, cannot be taken very far. The drama presents what is very much a 'pure' model of social intercourse, and the dialogue bears a very limited resemblance to what actually takes place in 'everyday' linguistic encounters. Compare for example, the following two passages, the first from a relatively idiomatic modern dramatic text (Sam Shepard's *The Tooth of Crime*) and the second from the transcript of an actual café conversation:

A

BECKY.   What happened to Jack?

BOSS.   We ran the session.

BECKY.   Here's your drink.

BOSS.   Thanks. Listen, Becky, is Cheyenne ready to roll?

BECKY.   Yeah. He's hot. Why?

BOSS.   Maybe we could just do a cruise. No action. Just some scouting. I'm really feelin' cooped up in here. This place is drivin' me nuts.

BECKY.   Too dangerous, Hoss. We just got word that Eyes sussed somebody's marked you.

BOSS.   What! Marked *me*? Who?

BECKY.   One a' the Gypsies.

BOSS.   It's all comin' down like I said. I must be top gun then.

BECKY.   That's it.

B

c. excuse me ↗   I hate to do this but I'm bringing it back 'cause it's stale ↘

S. ow well I'll make you another one ↘

C. ok ↘   thanks a lot ↘   I I kinda feel bad doing that but

D. I guess so eh ↗   (laughter) well it's your own fault ↗

C. I do ↘

S. is that more to your liking ↗

C. yeah ok well I feel rotten bringing it back ↘

D. well no ↗

overlap {
S. well if you're not satisfied you should why should why should you eat something you've paid for

C. I know

S. if you

C. I know

S. don't want it 'cause it's not . . . fresh

(Gregory and Carroll 1978, pp. 101–2)

It will be immediately evident that the Shepard passage is altogether better ordered and more coherent than the transcript, but it might be worthwhile to identify some of the differences involved and, more generally, to consider the major ways in which the dramatic exchange differs systematically from any 'real-life' equivalent.

1   *Syntactic orderliness.* Dramatic dialogue generally proceeds through syntactically complete or self-sufficient utterances, while 'everyday' exchanges are less neatly segmented. While passage B progresses through incomplete and dangling sentences, false starts and repetitions ('you should why should why should you'), passage A, although scarcely elaborate syntactically, falls into well-demarcated units. This has to do not only with the 'composed' quality of the dramatic dialogue but with the requirements of comprehensibility and, as it were, *followability*, that constrain the drama: 'If the actor on stage spoke as people do in "real life", with frequent *non sequiturs*, false starts, allusions, digressions, sentence fragments, etc., . . . the audience would suspect that the actor had failed to learn his lines; and, more importantly, perhaps, the audience would be unlikely to be getting the information it needs to get' (Gregory and Carroll 1978, p. 43). The relative orderliness of the dramatic text similarly accounts for its *repeatability*. Everyday

exchanges are extremely difficult to re-enact in their fragmentariness and inconsequentiality, while dramatic discourse is fully contextualizable in a potentially unlimited number and variety of performances.

2   *Informational intensity.* Much of our ordinary conversation comprises what the anthropologist Malinowski termed 'phatic communion', verbal signalling which 'serves to establish bonds of personal union between people brought together by the need of companionship and does not serve any purpose of communicating ideas' (1930, p. 315). The 'social' function of conversation, that is, usually predominates over its descriptive or informational function: what is actually said is very often of less importance than the fact of saying something, and in consequence the semantic information in social exchanges is frequently low, especially when the participants have already formed a relationship. In the drama, on the contrary, the information-bearing role of language is normally constant: every utterance counts, everything said is significant and carries the action and 'world-creating' functions forward in some way. 'Phatic' signals, serving largely to establish or maintain contact, keep the conversation going, provide feedback to the speaker, rather than furnish information (in B such elements as 'ow well', 'I guess so eh', 'yeah ok well', 'well no', 'well', 'I know . . . I know') tend to be greatly reduced in the drama. Even characters – like Shepard's – who have a supposedly established relationship exchange informationally rich utterances.

3   *Illocutionary purity.* By the same token, dramatic dialogue is illocutionarily purer than 'real-life' exchanges. If much of social intercourse is taken up with keeping itself going and maintaining the relationships involved, the kinds of speech act performed will often be indistinct and of relatively little import. In the drama, as we have seen, the illocutionary progress of the dialogue is essential to the development of the action. This is true especially at the level of macro-speech acts, which in the drama form far better-structured and more coherent global units than any conceivable extra-dramatic version, each individual illocution generating the next in a dynamic chain.

4   *Floor-apportionment control.* One of the more evident differences

between the two passages given above is the relative orderliness with which Shepard's characters alternate as speakers. There are none of the overlaps and interruptions which conspicuously characterize B. The much-studied issue of *floor-apportionment* – the determination of turns at talking (see Sacks *et al.* 1974; Goffman 1975; Pratt 1977) – rarely arises in the drama in so far as the dialogue is traditionally articulated into well-defined contributions or speeches, one following the other (and indeed *generated* by the other) in a logical and comprehensible fashion: '[in the drama] there is a cross-turn scripting. Every statement – save perhaps the first – made by a character can be one that was "set up" by the prior speaker' (Goffman 1974, p. 510). The possibility of 'competition' through overlap and interruption is again limited for obvious reasons of 'followability', but in any case turn-taking rights are established on dramaturgical grounds rather than on democratic conversational principles. It is predetermined that the protagonist will have more and longer 'turns' than minor characters, that the most important information-bearing or world-changing speeches will be allowed to unfold without interruption, without the speaker's having to request special 'rights', etc. Thus the kind of battles for the floor which occur in extra-dramatic conversation, whereby potential next-speakers attempt to 'book' the right to talk by overlapping or echoing the current speaker, asking permission to interrupt, overriding other would-be speakers, etc. (see Sacks *et al.* 1974), are circumvented in the drama through the need to focus on the major figures, to allow them as much talking space as they require (even in the form of monologuing) in order that they fulfil their dramatic functions, to follow their contributions one at a time, etc.

Textual coherence

What accounts for these systematic differences is, in short, the degree of textual control to which dramatic discourse is subject. While a spontaneous conversation can be considered as a text to the extent that it forms a distinct unit more or less coherently structured semantically and pragmatically (the speakers share the same objects and topics of discourse, their utterances are linked co-referentially, etc.; see Petöfi and Rieser 1973; Van Dijk 1972, 1975, 1977; Dressler 1977), it is clear that the textual constraints governing its progress are far looser than those regulating dramatic dialogue. Accordingly, digressions, redundancies, non sequiturs, sudden changes of topic and even an over-all inconclusiveness are often permitted without detriment to the 'purpose-success' of the conversation. Dramatic dialogue, on the other hand, is normally powerfully constrained throughout by various levels of textual coherence. These levels can be summarized as follows:

Proairetic ('action') coherence. The dialogue bears, in the form of both the speech acts performed through it and the extra-linguistic actions reported by it, the chief responsibility for manifesting the proairetic dynamic of the drama. This imposes a strict temporal ordering and an underlying action structure on the progress of the speech acts which in non-dramatic texts are less binding.

Referential coherence. In its 'world-creating' role, the dialogue is subject to greater referential and co-referential controls than spontaneous texts. The necessity of creating and maintaining a consistent universe of discourse whose elements the audience can readily identify entails a limited and more or less stable range of dramatic 'referents' whose properties are maintained, unless otherwise indicated.

Discourse coherence. Each exchange or monologue within the drama, according to the 'followability' requirement, will be geared towards a clear 'topic' of discourse (or overall 'theme'), changes in which will be plainly signalled. Similarly, the individual 'objects' of discourse (referred to in the course of the exchange or monologue) will be introduced in a strategic order, rather than at random (as is often the case in ordinary conversation).

Logical coherence. In addition to the consistency of the propositional content of the dialogue with respect to the dramatic world at large, individual characters may come to create more or less coherent 'sub-worlds' in the course of the play. The propositional attitudes expressed by the characters in referring to the 'actual' dramatic world or alternative 'possible' worlds of their own creating will normally indicate reliably the status of the 'world' in question (as the world of the speaker's wishes, fantasies, etc.). The modalities involved (deontic, boulomaeic, etc.) may come to be characteristic of the dramatis persona (see next section).

Rhetorical and stylistic coherence. A powerful dramatic text will create its own 'idiolect', an overall style characterized by recurrent syntactic and rhetorical patterns, lexical iteration (repetition and variation of the same words and phrases), dominant illocutionary modes, etc. Individual dramatis personae may be distinguished by similar patterns – a favourite type of speech act, a characteristic rhetorical figure or group of figures, a distinct personal lexicon, etc. The drama will often develop as a configuration of opposing rhetorical forces, manifested by one or sometimes more than one character (not every figure will represent a distinct rhetorical power).

Semantic coherence. Continuity at the level of the denoted and connoted signifieds of the drama arises through the operation of *isotopies*, i.e. the 'homogeneous semantic levels' at which 'whole texts are situated' (Greimas 1966, p. 53). Isotopies are formed, according to Greimas, through the recurrence of *semes*, the basic 'atoms' of meaning whose reappearance creates contextual restrictions on meaning (or *classemes*). Thus the sentence 'I love English runners' will be taken to refer (a) to athletes or (b) to green beans, depending on whether the isotopy of 'sport' or 'food' is at work. Isotopies account for the coherent decoding of texts. Where there is more than one possible level of consistent interpretation (e.g. in Middleton's *A Game at Chess* where the isotopies 'game' and 'political system' are simultaneously operative), the text is said to be *pluriisotopic*.

TOWARDS A DRAMATOLOGICAL ANALYSIS

Uniting the analytic criteria

In this chapter a somewhat eclectic range of analytic criteria has been brought together in order to throw light on dramatic discourse. It is suggested that the pragmatic, semantic and rhetorical perspectives outlined here are more directly pertinent to the understanding of the language of the drama than are traditional literary-critical considerations or, indeed, the available 'narratological' approaches. A fully *dramatological* analysis of a play – an analysis which respects the characteristic axes along which the drama and its meanings unfold – cannot ignore the interpersonal, interactional and contextual factors discussed here.

But in what way can these diverse categories be economically united so as to permit a coherent breakdown of dramatic dialogue and its semiotic functions? An attempt is made below to formulate a preliminary analytic 'grid' or, better, 'score', designed to meet this purpose.

A dramatological score

The eighteen-column scheme given below represents what is very much a micro-segmentation of the text in question, the first seventy-nine lines of Hamlet. Each segment of discourse – distinguished on the basis of a change in deictic orientation and/or illocutionary force – is broken down into its constituent 'parts' or semiotic functions, according to the pragmatic, rhetorical and semantic axes along which it operates. Each column is founded on one of the categories discussed in this or other chapters.

The score can be read horizontally, so as to determine the different levels at which a given segment works simultaneously, or vertically, in order to establish the patterns running throughout the passage, the strategies of a given speaker, the development of the interaction and so on. The diagram does not represent, in itself, an interpretation of the text, although certain columns (notably the final two) are more directly hermeneutic in nature, and thus more open to discussion, than others. Nor does such a breakdown account for the macro-proairetic levels of szujet and fabula, which, quite clearly, must be taken into consideration in any interpretation of the play. It is limited, rather, to that aspect of the text most neglected in the past, the discourse – and so the micro-proairetic – stratum. As such it aims to provide a more precise instrument than those traditionally adopted for the anatomy of language, action, character, interrelationships and the very construction of the fictional world in the drama.

The columns

1 *Verse*. The line references are to the *Complete Works*, ed. W. J. Craig, London, OUP, 1905.

2 *Segment.* This does not necessarily coincide with a line or an individual speech, but registers a new deictic-illocutionary unit.

3 *Speaker.*

4 *Listener(s).* The first name given is that of the actual addressee; names in parentheses indicate the characters present and presumably participating as listeners but not directly addressed.

5 *Deictic orientation.* Explicit deictic references are represented symbolically as follows:

- **●** Person-deixis (*I/you/we/he*, etc.)
- **●͟**³ Proximal deictic orientation towards speaker (*I*)
- **●͟ᴾᴸ͜** Plural proximal deictic orientation towards speaker (*we*)
- **●‑** Orientation towards listener (*you*)
- **♦** Distal deictic orientation towards third person (*he/she/they*)
- **□** Spatial deixis
- **ϙ** Proximal deictic orientation towards context (*here*)
- **ḥ** Distal deictic orientation towards an elsewhere (*there*)
- **☉** Temporal deixis
- **♀** Proximal deictic orientation towards context time (*now*)
- **☿** Distal deictic orientation towards other time (*then*)
- **▲** Functional deixis
- **↑** Orientation towards current activity (e.g. towards *guard* below)
- **⊥** Orientation towards absent activity
- **■** Object deixis (N.B. the Ghost is indicated as object in the passage analysed)
- **⬛** Proximal orientation towards object present in current situation (*this/these*)
- **♦** Distal orientation towards removed or absent object (*that/those*)

6 *Tense.* Orientation towards present, past, future. Symbols as follows: Pres.: present; P.P.: present perfect; Pas.: past; Fut.: future; Subj.: subjunctive ('Long live . . .') Imp.: imperative. (The latter two, naturally, are not tenses but register particular attitudes.)

7 *Channel.* This is a somewhat heterogeneous column including the dominant physical channels along which the characters operate (acoustic or visual), together with physical, psychological, emotional and ideational states expressed by the speaker, references

entailing movements, etc. It registers the axes along which the communication unfolds (physical, mental and emotional), the involvement of the speaker's body in the communication and the individual characters' biases (towards the physical world, towards cerebration, towards their own bodies or their own emotional condition). In the passage analysed, it is interesting to note the alternation between the acoustic channel (associated with the unknown and with danger) and the visual (associated with the apparition of the Ghost). Cerebration is associated consistently with Horatio. Symbols:

§   Acoustic channel (emphasis on the act of hearing/speaking)
👁   Visual channel (emphasis on the act of looking, seeing)
†   The body (references to the speaker's or interlocutor's physical involvement in the scene)
‡†   Movement (reference entailing a definite kinesic event)
♡   Emotional state (reference to attitude or reaction)
◻   Cerebration (ideational bias, expression of concepts)

8   *Topic/object of discourse.* By 'topic of discourse' is meant the global theme or central concern of the exchange. Thus the passage analysed manifests three main topics: the guard itself, the Ghost and, finally, the background events explaining the present situation. The 'object of discourse', instead, is the individual person, object, event or notion referred to within each segment. Thus, within a given global topic, many objects will appear. These objects constitute the dramatic universe of discourse.

9   *Illocutionary force.* Searle's taxonomy has been adopted. There will inevitably be instances of ambiguity, but the *apparent* force of the utterance is indicated. Macro-speech acts do not arise in the passage analysed, but would require a separate annotation. The first symbol in the pair is taken from Searle (1975b) and the second invented in order to indicate more precisely the act-type involved. Symbols:

!   Directives
!!   Command

!? Question
!√ Invitation/request
⊢ Representatives
⊢‖ Assertion
⊢+ Affirmation
⊢− Negation
⊢≏ Hypothesis
E Expressives
E∪ Thanks
E⊃ Greeting/salute
E∩ Apology
C Commissives
CP Promise
CV Vow
C∪ Undertaking
D Declarations

Where the illocutionary force is given in parenthesis, an indirect speech act is indicated, while the first symbol indicates the apparent force involved. Thus ⊢‖(E∪) indicates an assertion which is also an indirect expression of thanks. One speech act which solicits another directly is represented by ▶ (thus a command is given as !!▶!!). A diagonal bar separating symbols indicates two acts within a single segment.

10 Explicit performative. A speech act whose illocutionary force is specified through a performative verb ('I order you . . .'). The presence of such a verb is indicated by a + sign.

11 Perlocutionary effect. If a given command, say, is obeyed, it achieves a perlocutionary effect, indicated by a + sign. If it is not obeyed, the failure to achieve the effect is indicated by a − sign. Where it is rendered null and void (impossible to carry out, for example), an X sign appears.

12 Implicatures/rhetorical figures. Unspoken meanings founded on the cooperative principle and the major context-bound figures of speech are indicated.

13 Modality/propositional attitudes. This is a 'logical' column concerned with the attitude expressed by the speaker towards the

propositional content of the utterance (belief, possibility, etc.) and thus the logical modality governing the segment. It indicates the speaker's stance both towards the dramatic world and towards his own discourse, and the terms in which the fictional world and alternative possible worlds are constructed. Symbols:

p	Alethic necessity (it is the case that p)
~p	Alethic necessity (negative) (it is not the case that p)
pos. p	Alethic possibility (it is possible that p)
?p	Alethic possibility: interrogative (is p?)
Hp	Alethic possibility: hypothesis (if p)
prob. p	Alethic probability (it is probable that p)
~ pos. p	Alethic impossibility (it is not possible that p)
Kp	Epistemic certainty (I know that p)
~Kp	Epistemic doubt (I do not know if p)
Bp	Doxastic modality (I believe that p)
~Bp	Doxastic modality (negative) (I do not believe that p)
Wp	Boulomaeic modality (I want/wish that p)
~Wp	Boulomaeic modality (negative) (I do not want/wish that p)
Op	Deontic modality of obligation (You must p)
~p	Deontic modality of non-obligation (You need not p)
O ~ p	Deontic modality of prohibition (You must not p)
Pp	Deontic modality of permission (You may p)

Where one modality incorporates another, square brackets are used. Thus W[kp] indicates 'I want to know p'. Round brackets indicate implicit modalities.

14 *Anaphora.* Two kinds of anaphoric reference are indicated: internal or endophoric reference (⇒) to an antecedent in the linguistic co-text (given in quotation marks) and external or exophoric reference (⇐) to an extra-linguistic 'it' or 'he' not present in the current situation and not specified in the co-text (N.B. the Ghost, never named as such, is continually referred to as an unspecified 'it'.) The presumed object of the reference is given in parentheses.

15 *Metalanguage.* This column includes all references to messages, the

code, idiolect, the act of speaking or listening, silence, language at large, etc. Every time, that is, language serves as object of discourse, it is annotated. Symbols:

M   Reference to message
C   Reference to code
I   Reference to idiolect or style
R   Reference to particular rhetorical or stylistic features
T   Reference to type of speech act (e.g. to the narrative 'story' in the passage analysed)
◒   Reference to the act of speaking
ᛕ   Reference to the act of listening
S   Reference to silence, non-speaking
L   Reference to language at large

16 *Other functions.* Any semiotic function (such as the 'phatic') not indicated elsewhere.

17 *Lexemes/isotopies/semantic paradigms.* This is a broadly 'semantic' column designed to indicate the chief levels of semantic and lexical coherence running throughout the passage. Important or repeated lexemes, consistent isotopies and paradigmatic connotations are indicated. Clearly this is an interpretative section, and includes factors external to the scene in question. (The paradigms of 'sickness' and 'hurry', for example, are important to the play as a whole. To this extent the selection of significant elements is made retrospectively.)

18 *Cultural codes.* This section is closely related to the previous one, and is designed to indicate the chief social, ideological, religious, moral, epistemological and intellectual norms invoked in the dialogue.

1 V.	2 Seg.	3 Spe.	4 List.	5 D.O.	6 T.	7 Ch.	8 Topic/object	9 I.F.	10 E.P.
1	Who's there	Bar.	Fran.	⌂	Pres.	❦	T: *Guard* O: Other	!?	
2	Nay . . . me	Fran.	Bar.	●⊃	Imp.	❦	„	⊢ —	╱ !!
2	stand . . . yourself	Fran.	Bar.	●-	Imp.	❦	„	!!	
3	Long . . . king	Bar.	Fran.		Subj.	❦	O: King	E ⊃	
4	Barnardo?	Fran.	Bar.			❦	O: Bar.	!?	
5	He	Bar.	Fran.	● (= ●⊃)		❦	O: Self	⊢ +	
6	You . . . hour	Fran.	Bar.	●-	Pres.		O: Time	⊢ ‖ (E ∪)	
7	'Tis . . . twelve	Bar.	Fran.	♀	P.P.	❦	O: Time	⊢ ‖	
7	get . . . Francisco	Bar.	Fran.	●-	Imp.		O: Fran./ sleep	!!	
8	For . . . thanks	Fran.	Bar.	♠			O: Guard- change	E ∪	+
8	'tis . . . cold	Fran.	Bar.		Pres.	↟	O: Atmos- phere	⊢ ‖	
9	And . . . heart	Fran.	Bar.	●⊃	Pres.	♡	O: Psyche	⊢ ‖	

11 P.E.	12 Implic./ rhet.	13 Mod.	14 An.	15 Met.	16 Other functs.	17 Lexs./ isotops.	18 Cultural codes
−		W[kp]			Phatic function	Identity *there* (unknown)	
		Op		●	„	Identity	
+		Op		●	„	„	
	Impl.: 'Friend'	Wp			Conventional signal	*king*	National-patriotic
+		? p			Nomination	Identity	
		p	⇒ 'Barnardo'			„	
	Impl.: 'Thanks'	p				Temporality	
	Impl.: 'It's late'	p				„	Magical (midnight)
+		Op			Nomination	Sleep	
		p					
		p				*cold* (tomb)	
		p				*sick* (disease)	

1 V.	2 Seg.	3 Spe.	4 List.	5 D.O.	6 T.	7 Ch.	8 Topic/ object	9 I.F.	10 E.P.
10	Have . . . guard	Bar.	Fran.	•-	P.P.	ℰ	O: Guard/ atmos- phere	!?	
10	Not . . . stirring	Fran.	Bar.			ℰ	O: Atmos- phere	⊢‖	
11	Well . . . night	Bar.	Fran.				O: Time	E⊃	
12– 13	If . . . watch	Bar.	Fran.	•-	Pres. (fut.)		O: Hor./ Mar./ guard	⊢≏	
13	bid . . . haste	Bar.	Fran.	⚫	Imp.		O: Hor./ Mar./ urgency	!! ▶ !!	
14	I think . . . them	Fran.	Bar.	⚫	Pres.	ℰ	O: Hor./ Mar.	⊢‖	
14	Stand ho!	Fran.	Hor./ Mar. (Bar.)		Imp.	ℰ	O: Other	!!	
14	Who . . . there	Fran.	Hor./ Mar. (Bar.)	⌔	Pres.	ℰ	O: Other	!?	
15	Friends . . . ground	Hor.	Fran. (Bar./ Mar.)	⚏		ℰ	O: Hor./ Mar./ Denmark	⊢‖ (E⊃)	

11 P.E.	12 Implic./ rhet.	13 Mod.	14 An.	15 Met.	16 Other functs.	17 Lexs./ isotops.	18 Cultural codes
+		? p				quiet (tomb)	
		~ p				quiet (tomb)	
		Wp					
		Hp			Nomination		
×		O[op]	⇒ 'Horatio and Mar-cellus' ☞			haste	
		Bp	⇒ 'Horatio and Mar-cellus'				
+		Op					
+		W[kp]			Phatic function	Identity *there* (unknown)	
		p			„		National-patriotic

1 V.	2 Seg.	3 Spe.	4 List.	5 D.O.	6 T.	7 Ch.	8 Topic/ object	9 I.F.	10 E.P.
15	And . . . the Dane	Mar.	Fran. (Hor./ Bar.)			ℂ	O: Hor./ Mar./ Denmark	⊢‖ (E ⊃)	
16	Give . . . night	Fran.	Hor./ Mar. (Bar.)	●-	Subj.		O: Hor./ Mar./ time	E ⊃	+
16	O . . . soldier	Mar.	Fran. (Hor./ Bar.)		Imp.		O: Fran.	!! (E ⊃)	
17	Who . . . you	Mar.	Fran. (Hor./ Bar.)	●-	P.P.		O: Fran./ guard	!?	
17	Barnardo . . . place	Fran.	Mar. (Hor./ Bar.)	●⊃	Pres.		O: Fran./ Bar./ guard	⊢‖	
18	Give . . . night	Fran.	Mar. (Hor./ Bar.)	●-	Subj.		O: Mar./ time	E ⊃	+
18– 19	Say . . . there	Bar.	Hor. (Mar.)	⌁	Imp./ Pres. ℂ		O: Hor.	!!/ !?	
19	A piece . . . him	Hor.	Bar. (Mar.)	● (= ●⊃)		†	O: Hor.	⊢‖ (⊢ +)	
20	Wel- come . . . Marcellus	Bar.	Hor./ Mar.				O: Hor./ Mar.	E ⊃	

11 P.E.	12 Implic./ rhet.	13 Mod.	14 An.	15 Met.	16 Other functs.	17 Lexs./ isotops.	18 Cultural codes
		p			Phatic function	*Dane*	National-patriotic Heroic
		Wp					
		Op				*honest soldier*	Ethical Military
+		W[kp]				Identity Substitution	
		p			Nomination	Substitution (usurpation)	
		Wp					
+		Op /?p		●	Phatic function/ Nomination	Identity *there*	
	Impl.: 'I am cold'	p	⇒ 'Horatio'			Incompleteness	
		p			Nomination		

1 V.	2 Seg.	3 Spe.	4 List.	5 D.O.	6 T.	7 Ch.	8 Topic/ object	9 I.F.	10 E.P.
21	What . . . tonight	Hor.	Bar. (Mar.)		P.P.	👁	T: Ghost O: Un- known/ time	!?	
22	I . . . nothing	Bar.	Hor. (Mar.)	●⤳	P.P.	👁	O: Bar./ sighting	⊢ ‖ (⊢ −)	
23– 24	Horatio . . . of him	Mar.	Bar. (Hor.)	Pl ●⤳ ●	Pres.	◯	O: Hor./ psyche	⊢ ‖	
25	Touching . . . of us	Mar.	Bar. (Hor.)	Pl ●⤳		👁	O: Hor./ sightings	⊢ ‖	
26	Therefore . . . along	Mar.	Bar. (Hor.)	●⤳ ●	P.P.	♀	O: Hor.	⊢ ‖	
27	With us . . . this night	Mar.	Bar. (Hor.)	Pl ●⤳ ♀		👁	O: Time	⊢ ‖	
28	That . . . come	Mar.	Bar. (Hor.)		Subj.	👁	O: Ghost	⊢ ⌢	
29	He . . . to it	Mar.	Bar. (Hor.)	● ●⤳	Cond.	👁	O: Hor./ Ghost	⊢ ‖	
30	Tush . . . appear	Hor.	Mar. (Bar.)	●	Fut.	👁	O: Ghost	⊢ ‖	
30	Sit . . . awhile	Bar.	Hor. (Mar.)	●−	Imp.	⇡⇣	O: Hor.	!!	
31	And let . . . ears	Bar.	Hor. (Mar.)	Pl ●⤳ ●−	Imp.	👂	O: Hor./ story	!√	
32	That are . . . story	Bar.	Hor. (Mar.)	Pl ●⤳	Pres.	👂	O: Story	⊢ ‖	

11 P.E.	12 Implic./ rhet.	13 Mod.	14 An.	15 Met.	16 Other functs.	17 Lexs./ isotops.	18 Cultural codes
		? p	⇒ ?(Ghost)		Evasion of nomination	*thing* (unnamable) *again* (→ past)	
		p				Spectacle	
		p[~Bp]	⇒ 'Horatio'		Nomination	Illusion	Rational-sceptical
		p	⇒ (sightings)			Un-namable	
		p	⇒ 'Horatio'			Invitation	
		p				Spectacle	
		Hp	⇒ (Ghost)			Spectacle	
		Poss. p					
		~poss. p					Rational-sceptical
+		Op					
+	Hyper-bole	O[Pp]		◐/			Military
		p	⇒ 'ears'	/T			Military

1 V.	2 Seg.	3 Spe.	4 List.	5 D.O.	6 T.	7 Ch.	8 Topic/object	9 I.F.	10 E.P.
33	What . . . seen	Bar.	Hor. (Mar.)	PI ●⊃	P.P.	👁	O: Ghost/ sightings	⊢‖	
33	Well . . . down	Hor.	Bar./ Mar.	PI ●⊃	Imp.	⫯⫯	O: Selves/ sitting	!√	
34	And let . . . this	Hor.	Bar./ Mar.	PI ●⊃	Imp.	☽	O: Story	!√	
35– 37	Last night . . . heaven	Bar.	Hor. (Mar.)	■	Pres. / Pas.P.👁		O: Time of story/ star		
38	Where . . . burns	Bar.	Hor. (Mar.)	♀■	Pres.	👁	O: Star	⊢‖	
38	Marcellus . . . myself	Bar.	Hor. (Mar.)	●⊃			O: Bar./ Mar.		
39	The bell . . . one	Bar.	Hor. (Mar.)	⏱		☽	O: Time of story	⊢‖	
40	Peace . . . off	Mar.	Bar. (Hor.)		Imp.	☽	O: Mar./ story	!!	
40	look . . . again	Mar.	Bar./ Hor.	●	Imp. / Pres. 👁		O: Ghost	!!	⊢‖
41	In the . . . dead	Bar.	Mar./ Hor.		Pres.	👁	O: Ghost/ Old Hamlet	⊢‖	
42	Thou . . . scholar	Mar.	Hor. (Bar.)	●–	Pres.		O: Hor.'s learning	⊢‖	

11 P.E.	12 Implic./ rhet.	13 Mod.	14 An.	15 Met.	16 Other functs.	17 Lexs./ isotops.	18 Cultural codes
		p					
+		Op					
+		O[Pp]	⇒ (apparition)	◠ ℭ			
		p	⇐ 'star'		'Iconic' evocation;	heaven Macrocosm	
		p	⇐ 'star'		pseudo-		
					narrative oriented → now		
		p					
		Op		S	Iconization of narrative referent		
		Op / p	⇒ (Ghost)				
		p	⇐ 'king'			Simulacrum king dead	
		p					Scholastic

1 V.	2 Seg.	3 Spe.	4 List.	5 D.O.	6 T.	7 Ch.	8 Topic/object	9 I.F.	10 E.P.
42	speak ... Horatio	Mar.	Hor. (Bar.)	▪	Imp.	𝄃	O: Hor./ Ghost/ address	!!	
43	Looks ... king	Bar.	Hor. (Mar.)	▪	Pres.	👁	O: Ghost/ Old Hamlet	!?	
44	Most like ... wonder	Hor.	Bar. (Mar.)	▪ ●	Pres.	👁 / ♡	O: Ghost/ Hor.'s reaction	⊢‖	
45	It ... spoke to	Bar.	Hor. (Mar.)	▪	Cond.	𝄃	O: Ghost's desire	⊢‖	
45	Question ... Horatio	Bar.	Hor. (Mar.)	▪	Imp.	𝄃	O: Ghost/ Hor./ address	!!	
46	What ... night	Hor.	Ghost (Mar./ Bar.)	● ☿	Pres.	𝄃	O: Ghost/ time	!?	
47– 49	Together ... march	Hor.	Ghost (Mar./ Bar.)	▪	Past	👁	O: Ghost/ Old Hamlet	⊢‖	
49	/by heaven ... speak	Hor.	Ghost (Mar./ Bar.)	●	Imp.	𝄃	O: Ghost/ reply	!!	+
50	It ... offended	Mar.	Hor. (Bar.)	▪	Pres.	♡	O: Ghost's reaction	⊢‖	
50	See ... away	Bar.	Hor. (Mar.)	▪	Pres.	👁	O: Ghost	⊢‖	

11 P.E.	12 Implic./ rhet.	13 Mod.	14 An.	15 Met.	16 Other functs.	17 Lexs./ isotops.	18 Cultural codes
+		Op	⇒ (Ghost) ⊂⊃				
+		? p	⇒ (Ghost)			Simulacrum *king*	
		p	⇒ (Ghost)				
		(prob.) p	⇒ (Ghost)	☞ / ⊂⊃	Projection on to Ghost		
+		Op	⇒ (Ghost) ⊂⊃				
−		W[kp]				*usurp*	
		p	⇐ 'form'			Simulacrum *king*	Military Heroic
−		Op		⊂⊃	Phatic function	*heaven*	
		(prob.) p	⇒ (Ghost)		Projection on to Ghost		
		p	⇒ (Ghost)				

1 V.	2 Seg.	3 Spe.	4 List.	5 D.O.	6 T.	7 Ch.	8 Topic/ object	9 I.F.	10 E.P.
51	Stay . . . speak	Hor.	Ghost (Mar./ Bar.)	●⇀ ●⁃	Imp.	⊕	O: Ghost/ reply	!!	+
52	'Tis gone . . . answer	Mar.	Hor./ Bar.	▪	Pres.	👁/ ⊕	O: Ghost	⊢‖	
53	How now . . . pale	Bar.	Hor. (Mar.)	●⁃	Pres.	♡/ ⚲	O: Hor.'s appear- ance	⊢‖	
54– 55	Is not . . . you don't	Bar.	Hor. (Mar.)	●⁃	Pres.	◯	O: Ghost/ psyche	!?	
56– 58	Before . . . eyes	Hor.	Bar./ Mar.	●⇀	Cond.	◯/ 👁	O: Ghost/ psyche	⊢‖	
58	Is it . . . king	Mar.	Hor. (Bar.)	▪	Pres.	👁	O: Ghost/ Old Hamlet	!?	
59	As thou . . . thyself	Hor.	Mar. (Bar.)	●⁃	Pres.	👁	O: Ghost/ Mar.	⊢‖ (⊢ +)	
60– 63	Such . . . ice	Hor.	Mar./ Bar.	●	Past	👁	O: Old Hamlet/ wars	⊢‖	
64	'Tis strange	Hor.	Mar./ Bar.		Pres.	◯	O: Simi- larity	⊢‖	
65	Thus . . . hour	Mar.	Hor. (Bar.)	⏱			O: Time past/ present		

11 P.E.	12 Implic./ rhet.	13 Mod.	14 An.	15 Met.	16 Other functs.	17 Lexs./ isotops.	18 Cultural codes
−		Op		⌣	Phatic function		
		p		S			
		p					
+		?p(Bp)	⇒ (Ghost)				
		H[~ poss. p]	⇒ (Ghost)				Rational-sceptical
+		? p	⇒ (Ghost)			Simu-lacrum	
		p				Identity	
		p	⇒ (armour) ⇒ (Old Hamlet)			*dead*	Military-heroic
		p	⇒ (simi-larity)		Epic Pseudo-narrative	The in-explicable	
			⇒ (appari-tion)				

1 V.	2 Seg.	3 Spe.	4 List.	5 D.O.	6 T.	7 Ch.	8 Topic/object	9 I.F.	10 E.P.
66	With ... watch	Mar.	Hor. (Bar.)	●⊃ ●–	P.P.	👁	O: Ghost/ guard	⊢‖	
67– 69	In what ... state	Hor.	Mar. (Bar.)	●⊃	Pres.	◯	O: Ghost/ psyche	⊢‖	
70	Good ... down	Mar.	Hor./ Bar.	♀	Imp.	ⵗ	O: Selves/ sitting	!!	
70	and tell ... knows	Mar.	Hor./ Bar.	●⊃	Imp.	⸦	O: Explanation	!!	
71– 72	Why ... land	Mar.	Hor./ Bar.	↑	Pres.		T: Background O: Guard	⊢‖ (!?)	
73– 78	And why ... day	Mar.	Hor./ Bar.	▲	Pres.		O: Preparations	⊢‖ (!?)	
79	Who ... me	Mar.	Hor./ Bar.	●⊃	Pres.		O: Explanation	!?	

11 P.E.	12 Implic./ rhet.	13 Mod.	14 An.	15 Met.	16 Other functs.	17 Lexs./ isotops.	18 Cultural codes
		p	⇒ (Ghost)				Military
	Hen-diadys	~Kp / Bp	⇒ (appari-tion)			Macro-cosm state	National-istic Super-natural
+		Op					
+		Op (W[kp])	⇐ 'that knows'	👄			
+		W[kp]	⇐ 'nightly'		'Iconic' evocation of		
+		W[kp]	⇐ 'daily cast' 'im-press'		macro-situation		
+		W[kp]	⇐ 'can inform'	👄			

6

CONCLUDING COMMENTS: THEATRE, DRAMA, SEMIOTICS

DRAMATIC TEXT/PERFORMANCE TEXT

An elementary distinction has been drawn throughout this book between two kinds of text and thus two possible objects of semiotic analysis. Approaches to each have been considered, without, however, any premature attempt at a synthesis. But the question inevitably arises: in what ways are the dramatic text and the performance text related – what are the points of contact between them?

Literary critics have usually implicitly or explicitly assumed the priority of the written play over the performance, the latter being more often than not described as a 'realization' (actual or potential) of the former. The written text constrains the performance in obvious ways – not only linguistically in determining what the actors say, and proairetically in establishing the structure of the action, but also, in varying degrees, across the range of theatrical codes by indicating movement, settings, music and the rest. Since, chronologically, the writing of the play precedes any given performance, it might appear quite legitimate to suppose the simple priority of the one over the other.

But it is equally legitimate to claim that it is the performance, or at least a possible or 'model' performance, that constrains the dramatic text in its very articulation. The 'incompleteness' factor considered in the last chapter – that is, the constant pointing within the dialogue to a non-described context – suggests that the dramatic text is radically conditioned by its performability. The written text, in other words, is determined by its very need for stage contextualization, and indicates throughout its allegiance to the physical conditions of performance, above all to the actor's body and its ability to materialize discourse within the space of the stage. As Paola Gulli Pugliatti has said, the dramatic text's units of articulation 'should not be seen as "units of the linguistic text *translatable* into stage practice"', but rather as 'a linguistic transcription of a stage potentiality which is the motive force of the written text' (1976, p. 18).

What this suggests is that the written text/performance text relationship is not one of simple priority but a complex of reciprocal constraints constituting a powerful *intertextuality*. Each text bears the other's traces, the performance assimilating those aspects of the written play which the performers choose to transcodify, and the dramatic text being 'spoken' at every point by the model performance – or the n possible performances – that motivate it. This intertextual relationship is problematic rather than automatic and symmetrical. Any given performance is only to a limited degree constrained by the indications of the written text, just as the latter does not usually bear the traces of any *actual* performance. It is a relationship that cannot be accounted for in terms of facile determinism.

A UNITED ENTERPRISE?

These considerations lead us back to the issue raised in Chapter 1: to what extent does the broad and heterogeneous range of objects and concepts, rules and practices, structures and functions discussed in this book make up a single field of investigation? Can a semiotics concerned at once with theatrical communication and dramatic principles, performance and written play, hope to be a coherent project?

At the present, and still largely nascent, stage of work in these areas, a reassuring unity of aims and methods can scarcely be said to prevail, and much of the basic groundwork of establishing agreed objectives and common analytic criteria for purposes of empirical research remains to be done. In particular, there appears to be little dialogue at present between semioticians working on the performance and its codes and those whose principal interest is in the dramatic text and its rules. But it is very difficult, on the other hand, to conceive of an adequate semiotics of theatre which takes no account of dramatic canons, action structure, discourse functions and the rhetoric of the dialogue, just as a poetics of the drama which makes no reference to the conditions and principles of the performance has little chance of being more than an eccentric annexe of literary semiotics.

The aim of this book has been to sketch out in a very provisional fashion the territory of a dialectical and, at present, unsettled enterprise – a semiotic poetics concerned with the widest possible range of rules governing our understanding of theatre and drama – but without claiming that this constitutes, as yet, a comfortably established intellectual field. What emerges is an area of inquiry whose complexity may be daunting but whose very openness makes it peculiarly inviting and challenging.

'POST'-SCRIPT: POST-SEMIOTICS, POSTHUMOUS SEMIOTICS, CLOSET SEMIOTICS

In writing a new chapter for a new edition of this volume, I feel somewhat like an intruder in another author's text. Time, as Samuel Beckett tells us in *Proust* and as he goes on to show us in *Krapp's Last Tape*, drives huge wedges between yesterday's version of our identities and today's, making it difficult to dialogue with our former selves and to construct a line of continuity between past and present. It is therefore a hard task to add an afterword to a book at a distance of more than twenty years, and this is especially the case in a study that is so much of its time. This volume, first published in 1980, was written at the end of the 1970s, and looks back over a body of work produced under the influence of an intellectual movement – structuralism, together with its 'successor' semiotics – that has long since lost its cultural pre-eminence. Moreover, developments that have taken place in the fields of literary and performance studies since 1980 – from what was generically known as post-structuralism to new historicism and cultural materialism – have gained much of their energy precisely from the questioning or even from the outright refusal of semiotics in its structuralist guise. This makes any linear 'evolutionary' narrative about the transition from 'formal' semiotics (as it has been called) to the various 'post'-structuralist or 'post'-semiotic theories extremely arduous. And it renders any attempt merely to update this book in a 'what happened next' fashion – as if adding the latest data to a technical handbook – quite fatuous.

At the same time, there are several reasons, I believe, for wishing to write a post-script (as opposed to a 'continuation') to this book at a distance of twenty-two years. The first is that it may be worthwhile, as an exercise in intellectual history, to reflect upon why the 'semiotic moment', which some years ago seemed so vigorous, came to lose its cultural and academic prominence, particularly with regard to drama and performance. A second reason is that the very discontinuities that have characterized developments in literary and theatrical theory over the past two decades nonetheless presuppose and sometimes – however critically – set out from ideas of the kind examined in this volume, for example with regard to the nature of the sign and of signification. It may thus be of interest to the reader who wishes to 'locate' this study within the map of contemporary theory to know in what ways later critical movements have defined themselves with reference to semiotics.

The main reason, however, for undertaking a new chapter at such a temporal distance is that the original aim of the book, namely to take theatre and drama seriously and to discuss possible ways of coming to terms with the great richness and complexity of performance, remains valid today, even if some of the theoretical and methodological apparatus discussed here may now appear questionable or dated. Yuri Lotman's claim that theatre is the ideal laboratory for semiotic investigation – on the grounds that 'Theatrical performance offers such an array of varied and complex elements that it could be defined without any difficulty as an encyclopaedia of semiotics' (1981: p. 1) – is still true and still powerful. The desire to do justice to such complexity within a combined, if not necessarily unified, investigative enterprise may be – in the view of 'post'-semiotic theory – a positivistic dream or an imperialistic fantasy, but it has not altogether lost its appeal. If nothing else, this book testifies to this desire and invites the reader to reflect on the formidably abundant phenomenology of theatre, while putting at his or her disposal a range of methodological tools from a number of often heterogeneous sources (rather than any monolithic 'theory') aimed to deal with such abundance. Whether these tools, with their sometimes baroque complexities of method and of terminology, offered a convincing way of dealing with the riches of theatrical discourse is another matter, and one that this chapter proposes to ponder.

My aim in this post-script is therefore not so much to renew or to upgrade the semiotics of theatre and drama as to throw retrospective light upon the enterprise by discussing its destiny in the supposedly 'post'-semiotic era. In reality, the years following the publication of this book – particularly the early 1980s – witnessed quite contradictory tendencies. Just as post-structuralist theorists were announcing the death of semiotics, newspaper critics and other non-academic persons interested in the drama, including the occasional theatre director, began to take note of its existence and to defend themselves from what they considered a threat from an alien intellectual planet. The success of theatre semiotics – in terms of visibility – thus coincided ironically with its well-publicized demise. The 1980s and early 1990s also brought about what we might term the institutionalization of semiotics, in the sense that it started to make its (again supposedly posthumous) mark on encyclopedias, dictionaries and the like as an established force within theatre studies. Nor has there been a lack of 'continuations' or attempted revivals, such as studies more or or less similar to this one – but published later – offering theoretical overviews of the field, or further (and sometimes critical) applications of semiotic theory to drama and performance. Within literary and dramatic theory itself, finally, semiotics met with a mixed and in some ways paradoxical reception: post-structuralism came to absorb semiotic concepts in the very endeavour to 'overcome' them, so that a sometimes hidden semiological agenda – what we might call a closet semiotics – has characterized a good deal of critical discourse on the drama over the past few years. It might be helpful to bring some of this secret, and not always coherent, semiology to light. The following discussion is accordingly organized under four headings: Reactions, Institutionalizations, Extensions and Disseminations.

REACTIONS: THE THREAT FROM OUTER THEATRICAL SPACE

Publishers are known to aver that the impact of a book or other publishing venture is measured not in the contents of reviews and responses but in the sheer number of column inches dedicated to it in the press. In these terms, the semiotics of theatre and drama as a branch of academic publication achieved its greatest degree of prominence, at least in English-speaking countries, in the 1980s when a number of newspaper critics felt somehow obliged to acknowledge, however grudgingly and sceptically, the existence of a new intellectual discipline on their distant professional horizon. Apart from reviews proper, signs of this awareness may be found in discussions by non-academic theatre critics of the state of their art.

In 1988 the well-known theatre critic John Elsom contributed an entry to the *Cambridge Guide to World Theatre* on European drama criticism, at the end of which he discusses the current (declining) state of newspaper reviewing and identifies one of the causes of its malaise: 'What may also be a contributory factor to the decline of [journalistic] theatre criticism lies in the fact that one powerful, intellectually cogent and embracing form of criticism has had no impact on journalism whatsoever, nor can it have. It derived from the universities and the systematic study of language' (1988, p. 251). Elsom names the powerful, cogent and rival form of criticism as 'semiology', and goes on to explain why it has failed to interact with newspaper criticism, or vice versa (although he does mention the exception of Carlos Tindemans who succeeded both in journalism and as a Professor of Semiotics at Antwerp University): 'But for everyday journalism, semiology is far too cumbersome and exacting a science to be of much practical help, although sometimes it offered a useful corrective to the prejudices and slipshod opinions of theatre critics. Indeed, after the arrival of the semiologists, no journalist critic could claim to be in the vanguard of opinion' (p. 251). Elsom, despite his reservations, paints a rather glamorous picture of semiotic criticism, with its methodological rigour and its supposed cultural kudos ('the vanguard'), at a time when such glamour had more or less faded within academic circles.

The sense of ambivalence that Elsom expresses marks the extent to which the need to renew our understanding of theatre was felt, especially on the part of those professionally engaged in the field, while at the same time it signals the real problem of a lack of dialogue between semiotics and non-academic critical discourse. Unquestionably this was in part a matter of terminology – the 'technical' vocabulary of semiotics that deterred not only journalists but also other non-academic (and many academic) readers – but it was above all due to differences in critical goals. Newspaper critics have as their primary aim the evaluation of a given play or performance (good, bad or indifferent), semioticians its description and analysis. The real difficulty for reviewers was not that theatre semiotics was 'far too cumbersome and exacting' but that it offered little help in the day-to-day business of assigning points for merit.

The differences between the two critical spheres emerge quite clearly in the reflections of an eminent reviewer, Irving Wardle, erstwhile theatre critic for The Times. In his stimulating volume Theatre Criticism (1992), Wardle identifies as the crucial limits of semiotic criticism – from the point of view of a practising theatre journalist – both its offputting predilection for the naming of parts and the distance it assumes with regard to the object of analysis: 'This [the objective fallacy] is also the drawback of theatrical semiotics, which has developed a new language of performance analysis, and whose subtle practitioners regard run-of-the-mill reviewers as stone-age hunters still assaulting their prey with flint arrows. It is true that semiotics enables you to name things for which no names previously existed. The act of naming is a basic means of apprehending reality . . . But to speak of "deictic strategies" and "illocutionary acts", and to draw distinction between the énoncé and the énonciation is not like asking readers to look up an unfamiliar word. Semiotic terminology is a closed system that seems to have been devised with the express purpose of discouraging intruders' (p. 57). Wardle, without naming names, criticises works like this book (perhaps primarily this book, and in particular the 'dramatological score' presented in its finale) for their systematic and strategic failure either to make or facilitate aesthetic judgements: 'Intelligibility aside, there is another barrier against its general critical use: namely that despite structuralist claims to have supplanted the author, semiotic performance analysis is more dependent on the object of its scrutiny than the most slavish piece of plot synopsis. It may present an X-ray of dramatic micro-sequences, or break down the opening scene of *Hamlet* into alethetic [sic] possibilities, doxastic modalities, lexemes and isotopies, but it leaves you with no idea whatever of whether the scene is any good or not.' (p. 57). Certainly the 'score' to which Wardle alludes is – as I was fully aware at the time I wrote the book – the most easily criticised part of this study, precisely because it is (literally) so visible and so uncompromising in its attempt to bring many of the proposed analytic criteria together in a 'dazzling' final scene or scheme. As such it is also probably the most 'dated' aspect of this volume. Fernando de Toro observes in his own self-critical and retrospective preface added to the 1995 English edition of his *Theatre Semiotics* (first published in Spanish in 1987), 'It seemed after a while that producing diagrams and arrows had been unnecessarily obtrusive and did not get us anywhere.' (p. 2). Wardle would doubtless agree.

Be that as it may, Wardle is unequivocally explicit about the true object of his frustration: the semiotician's determinedly non-judgmental stance. The problem of withholding – or at least not necessarily expressing – immediate evaluations ('*Hamlet* 1.1.? Great scene! You must read/see it') is of course by no means limited to semiotics but regards any investigative or hermeneutic enquiry that does not aim simply to provide good/bad verdicts or top-ten hit parades. Having said this, however, and despite his evident disappointment, Wardle at least gives semiotics a hearing, and it is to his credit that he should take the trouble to struggle with such an 'alien' discipline at all. Perhaps reviewers, precisely because they are faced by the necessity of interpreting and evaluating performances, looked towards new instruments of analysis with greater interest and hope than many literary academics concerned more generally with critical theory. Hence also their disappointment at the 'difficulty' and apparent remoteness of such instruments. 'Criticism' concludes Wardle, 'would be enriched if it could absorb the insights of semiotics', but adds, paraphrasing Shaw, 'you should master the aesthetic theory and technical vocabulary, and then throw the lot away before you begin to write.' This is not altogether bad advice, although how many reviewers would be willing to 'master the aesthetic theory' before throwing it away is an open question.

The degree of suspicion expressed by theatre critics towards the 'new' critical language is multiplied exponentially in the pronouncements of theatre practitioners proper, especially directors. A good example of such directorial hostility may be found in the published proceedings of an event known as The Alsager Seminar on Semiotics and Theatre, which took place in 1983. This meeting had the peculiar distinction of being perhaps the first theatre semiotics conference from which theatre semioticians appear to have been strategically excluded, leaving the field free for directors, actors, critics and drama teachers to agree ritualistically, as it were by way of exorcism, that even if they did not quite know what the semiotics of theatre was, they were sure they did not really need it, thank you. Among those who turned down semiotic performance analysis – on the basis of an introductory talk by the apparently self-elected semiotics spokesperson Martin Esslin (an illustrious drama critic but not previously known in this role) – was the Royal Shakespeare Company director John Caird, who stated categorically, 'It seems to me, from what I've heard . . . that semiotics, semiology, is an intellectual tool . . . If all we are getting is a description, all we can do is see the thing ourselves, and make our own judgement about it. I don't need someone to describe the Mona Lisa to me, it doesn't help me at all.' (D. 29). So much – one might respond – for art criticism as well as theatre criticism or indeed any form of critical discourse.

The declared reason for the director's scepticism is analogous to that of the reviewers (although Caird, unlike Wardle, has never read a word of semiotic theory), namely that 'semiotics, semiology' does not provide him with tools for his trade: 'it doesn't help me at all'. Now theatre practitioners, especially English and American ones, are notoriously resistant to what they consider 'intellectual' approaches to theatre, and certainly semiotic analysis – or any other mode of 'description' as Caird scathingly defines it – does not have to justify itself in terms of its usefulness to the Royal Shakespeare Company. But there is unquestionably a broader cultural issue involved here. The semiotics of drama was born in Europe and in some ways born out of European theatrical practice. Early structuralist approaches to performance analysis were close, for example, to the self-analytical epic theatre of Brecht, just as the latter's concept of *Verfremdungseffekt* (alienation effect) grew, as we have seen (pp. 15–16) out of the Russian formalist notion of *ostranenie* or defamiliarization. Such a dialectic between practice and analysis is possible only within a tradition, such as the German theatrical tradition, in which theoretical and analytic approaches are not considered detrimental to directorial creativity (not by chance the figure of the dramaturg, an integral part of German theatre, has no real equivalent in English and American theatre). The studied indifference of John Caird is quite far from the attitude of German, French or Italian practitioners (directors, for example, like Peter Stein, Antoine Vitez or Giorgio Strehler) who, especially in the 1980s, openly encouraged theoretical and cultural debate and the kinds of 'description' that were so unhelpful to the RSC.

This raises a further issue regarding the relationship between theatrical and critical practice. Mainstream British and American theatre has always tended towards a pragmatic – and hence methodologically conservative – approach to the business of 'putting on' plays, seeing the director less as *auteur* on the European model than as skilled go-between serving the dramatist and actors. Exceptions among English-speaking directors, such as Peter Brook or Robert Wilson, have often fled to Europe. It is evident that this conception of staging as skill or craft does not leave much room for distanced reflection, let alone for theorization. This is one of the reasons why semiotic performance analysis, being itself an 'avant garde' and methodologically anti-traditionalist endeavour, tended to look for its objects and for its ideal models of theatricality precisely in avant garde, anti-traditionalist forms of theatre, in the hope of bringing about a 'natural' alliance or symbiosis between practice and theory. Thus it inevitably favoured certain kinds of director's and choreographer's theatre which was decidedly authorial and in a sense 'textual', i.e. where the performance was conceived as a coherent and well-controlled mode of discourse and could thus be read as a text. The points of reference in this alliance between textualized performance and textual reading were not John Caird or Trevor Nunn but Robert Wilson, Richard Foreman, the 'early' Grotowski, Ariane Mnouchkine, Luca Ronconi, European and American performance art, and so on.

Perhaps the best examples of performance analyses going hand-in-hand with theatrical experiment are the contributions to *Les voies de la création théâtrale* – especially the first (1970) volume with its splendid description by Serge Ouaknine of Grotowski's seminal *The Constant Prince* – which were not taken into consideration in this volume because they are in a sense 'pre-theoretical'. Ouaknine brought to his description-reconstruction of the performance an annotational rigour analogous to the austere dedication that Grotowski asked of his actors, just as the descriptive method – involving all possible degrees of symbolic and iconic notation, from verbal description and reported dialogue to schemes of stage movement and of interpersonal proxemic relations to actual photographs – has its own 'performative' visual richness, constituting, I think by general consent, the single most impressive endeavour to leave a digital-analogical trace of a by now long-lost theatrical event.

This doubtless goes to underline the fact that semiotic analysis (or even 'pre'-semiotic analysis, as in the case of Ouaknine) not only started life but remained culturally 'other' with regard to the mindset of the Anglo-Saxon theatre world. In reality, semioticians of drama shared with theatre practitioners not only a passion for dramatic art but also, often enough, a vocation for pragmatic 'bricolage', as Levi-Strauss terms it, namely a willingness to devise such methods as served the occasion, be they verbal, iconographic, terminological or techno-logical. What theatre semiotics and theatre practice did not have in common was precisely a semiotic medium, i.e. a shared language.

INSTITUTIONALIZATIONS: THE SEMIOTICS OF THEATRE AND DRAMA ON THE MAP

One of the signs of academic canonization – in the sense of admittance to the canon of 'officially' recognized disciplines – is presence within maps or guides to the field of studies in question. Another and more tangible sign is the creation of academic posts. If theatre semiotics was not unduly successful in generating jobs, being considered at best a somewhat eccentric branch of literary or drama criticism (and despite the provocative title of Brean Hammond's contribution to the Alsager Seminar: "Theatre Semiotics: An 'Academic Job Creation Scheme'?"), it did make some impact on the guides to theatre and drama studies. I have already mentioned the 1988 *Cambridge Guide to World Theatre* with its albeit brief and ambivalent allusion to 'semiology'. Far more substantial attention is paid to semiotic concepts in Patrice Pavis's well-known *Dictionnaire du théâtre*, first published in 1980 and translated into English in 1998 (as *Dictionary of the Theatre: Terms, Concepts, and Analysis*). As well as lengthy general entries on semiology and the theatrical sign, Pavis's encyclopaedic *Dictionnaire* includes more specific discussions of Theatrical Codes, Connotation, Deixis, Énoncé and Énonciation, Icon, Index and Symbol, Isotopy, Ostension and the like. These are mixed, in a stimulating and innovative fashion, with more traditional dramaturgic and literary critical categories, from Prologue to Exposition to Dénouement.

It might be said that Pavis, being himself an eminent theatre semiotician, is not representative of theatre specialists at large. A perhaps more surprising attempt to include semiological criteria in a general lexicon of theatrical terms is Terry Hodgson's valuable 1988 reference book *The Batsford Dictionary of Drama*, which includes entries on Semiology/ Semiotics, Sign, Signifier/Signified and Structuralism, as well as more 'technical' definitions of Deixis, Foregrounding, Icon, Index, Intertextuality, Isotopy, Ostension and Proxemics. Again these terms are found alongside more familiar dramaturgic lemmas, from Act to Zany.

Particular mention needs to be made here of Marvin Carlson's influential *Theories of the Theatre* (1984), subtitled *A Historical and Critical Survey, from the Greeks to the Present*. Carlson's lucid discussion of semiotic theories of theatre (pp. 493–512) attributes to them – rather like Elsom's sketchier account – an academic pre-eminence that, if indeed it existed, was not to last for long: 'In the early 1980s, semiotics seems well established as the dominant new approach to theatrical theory, though only a handful of major writings have yet appeared in English.' He adds, however, somewhat prophetically, that 'Poststructuralism, which has mounted so stimulating a challenge to semiotics and structuralism in recent non-theatrical literary theory, has as yet inspired little theatre-oriented work' (p. 512; on poststructuralism, see below). Carlson returns to linguistic-semiotic approaches to theatre in his more recent critical compendium *Performance: A Critical Introduction* (1996), which dedicates a highly informative chapter to speech-act theories of performance (pp. 59–77). Again he emphasises the innovative – indeed, 'revolutionary' – effect of such approaches: 'speech-act theory has joined with the new performative interest in the social sciences in general to effect a major change, one might say a revolution, in the areas of literary studies most associated with performance.' (p. 75). Semiotics has apparently gained a place on the performance map, although like more geo-political maps this representation of the world of theatre studies is necessarily unstable (for another general introduction to theatre theories which refers extensively to semiotics, see Fortier [1997] pp. 22–8).

EXTENSIONS: THEORETICAL MODELS AND CRITICAL APPLICATIONS

Despite the dominance of post-structuralism and other supposedly post-semiotic critical movements, the 1980s and 1990s witnessed a number of publications that seemed to perpetuate the semiotics of theatre and drama more or less within the structuralist tradition. One of the causes of such a double time scheme was translation: various important guides to the field, originally published years earlier, appeared somewhat belatedly in English. Perhaps the most emblematic of these late – and, in the event, almost retrospective – volumes is Fernando De Toro's already-mentioned *Theatre Semiotics*, published in English in 1995. De Toro's preface betrays a sense almost of embarrassment at the appearance of his study in a greatly changed intellectual climate: 'the whole semiotic and structuralist paradigm, which has been with us since the Russian Formalists', he claims, 'came tumbling down strenuously with the emergence of the Post-Structuralists and Deconstructionists' (p. 2). This turns the translated version of his study into what is virtually a commemorative volume for a posthumous science: 'the discipline of Theatre Semiotics', he affirms somewhat drastically, 'came and went with great speed. By the late 1980s the discipline had been exhausted and the best proof of this is that [in 1995] only three new books and very few articles have been published since 1987' (p. 2). By this account even the original 1987 publication in Spanish arrived after the event.

De Toro's paradoxically self-punishing self-presentation is probably excessively severe, attributing extraordinary powers of destruction or deconstruction to 'the Post-Structuralists' who had succeeded, in a violent but bloodless revolution, in sweeping away fifty years of European critical thought. Just as to characterize his own book as an object of merely antiquarian interest, addressed 'to those who would like to know something about this ["dead"] discipline', is unduly harsh. De Toro's study provides useful, and not necessarily post-mortem, discussions of discourse and performance, and has two particularly interesting chapters on aspects of semiotic enquiry relatively absent from earlier studies, namely 'Theatre Reception' (Chapter IV) and 'Theatre History and Semiotics', with particular and lively reference to Latin America (Chapter VI). The attempt here to historicize and politicize the application of descriptive tools goes some way to answering precisely the post-structuralist critique of 'formalism'.

No such critical or self-critical qualms appear in the 1993 translation of Erika Fischer-Lichte's *The Semiotics of Theater* – originally published ten years earlier – which remains relentlessly and unrepentantly formalistic. Setting out from the Prague School structuralist tradition, Fischer-Lichte sets as her main task the naming of performance layers, which in her view means the naming of signs. Thus she gives us sections on 'The actor's activities as a sign', 'The actor's appearance as a sign', 'Spatial signs', etc., which are then further divided hierarchically into sub-layers: 'mimic signs', 'gestural signs', and so on. This labour is largely empirical and intuitive, since what she identifies as 'signs' are simply the items of the performer's stock in trade: 'hairstyle', 'costume', 'props'. Little attempt is made to examine whether, for example, the 'signs' of hairstyle constitute not merely units but a language or discourse as such. Moreover, the attempt to segment the performance vertically in its phenomenal wholeness, as if it were a layer cake, leads semiotic analysis not only to stratify the performance but to reify it as, in Mukarovský's terms, an 'aesthetic object'.

The risk is that of statically freezing theatrical performance, and thereby sacrificing precisely what best characterizes it as a cultural and phenomenological experience, namely its open, dialectical character as a work or production – rather than product – ever in progress and ever in process. What is particularly worrying in Fischer-Lichte's name-that-sign procedure is the concept of the 'sign' itself, which is insufficiently problematized. In addition to cataloguing component performance signs, the author poses herself the unenviable task of identifying that semiological philosopher's stone, the 'specificity of the theatrical sign' (pp. 129–31). This means discovering the peculiar ingredients of the performance slice. Disappointingly, her definition of such specific ingredients simply takes up familiar 1930s Prague School concepts such as the 'mobility' and 'polyfunctionality' of the stage sign. But it is surely the very notion of the single theatrical sign unit, with its atomistic and positivistic implications, that needs to be questioned. Fischer-Lichte's study has the undoubted merit of methodological (although not discursive) simplicity: dealing in the currency of single signs makes transactions easier for students, for example. It is, however, singularly lacking in illustrative references either to actual texts or to particular productions. This is unfortunate, since the liveliest chapter is one that deals with a specific historical codification of a particular sign system, namely gesture in eighteenth-century German theater (chapter 6).

An alternative solution to handling the embarrassment of semiotic riches in the theatre is to worry less about the cohesion of the theatrical cake than about the coherence of the theoretical model applied to it. This is a more demanding undertaking, and one that Marco De Marinis addresses with formidable rigour in his important volume *The Semiotics of Performance* (1992, first published in Italian in 1982). If Fischer-Lichte's study is insufficiently self-questioning, De Marinis's book is consistently self-interrogating, with the result that it might fairly be described as a metatheoretical discourse, or metasemiotics. It is more sophisticated in its attempt to set up an adequate model for what the author terms the 'textual analysis of performance'. Here we have moved far beyond the typology of the sign and into the realm of discourse, or of texts.

De Marinis shares with Fischer-Lichte certain inevitable semiological buzz-words, especially 'code' and 'text' itself, but there any resemblance ends. De Marinis's position is determinedly contextual and thus pragmatic: instead of single signs we have cultural contexts, macro-speech acts and model spectators. Indeed, the two volumes argue at a distance. Where Fischer-Lichte remains faithful to the structuralist notion of the performance as a 'transformation' of the 'literary' dramatic text (pp. 191–206), De Marinis dedicates his whole first chapter to repudiating this literary critical notion of the 'priority' of the script over the performance. 'There is still a widespread tendency among theorists', he complains, 'to place the dramatic text in a position of privilege and absolute superiority vis-à-vis its transcoding into performance' (p. 15). De Marinis has, or perhaps had a point, as Fischer-Lichte's work suggests, although his 'still' sounds a little anachronistic: he refers back to work in the early Seventies which endeavoured, for example, to posit the written text as a Chomskyan 'deep structure' within the performance. The old belief in the supremacy of the written text over the performance has surely receded in recent years for cultural rather than theoretical reasons: in an increasingly 'performative' and decreasingly literary culture, it is performance, and certainly not the maligned written play, that is the supreme object of semiotic desire and cultural kudos.

Be that as it may, it is De Marinis's attack on the literary critical colonization of performance that gives his book its polemical edge. So much so that the author seems to be engaged in what one might call the 'wars of the texts'. Which is to say wars between texts (dramatic text versus performance text) and wars over texts (over the dramatic text and its status, over the performance and its putative textuality). They are essentially wars of liberation. This book derives much of its ideological and expository energy from the notion of freeing its terrain from forces of oppression. The performance itself has to be liberated from the invading textuality of literature, and has thus to be fully recognized as a text in its own right, subject to specific and autonomous laws of textuality.

De Marinis's main project, however, focuses not on the repudiated dramatic text but on the performance itself. The definition of the performance as text is common to both his and Fischer-Lichte's volumes and to the semiotics of theatre in general (as in this volume). Fischer-Lichte's justification of the notion of 'theatrical text' is more voluntaristic than logical; she wills it into being simply because she wants to conduct 'textual analysis': 'In epistemological terms, the performance can . . . be defined as a text and, since the signs it uses have been found to be theatrical signs, it can be defined as a theatrical text. Performance analysis can therefore be construed as a particular mode of textual analysis and conducted as such' (p. 173). Instead, in what is probably his shrewdest strategic move, De Marinis first argues for the theoretical necessity of the performance as text and then goes on to distinguish the performance as such, in its crude materiality, from the analyst's textual construct: 'It should be clear that the concepts of /theatrical perform-ance/ and /performance text/ do not completely coincide. /Theatrical performance/ involves theater as a material object, the phenomenal field that is immediately available to perception and to an analytical approach. /Performance text/ refers to a *theoretical object* . . . or to the theatrical event considered according to semiotic-textual pertinence, assumed and "constructed" as a performance text within the paradigms of textual semiotics' (p. 48: the use of phonetic brackets is a semiotic tic borrowed from De Marinis's master, Umberto Eco).

To elect the performance text as 'theoretical object', rather than phenomenal object, is a perfectly legitimate option, and one that gets De Marinis out of all kinds of descriptive and analytic trouble. Having set aside the actual /performance/, he can get on with the business of constructing his own theoretical model of the /text/, something that he does very ably. Here, too, the reader will find few examples of actual /performances/, and still fewer mentions of particular /dramatic texts/, but in this case the absence is deliberate, a guarantee of the theoretical purity of the model. De Marinis's competence in text theory is certainly impressive, and his study has important things to say about audiences – even if they are Econian /model spectators/ rather than their phenomenal and material counterparts – about theatrical conven-tions, about theatrical intertextuality, and in general about the prag-matics of stage communication. It is difficult to imagine a more refined and exhaustive reflection on the *possibility* of conducting a textual analy-sis of performance, even if it is not the book's aim to offer such analyses.

Not all the more recent book-length guides to theatre semiotics in English are translations, however. Elaine Aston and George Savona's *Theatre as Sign System*, published in English in 1991, undertakes the dif-ficult task of making the subject more readily accessible to students, both through the language employed and through the use of a large number of illustrative examples. The authors' opening gambit is to take theatre semiotics 'not as a theoretical position, but as a *methodology*' (p. 1): an effective strategic move, since it clears the air of such theoretical and ideological issues as the structuralist versus post-structuralist dichotomy. Responding to what they perceive as 'the palpable hostility towards semiotics' within British academic departments (p. 1), they announce their intention to remedy this situation by curing the discipline of its habitual vices, especially linguistic, thereby espousing the very criticisms that their hostile colleagues have levelled against earlier studies such as this one: 'At one level, some of the criticism which theatre attracts is, in our view, justified. The dangers of establishing a jargon-laden language accessible only to academics, of a dialogue between theoreticians and theoreticians, have not always been heeded . . . The degree of obfuscation has been such that the benefits of the "findings", of understanding theatre as a sign-system, have tended to be eclipsed and the considerable advantages of studying theatre through a semiotic approach overlooked.' (pp. 1–2). Their prime example of a 'jargon-laden' text that literally obscures the merits of the semiotic approach is the present volume: 'While this has filled a need for published documentation of theatre semiotics, it has nevertheless been greeted by students of theatre at first-degree level or below, as complex, difficult, and obscure to the point of inaccessibility.' (p. 4)

Aston and Savona therefore elect themselves as linguistic mediators between the available texts in English and a bemused readership of first-degree or below students and their apparently even more bemused or hostile teachers, aiming 'to provide in this volume an introduction or guide to some of the more useful "findings" theatre semiotics has to offer, and to do so in relatively straightforward terms.' (p. 2). What they offer is more or less faithful to this project, in the sense that it does not go much beyond – in conceptual or methodological terms – the body of work produced in the Seventies and early Eighties, but does its best to make it seem less forbidding through a mixture of quotation from the work in question and explicatory paraphrase. Their guide has the merit of not shunning analytical criteria on the grounds of mere linguistic difficulty, although whether the result is necessarily much more 'accessible' than other studies is a moot point.

The volume is somewhat schematically divided into two parts, 'Text' and 'Performance' (which suggests a division of the investigative field that other semioticians, such as Patrice Pavis, endeavour to avoid). The 'textual' half of the book has useful and well-illustrated sections on plot structure, character functions and dialogue, while the 'performance' half is dedicated to such questions as signs and codes, stage directions, the reading of the stage image, the performance as text. One of the more refreshing aspects of this introductory guide is that, unlike De Toro's volume for example, its tone is decidedly upbeat and its conclusion optimistic, which is to say future- rather than past-oriented: 'The field of theatre semiotics is in many respects still wide open for investigation, and our understanding of theatre as a sign-system is still nascent. The semiotic method has yet to fulfil its potential as a challenging and a highly rewarding approach to the study of drama and theatre.' (p.180).

If Aston and Savona's contribution, despite its anti-obscurity premise, avoids the worst traps of over-simplification, Martin Esslin's The Field of Drama (1987) falls happily into them. One might not even suspect that this more or less traditional overview – of what J. L. Styan, in his classic study, called The Elements of Drama (1960) – had anything at all to do with semiotics, were it not for the fact that Esslin affirms in his introduction his interest in the subject and his intention to make it more palatable to his readers. It appears that the above-mentioned Alsager seminar, which failed to convert John Caird and other sceptics, represented something of a road to Damascus for Esslin, presumably because he was given the task of speaking for the absent semiologues, so much so that he now presents himself in the guise of what Aston and Savona term 'a born-again semiotician' (p. 1). Like them, he starts out by rehearsing the familar 'obscurity' topos – 'What struck me as unfortunate, however, from the outset was the obscure language and excessively abstract way in which the, in many cases, outstandingly brilliant exponents of semiotics presented their findings' (p. 11) – and then sets about purging the discipline of its excessive abstractions, which in his case means virtually the whole methodological and terminological apparatus. What remains is an ill-defined hold-all concept of the 'sign', while Esslin's one 'theoretical' contribution is a taxonomy of twenty-two sign systems (nine more than in Tadeusz Kowzan's list) which however turn out to be merely the most familiar tools of the performer's trade, such as costume and make up (pp. 103–5). This is not to say that the desire to increase both the readability and the didactic utility of text and performance analysis is misguided; it is simply to note that readability achieved at the cost of the analytic instruments themselves is surely self-defeating. A degree of complexity – read, in Esslin's terms, obscurity – may be a price to pay for the precision and incisiveness of the methodological tools as such.

Still on the subject of the incisiveness of methodological tools, the years since the original publication of this volume have witnessed important efforts to hone and enrich the heuristic and hermeneutic instruments available to analysts, especially with reference to the dramatic text. In Italy a research group led Alessandro Serpieri enquired, during the Eighties, into Shakespeare's dramatization of his narrative sources in the history and Roman plays, examining the processes of historical and ideological transformation and of dramaturgic 'transcodification' in the passage from one genre to another (Serpieri et al. 1988). What distinguishes this research is the attempt to move beyond static conceptions of textuality and to recover the sense of the drama as 'work', i.e. as a mode of rhetorical and historiographical production. In order to go about this task, moreover, Serpieri and his team set up, in the first of their four volumes, a veritable armoury of 'comparative' categories concerning the articulation of fabula, plot and discourse in narrative and drama respectively, allowing the two kinds of text to be placed side by side and the dynamics of their interaction to be closely investigated. The remaining volumes apply these categories – which are discussed under the headings 'fabula', 'plot', 'time', 'space', 'voice', 'point of view' and 'discourse' – to Shakespeare's dramatization of his sources, in progressive scene-by-scene readings of individual plays.

With regard to semiotic approaches to Shakespeare, Alessandro Serpieri's own contribution to the collective volume *Alternative Shakespeares* (1985) endeavours likewise to marry the textual with the historical: 'A semiotic reading of the dramatic text', he says, 'must be aware not only of the cultural pragmatics of its historical context, but also of the potential pragmatics of the stage relationships that are inscribed in the strictly verbal make-up of the text itself' (1985:122). A cogent example of such a historical-textual marriage is Serpieri's discussion of *Julius Caesar* (following Yuri Lotman's semiotics of culture) as the *mise-en-scène* of a clash between historical models or representations of the world-order, namely between the symbolic model (the classical and medieval world view 'with its centripetal ideology and its stabilizing rhetoric') and the syntagmatic model 'inaugurating the relativism of the modern age' (p. 126). This clash is examined in detail in terms of spatial oppositions and of antithetical rhetorical and deictic modes.

Attention to the spatial semiotics inscribed in the dramatic text – but with reference to specific historical, theatrical and indeed architectural problems – has also characterized research conducted at the Centre for Performance Studies of the University of Sydney. Tim Fitzpatrick – whose preliminary theoretical position is well articulated in his essay "Playscript Analysis, Performance Analysis" (1986) and in his own contribution to the issue of *Altro Polo* that he edited in 1989, dedicated to "Performance: From Product to Process" – applies semiotic criteria to such questions as the number of doors and stage hangings present in Elizabethan public playhouses, with reference, among other texts, to *Macbeth* (1995). Here, and in an article written together with his colleague Wendy Millyard (2000), Fitzpatrick questions Andrew Gurr's assumption that certain Elizabethan play texts demanded the use of three stage doors, and demonstrates, through a series of experiments in what we might term applied proxemics, the redundancy (both textual and performative) of the putative middle door. Such work represents an unprecedented demonstration of the potential utility of semiotic criteria in the field of historical theatre research.

Still on the level of the dramatic text and its investigation, an important advance is represented by Vimala Herman's *Dramatic Discourse* (1995), by far the most complete and detailed discussion to date of the application of linguistics to dramatic texts. Herman's approach is broadly speaking pragmatic and ethnographic. After a preliminary consideration of what she calls 'the ethnography of speaking', devoted to time and space in drama and their verbal registration through deixis, Herman turns her attention to the application of ethnomethodology and conversation analysis, with particular regard to turn sequencing, speech acts, politeness, and, in a lively final chapter, gender and talk. Her adoption and adaptation of 'conversational' criteria to dramatic discourse is predicated not on a notion of the theatrical mirroring of life but on the intuitively sound supposition that playwrights will inevitably exploit the principles of turns, of co-operation, of shared knowledge, etc., that govern everyday talk – something that we, as audiences, readily recognize – as the very basis of the interactional rhetoric of drama:

> it is a question of *mechanics*, in the exploitation by dramatists of underlying speech conventions, principles and 'rules' of use, operative in speech exchanges in the many sorts, conditions and contexts of society which members are assumed to share and use in their inter-actions in day-to-day exchanges. The principles, norms and conven-tions of use which underlie spontaneous communication in everyday life are precisely those which are exploited and manipulated by drama-tists in their constructions of speech types and forms in plays. Thus, 'ordinary speech' or, more accurately, the 'rules' underlying the orderly and meaningful exchange of speech in everyday contexts are the *resource* that dramatists use to construct dialogue in plays. (p. 6; for an earlier introduction to the application of discourse analysis to the drama, see Short 1981. The use of conversational models in the study of dramatic texts is also widely discussed in the collective volume *Interazione, dialogo, convenzione*, 1983).

Another significant contribution to the linguistic study of dramatic texts is David Birch's *The Language of Drama* (1991). Birch affirms at the outset that his approach is different from 'the more formal semiotic approaches . . . in a number of important ways', since what he offers is a 'politically committed' analysis concerned with the description of language structures 'as part of a *social semiotic*' (pp. 1–2). Birch's socially and ideologically aware perspective on dramatic language is in effect a useful corrective to the formalism of some earlier semio-linguistic approaches. What Birch proposes, to this end, is a conflictual model of verbal interaction in drama, as opposed to the co-operative model adopted in many studies: 'I am concerned', he says, 'with developing a theory of *drama praxis* which argues for a social theory of language based on conflict rather on the more usual co-operation, and for a social theory of drama based on the political and institutional uses to which texts can be put.' (p. 2) His volume has particularly useful chapters on 'Drama Praxis' (pp. 6–33), concerned with how ideolo-gies become involved in meaning-making; on 'Making Sense' (pp. 34–53), regarding strategies of interpretation; and on 'Cultural

Power' (pp. 131–150), devoted to discourses of gender and ethnicity. As for performance research, much of the most interesting work produced over the past two decades has concerned audience reception. In addition to Marco De Marinis's already-mentioned 'model' spectators (see also his 1984, 1985 and 1989 articles), 'real' or empirical spectators have come under scrutiny. One of the more effective instruments proposed to date for enquiry into (and stimulation of) spectator response is Patrice Pavis's questionnaire, designed for students of theatre with some knowledge of semiotics, which orients spectator attention by listing the main sign-systems involved in performance and by posing questions regarding the production of meaning on stage (1985b; for Pavis's work on reception, see also his 1983 and 1985a articles; on the same topic see Helbo 1985 and 1987, and various contributions to Fitzpatrick 1989a). Certainly the most ambitious and wide-ranging study of theatre audiences undertaken so far, however – although not primarily in semiotic terms – is Susan Bennett's 1990 volume, which usefully brings together perspectives from sociology, reception theory and theatre history.

Susan Bennett complains in her book of how little attention semioticians have paid to audiences. An analogous complaint is made by Marvin Carlson in his important study of the semiotics of theatrical architecture, 'an area', he says, 'that has as yet received almost no attention from theatre semioticians' (1989, p. 6). Carlson remedies this omission in his lucid essay in spatial and historical semiotics, which starts out from the question 'How do theatres mean?', and which proposes to examine 'how places of performance generate social and cultural meanings of their own which in turn help to structure the meaning of the entire theatre experience' (p. 2). Carlson provides detailed and historically well-documented discussions of the city conceived as theatrical space; of – at an opposite extreme – the theatre as 'jewel in the casket', i.e. as a space 'hidden' within a building expressing another function or purpose; of the playhouse as civic monument; of the facade theatre contributing to the overall signifying force of street architecture; and of the meanings of interior space and decoration within the playhouse. Mention should also be made, with regard to the 'places of performance', of Steven Mullaney's brilliant explorations of the interplay between the Elizabethan playhouse and its urban and ideological setting in The Place of the Stage (1988).

A particularly fertile terrain for the application and re-elaboration of theatre semiotics has been feminist theory and criticism. One reason for this is that feminist drama critics wish to expose the ideological codes at work in the production of (patriarchal) 'meanings' on stage, and find in semiotics a vocabulary adaptable to this purpose. Sue-Ellen Case's excellent introduction to the field (1988), for example, suggestively recasts the concept of performance text from the perspective of audience collaboration:

> The constitution of a performance text, separate but equal to the written one, implies new dimensions in the co-production of the text. The importance of the author's intent gives way to the conditions of production and the composition of the audience in determining the meaning of the theatrical event. This implies that there is no aesthetic closure around the text, separating it from the conditions of its production.

Case then goes on to consider the implications of this concept for feminist theatre studies:

> This semiotic constitution of the performance text is useful to a feminist poetics. Because the composition of the audience is an element in the co-production of the play's meaning, the gender of the audience members is crucial in determining what the feminist play might mean. (p. 117).

Of particular interest to Case is the stage image of women as an encoding of gender conventions, for example in the management of movement and body-to-body space, since 'Stage movement replicates the proxemics of the social order, capitalising upon the spatial relationships in the culture at large between women and the sites of power.' (pp. 117–18).

Gayle Austin, in her guide to feminist theories applied to dramatic criticism (1990) is similarly concerned with the way 'Each object, body, and gesture on stage is inscribed with cultural meanings', and she affirms that 'semiotics helps focus attention on the fact that these signs are not value-free. Feminist semiotics examines "woman as sign," finds that "woman" is a cultural construct, and attempts to deconstruct this sign'. (p. 76). Such concern with women on stage as ideologically determined sign vehicles takes the more specific form, in Elaine Aston's introduction to feminism and theatre (1995), of an enquiry into the female performer as text: 'Feminist intervention in understanding theatre as a sign system has also opened up the possibilities of analysing the female performer as the author of a potentially subversive site/sight in mainstream historical stages . . . The female performer as potential creator of an "alternative" text to the male-authored stage picture in which she is "framed", is then made available for consideration' (p. 32). Aston turns her attention elsewhere (1996) to feminist spectatorship, developing Jill Dolan's notion of the 'resistant spectator' (Dolan 1988) with specific reference to responses to performances of Sarah Daniel's play *Masterpieces*.

DISSEMINATIONS: THE 'POST'-SEMIOTIC DIASPORA OF THE SIGN

Not all recent critical modes or movements have been as receptive to semiotics as feminist theory. More or less radical critiques of semiotic approaches to theatre have come from neighbouring and potentially sympathetic fields such as the phenomenology of drama. Thus the American phenomenologist Bert States has criticized the semioticians' failure to respect the perceptual, and hence phenomenal, materiality and unity of performance in their anxiety to view it as a mode of textual or 'linguistic' articulation: "The problem with semiotics is that in addressing theater as a system of codes it necessarily dissects the perceptual impression theater makes on the spectator . . . Thus the danger of a [semiotic] approach to theater is that one is apt to look past the site of our sensory engagement with its empirical objects. This site is the point at which art is no longer *only* language.' (1985, p.7). The result, according to States, is a failure to engage directly with the theatrical experience.

An insufficient hold on the materiality of the phenomena it addresses is one of the charges brought against structuralist semiotics within post-structuralist critical movements such as cultural materialism, which has tended to regard any reduction of cultural production to the status of language as idealistic. Or to put it another way, the chief accusation of post-structuralist criticism towards semiotics has been that of excessive formalism. Christopher Norris gives a good account of this critique and of the desire to move 'beyond formalism' in his essay on "Post-structuralist Shakespeare" (1985):

> Post-structuralism is perhaps best characterized by its willingness to acknowledge this predicament [the 'repetition compulsion' of criticism.] The structuralist enterprise aimed at precisely this ideal: that criticism should aspire to a 'science' of the text which would finally uncover its variant 'grammars' of structure and style. This approach laid down a firm disciplinary line between literature and the systematic discourse of knowledge which sought to comprehend it. But such ambitions soon gave way as critics like Roland Barthes came to recognize the inadequacy of formalistic methods and the way in which textual signification exceeds all merely heuristic limits. (p. 61)

The post-structuralist critique of the sign began not within critical theory and practice but within the radical philosophical questioning of the history of western thought and its idealist metaphysical underpinnings by such thinkers as Foucault and Derrida. The latter's critique of structuralism and semiotics, like his formidable attack on speech-act theory, was not undertaken as a contribution to literary critical discourse, despite the great influence that it has exercised on recent criticism, but as part of a highly ambitious deconstructive project that took on many of the major bulwarks of twentieth-century philosophy. This project coincided, in Europe, with the questioning of the ideological and methodological limits of structuralism within the very human sciences that it had dominated for many years, as in the case of the erstwhile semiological critic Roland Barthes mentioned by Norris. The need to move beyond the classificatory and formalizing methods of structuralist poetics was both necessary and urgent. But it assumed such poetics as its background, as well as its target, so that the prefix 'post-' took on the meaning of going beyond rather than merely doing away with (structuralism), or at least the doing-away-with presupposed its object.

In Britain and the States, on the contrary, post-structuralism arrived on a critical scene where structuralism had never been dominant. The typical stance of post-structuralist criticism – i.e. the gesture of earnestly refuting the formalisms that had preceded it – was made in the absence of a powerful native tradition, making the most readily available target an enemy of straw, namely the moribund New Criticism. This not only created the problem of a lack of critical-historical 'background', but also turned the 'post' in post-structuralism into an often ideological stand rather than a dialectical process. One of the more questionable results of this was to 'desemiotize' a critical discourse that had not had the chance to absorb any of the lessons of semiotics, although there is no question that post-structuralist critical theory brought about an enormous injection of new intellectual energy into the study of literature and drama in English-speaking countries.

With regard to drama itself, particularly Renaissance drama, the most interesting and innovative development within what is generically known as post-structuralist criticism has been the advent, if not dominion, of new historicism, a movement that grew principally out of the impact in American universities – starting with Berkeley at the beginning of the Eighties – of the thought of Michel Foucault (see Richard Wilson's introduction to Wilson and Dutton [1992]). Foucault's philosophical and historical enquiries into 'the microphysics of power' fed into a new and highly productive interest in the relations between (among other things) the drama and political power structures in early modern England.

New historicism espouses the post-structuralist critique of the sign, and in particular expresses suspicion towards the tendency of structuralism – and of semiotics in the structuralist tradition – to propose universal and a-historical models, thereby avoiding any engagement with ideology. This suspicion runs, more or less explicitly, throughout the work of the 'founder' and most representative exponent of new historicist criticism, Stephen Greenblatt. Greenblatt proposed, in the introduction to his seminal volume *Renaissance Self-Fashioning* (1980), what he termed a 'poetics of culture', which he defines in his later *Shakespearean Negotiations* (1988) as the 'study of the collective making of distinct cultural practices and inquiry into the relations among those practices'; the aim of such a poetics, he says, is to determine 'how collective beliefs and experiences were shaped, moved from one medium to another, concentrated in manageable aesthetic form, offered for consumption' (p. 5).

The attempt to found a poetics not of literary and dramatic texts alone but of cultural phenomena at large, as part of what Greenblatt has called the 'circulation of energy' within Renaissance society, has proved an extremely fertile and in many ways liberating endeavour, and it has undoubtedly produced some of the best critical readings of Elizabethan drama in recent years, starting with Greenblatt's own brilliant engagements with Shakespeare and company. Above all, it has enabled a fruitful dialogue between dramatic texts and the institutions and events that shaped (and were shaped by) them, overcoming the determinism of the 'old' historicism and at the same time the a-historical closure of the various critical formalisms. The project, however, is not without its problems and its contradictions, and some of these have precisely to do with its somewhat tangential relationship with semiotics.

There is an often undeclared or 'closet' semiotics underlying new historicist discourse that might benefit from greater theoretical explicitness or (self-)awareness. This relatively hidden semiological agenda comes to light, for example, in the almost unspoken debts – or at least affinities – of Greenblatt's cultural poetics towards the cultural semiotics of Yuri Lotman. Not by chance, in his influential 1987 essay "Towards a Poetics of Culture", Greenblatt adopts Lotman's expression 'the poetics of everyday behaviour' (as he acknowledges in a footnote, p. 8). Lotman's work on the cultural models governing different historical societies and epochs is indeed close to new historicist poetics, with the difference that Lotman's project to read cultures as 'texts' is continually self-interrogating on a theoretical and methodological plane, whereas new historicism often takes its theoretical precepts as givens.

A crucial example of such silence regards precisely the key concept for any poetics or semiotics, namely the text. While Lotman and other semioticians posed, with perhaps an excess of procedural scruples, the problem of the definition and confines of the text – in what ways can a culture, or a work of art or a performance be considered as a text? – new historicists tend to read all historical phenomena, from documents proper to bodies to events, as modes of textual production, without stating or questioning the terms of such 'textualization'. This is a vital matter, since it concerns the very possibility of a poetics taking non-linguistic objects into its sights. The risk – ironically, given the anti-formalist thrust of new historicism – is that of taking all historical phenomena as an open and boundless Text, an eminently readable Liber Historiae or great book of history, and thereby of reducing historically determined social formations to merely formal (or 'poetic') structures.

The 'textual' reading of culture takes on particular force with reference to the early modern body, object of a vast amount of post-structuralist critical attention (see Elam 1996). New historicists frequently (and silently) assume a general semiotic model, namely the principle of similitude or resemblance, elected by Foucault in The Order of Things as the governing paradigm of the sixteenth-century world-view: 'It was resemblance that largely guided exegesis and the interpretation of texts; it was resemblance that organized the play of symbols, made possible knowledge of things visible and invisible, and controlled the art of representing them.' (1971: 17). Here again is the idea of the great book, in this case the Liber Naturae, the Book of Nature in which all bodies – human and animal, worldly and heavenly – are potentially readable to the trained eye: 'There are no resemblances without signatures . . . This is why the face of the world is covered with blazons, with characters, with ciphers and obscure words – with "hieroglyphics" . . . And the space inhabited by immediate resemblances becomes like a vast open book; it bristles with strange figures that intertwine and in some places repeat themselves' (1971: 26–27). The interpretation of the world and the body is thus a matter of close reading, a search for textual resemblances: 'The sixteenth century', affirms Foucault, 'superimposed hermeneutics and semiology in the form of similitude' (1971: 29).

The most celebrated reading of the drama under the aegis of Foucault's semiology of similitude is without doubt Greenblatt's essay on Twelfth Night, "Fiction and friction" (1988). Drawing on Thomas Laqueur's 'one-sex' theory, according to which early modern anatomy viewed the female sex organs as similitudes or homologues of male organs, turned inside out – 'Women . . . are inverted, and hence less perfect, men. They have exactly the same organs but in exactly the wrong places' (Laqueur 1990: 26) – Greenblatt searches for sexual resemblances and textual resemblances, not least between dramatic and medical texts: 'we must historicize Shakespearean sexual nature', he asserts, 'restoring to it its relation of negotiation and exchange with other social discourses of the body' (1988: 72). This leads him to find homologies between Renaissance medical studies of hermaphrodites and Viola's androgynous sexuality (or still more the boy actor's trans-figured gender). The relationship between medical and theatrical discourses is an Eco-like 'shared code', in this case Foucault's 'set of interlocking tropes and similitudes' (1988: 86).

Greenblatt's dramatic-medical discourse of sexual resemblances – in addition to its unquestioning reliance on the controversial 'one sex' theory – takes Foucault's semiological 'episteme' as the whole and unequivocal historical truth. This is an assumption made in much recent work on the early modern body: compare David Kuchta's claim that the Renaissance semiotics of masculinity was based on 'a hier-archy of analogies, a system of resemblances between clothing and social position' (1993, p. 244). But as with any other great historical generalization, Foucault's Renaissance 'resemblance' cannot be taken as absolute, being one semiological discourse in a play of competing models of the world, namely the Neoplatonic model (or what Lotman calls the symbolic model: see above; on Neoplatonic semiology, see Elam 1984, p. 117).

From the point of view of the semiotics of theatre, perhaps the most serious limit of recent new historicist 'body' criticism in the field of early modern drama is its lack of any reference to performance. Para-doxically, historicist poetics tends to idealize the body by collapsing actor and role into a single trope within the similitudinous play of Renaissance discourses. Little attention is paid to the conditions and conventions constraining the performer's body on the Elizabethan stage, and still less to the practice of modern or contemporary per-formance. If the semiotic poetics of drama certainly needed a 'new' historicizing and an opening up to the ideological play of power, per-haps the new historicist poetics of culture needs a more explicit and a more self-critical semiotics.

'POST'-CONCLUSION: LIFE AFTER DEATH AND PREMATURE FUNERALS

Post-structuralism may not have decreed, therefore, the demise of semiotic analysis so much as a politicizing and indeed revitalizing of its objectives. It may be, therefore, that announcements of the death of the semiotic enterprise have been greatly exaggerated, as feminist criticism among other contemporary discourses would seem to suggest. Rather than as a monument to a defunct — or merely cold, or obscure, or otherwise inaccessible — academic activity, this volume might be taken as an account of research into the languages of drama and performance in one of its livelier historical phases. Whether or not it goes under the name of semiotics, this research will surely go on.

SUGGESTIONS FOR FURTHER READING

These are the original (1980) suggestions for further reading. These works remain important, but readers should also consult the Afterword for comment on recent publications.

A number of indications have been given in the text regarding major sources and useful points of reference. Here a brief and selective guide is offered to the material – some of it not referred to above – most directly relevant to the main areas of discussion in the book. Full references for this section and the rest of the text are given in the Bibliography.

SEMIOTICS AND SEMANTICS: GENERAL THEORY AND INTRODUCTIONS

In addition to the two 'founders' of modern semiotics, Peirce (1931–58) and Saussure (1915), a number of more recent introductions may be usefully consulted. The most ambitious attempt at a general theory of semiotics is Eco (1976), largely Peircean in outlook but drawing widely on linguistics, logic and information theory: essential reading. Barthes (1964a) gives a brief account of 'semiology' in the Saussurian tradition, represented also by Prieto (1966) and Mounin (1969). A rich and idiosyncratic reflection on 'signifying practices' at large is found in Kristeva (1968b) (see also the enjoyable introduction Heath *et al.* 1971), while Guiraud (1971) offers a readable, if simplified, exposition of the 'code' and its varieties. Key semiotic concepts are defined in the Greimas and Courtès dictionary (1978). A new general introduction is promised from the American semiotician Sebeok (to appear).

Indispensable to an understanding of Continental semiotics is the work of the linguists Hjelmslev (1943), Benveniste (1966), Greimas (1966, 1970) and Jakobson. The latter (1971b) casts a retrospective eye over the semiotic project and its development.

Literary criticism is one area in which semiotic approaches have flourished in recent years. Extensive and lucid accounts of the issues in a semiotic poetics are found in Culler (1975) and Hawkes (1977a). This is a field – among others – in which Soviet semiotics is outstanding. See in particular Lotman (1972), Lotman and Uspensky (1973) and the introductory guides in Shukman (1977). Literary communication and its complex codes are well treated in Segre (1969) and Corti (1976).

On communication – particularly human – in general, nothing has replaced Colin Cherry's classic introduction (1961).

Any semiotic theory must include a semantic theory. Lyons (1977) gives an excellent overview of linguistic, logical, pragmatic and other theories of meaning, together with a chapter on semiotics. Recent linguistic accounts include Katz (1972) and Leech (1974), while logical approaches are represented in Davidson and Harman (1972) and Kempson (1977).

SEMIOTICS OF THEATRE: PRAGUE SCHOOL CONTRIBUTIONS

Matejka and Titunik (1976) collects a wide range of Prague School writings on the semiotics of different art forms, including several major articles on theatre by Bogatyrev, Brušák, Honzl and Veltruský. Matejka's postscript is a useful survey. Another anthology, Garvin (1964), includes explications by Mukařovský (1932) and Havránek (1942) of 'foregrounding', together with Veltruský's important paper (1942) on 'subjectivity' on the stage.

Useful introductions to Prague School theatrical semiotics are found in Deák (1976) and Slawinska (1978).

SEMIOTICS OF THEATRE: GENERAL THEORY AND INTRODUCTIONS

Tadeusz Kowzan's pioneering work on theatrical sign-systems (1968) has been expanded into a book-length comparison between literature and stage spectacle (1975). The best general introduction to the problem of the theatrical sign is Pavis (1976), especially illuminating on the Peircean classification, while Pavis (1980a) gives extensive definitions of traditional dramaturgical and specifically semiotic terms. The anthology edited by Helbo (1975a) includes commentaries on the sign, the code and structural analysis in the theatre.

On the 'reading' of theatrical discourse at large, Ubersfeld (1977) is a rich and packed introduction. A dense and somewhat inaccessible 'textual semiotics' theory of theatre is found in Ruffini (1978); the same author surveys semiotic approaches to the theatre (1974a) and applies information theory to theatrical communication (1974b).

Among other introductions, Eco (1977) is the most readable and contains illuminating observations on 'ostension'. Barker (1976) and Durand (1975) expound different theories of theatrical structural analysis. Overviews of problems and possible approaches appear in de Marinis (1975), Ertel (1977) and Jansen (1977). A highly useful bibliographical guide is provided in Bettetini and de Marinis (1977).

Several journals have devoted issues or parts of issues to the semiotics of theatre, notably Sub-stance (1977), Degrés (1978), Biblioteca teatrale (1978), Versus (1978b, 1979) and Poetics Today (1981).

THE PERFORMANCE TEXT AND ITS ANALYSIS

Little work has been done by way of theorizing the 'textuality' of the performance. Apart from Ruffini (1978), already mentioned, Koch (1969), a comparison between the theatrical text and the linguistic and cinematic texts, and de Marinis (1978, 1979), an exploration of the principles of textual organization and coherence in the performance, are the only instances of note, although Paul Bouissac's work on the circus performance as text (1976a, 1976b) is of direct interest here.

Semiotic analyses of specific performances are also rare. Corvin

(1971) attempts to formulate the means to coherence and ambiguity in Robert Wilson's *Deafman Glance* and *Prologue*. In Kowzan (1976) the classification of sign-systems expounded in Kowzan (1968) is applied by students to individual performances. Kirby (1976) both describes and theorizes the structural principles of the work of the Structuralist Workshop.

BODY, VOICE AND STAGE SYSTEMS

Proxemic analysis is best approached through the work of its founder, Hall (1959, 1966). More recent developments are represented by Fabbri (1968), Watson (1970) and Key (1975). The results of the direct application of proxemic research to performance are examined in Argelander (1973).

The literature on gesture is more extensive. Apart from Birdwhistell (1971), still the fullest and most detailed introduction to kinesics, other significant essays in gestural communication include Efron (1941), Greimas (1968), Scheflen (1973), Bouissac (1973), Argyle (1974) and Bernard (1976). Kristeva (1968b) gives a critical view of kinesics. The application of kinesic studies to stage movement is discussed in Stern (1973) and Schechner and Mintz (1973). Other useful observations on theatrical gesture are found in Doat (1941), Marotti (1974) and Pavis (1981). Body motion in related performance forms, i.e. circus, dance and opera, is analysed in Bouissac (1968), Ikegami (1971) and Scotto di Carlo (1973). On non-verbal communication in general in the theatre, see Miller (1972).

Paralinguistic phenomena, first systematically approached by George L. Trager (1958), are discussed in La Barre (1964), Mahl and Schulze (1964), Davitz (1964), Abercrombie (1968) and Lyons (1977, pp. 63 ff.).

Visual stage systems such as lighting and scenery design have been relatively neglected by semioticians. Schefer (1969) examines the relationship between pictorial and stage codes in the Renaissance (see also Kernodle 1944), while the same relationship in the nineteenth-century Russian theatre is the subject of Lotman (1973). Polieri (1971) attempts to formalize the annotation of stage design in a scientific 'semiography'. A preliminary 'syntax' of stage lighting is provided by the stage designer Richard Pilbrow (1970). For a good general introduction to stage systems, see Cameron and Hoffman (1974).

AUDIENCE ROLES AND RECEPTION

Some principles of a projected aesthetics of theatrical reception are outlined by Pavis (1980b), drawing on the work of Jauss and others. (On the aesthetics of reception in general, see Jauss 1970; Segers 1978; Odmark 1980.)

The receptive and active roles of the spectator in theatrical communication are explored in Campeanu (1975), and the different theatrical 'transactions' into which the audience enters in Schechner (1969).

Sociological and other modes of research into audience response are described in Goodlad (1971, pp. 94 ff.) and in the journal *Empirical Research in Theater*.

SOCIOLOGICAL PERSPECTIVES

The above-mentioned Goodlad (1971) adopts a 'mass communications' approach to the social functions of 'popular drama'.

An intelligent sociological approach to the 'theatrical' conventions governing both onstage and offstage activity is adopted in Burns (1972). In Goffman (1956, 1961) the concepts of 'role' and 'performance' in social interaction are subtly explored, while Goffman (1974) deals extensively and brilliantly with the ways in which we define theatrical and other 'performance' situations.

On the sociology of theatre in general, and of the actor in particular, see also Duvignaud (1963, 1965). Burns and Burns (1973) collects classic essays in the sociology of drama and theatre, as well as literature.

Of considerable interest to theatrical semiotics is a large body of work on face-to-face interaction in society. For introductory readings, see Goffman (1967), Laver and Hutcheson (1972) and *Semiotica* (1978).

DRAMA AND THE DRAMATIC TEXT

A number of attempts have been made to found a structuralist or semiotic theory of the drama. The most ambitious is Schmid (1973), placing the drama within a general structuralist theory of genre which owes much to the Prague School tradition. The theory is applied to plays by Chekhov.

Slawinska (1959) offers an illuminating reflection on 'structure' across a range of dramatic elements (the event, situation, character, time, space, etc.).

Hjelmslev's 'glossematic' methodology is adapted to dramatic form in Jansen (1968a). Jansen (see also 1973, 1978) takes as his base unit the 'situation', defined by the entrances and exits of characters.

Marcello Pagnini, in an influential essay (1970), applies Barthes's 'narrative functions' to the fabula of the drama, in particular Hamlet, after a general reflection on the problems of segmenting the text. These problems, and the solutions offered to date, are examined in Guarino (1978). The segmentation of the dramatic text proposed by Serpieri (1978b) on the basis of the 'deictic-performative' unit, is developed and applied to a series of texts in Serpieri et al. (1978, 1981).

In Romania, a distinct logico-mathematical school of dramatic analysis has arisen under Solomon Marcus. Informational models are used to define character (see Marcus 1975; Dinu 1968, 1974) and the dynamic structure of scenes (Dinu 1972). For a general introduction to Marcus's model, see Brainerd and Neufeldt (1974) and Revzina and Revzin (1973).

Among recent Anglo-American theories, the account of structure in Levitt (1971) is traditionally dramaturgical (the suggested unit is the 'scene'), while Hornby (1977), after a reductive exposition of 'structuralism', applies such criteria as 'choice', 'sequence' and 'rhythm' to various texts.

Relations between dramatic text and performance are the concern of Veltruský (1941), Schechner (1973), Gullì Pugliatti (1976), Jansen (1978) and Serpieri et al. (1978).

Semiotic analyses of individual dramatic texts outnumber those of performances. Classical French drama has been a favourite area of investigation. Jansen (1967, 1968b) conducts a 'situation'-based analysis of *Andromaque* and *Lorenzaccio*. The intimate relationship between language and action in the latter is discussed in Kittang (1975), in Barthesian terms. Racine's *Phèdre* serves as the basis for a comparison between narrative and dramatic time in Guiraud (1969) and for a general theory of dramatic representation in Kaisergruber *et al.* (1972). The same play is approached through a pragmatic 'performative' model in Thomas (1973). Tragedies by Racine and Corneille are examined in Hjelmslevian terms in Aron (1968). Jaffre (1974) draws on speech-act and discourse-analysis notions in describing the ideological structure of the comedies of Molière, the ambiguity of whose *Dom Juan* is considered in Rastier (1971).

Among later French texts, those of Dumas *père* are taken in Ubersfeld (1968) as paradigms of Romantic drama, structured on conflicting 'spaces' (or worlds). Helbo (1974) gives a Jakobsonian account of the linguistic code in Montherlant's *Port Royal*.

The 'metatheatrical' strategies adopted in the plays of Pirandello, experimenting with the audience-stage relationship, are the subject of Genot (1968). Elsewhere, 'absurd' drama frequently figures as object of analysis. Corvin (1973) attempts to represent the semantic structure of Adamov's *La Parodie*. Nojgaard (1978) distinguishes different temporal levels in Beckett's *Krapp's Last Tape*, whose tension structure – together with that of Pinter's *The Dumb Waiter* – is diagrammatized in Caine (1970). Segre (1974) takes the stage directions in Beckett's *Act Without Words* as a text in their own right and considers their poetic function. A lively approach to Ionesco's comedies as experiments with the communication model is adopted in Revzina and Revzin (1971, 1975).

Shakespearian drama has been the preferred object of a number of Italian semioticians. Pagnini (1976) traces the 'specular' pattern in *A Midsummer Night's Dream* and *King Lear*. The semantic and rhetorical elements of the latter are broken down in Gullì Pugliatti (1976), while Valesio (1977) gives a bold reading of Cordelia's rhetorical stance. Serpieri (1978a) contains a penetrating rhetorical-cum-psychoanalytic account of *Othello*. The metalinguistic structure of *Romeo and Juliet* is extensively discussed in Rutelli (1978). Dodd (1979a) gives a detailed metadramatic reading of *Measure for Measure*. Outside Italy, Hawkes (1977b) makes some acute observations on the paralinguistic and kinesic factors in Shakespearian dialogue.

LANGUAGE IN THE DRAMA

Several studies have been devoted to the specific question of language and its roles in the drama. One of the earliest and most important, after the founding work of Veltrusky (1941, 1942) and Honzl (1943), is Ingarden (1958), a phenomenological view of linguistic functions, concerned with the ontological, proairetic and expressive status of the dialogue.

Larthomas (1972) attempts to define the 'specific' character of dramatic discourse through a 'stylistics of genres'. Elam (1977) explores the 'foregrounding' of dramatic language through such means as metalanguage and connotation. Dodd (1979b) distinguishes the 'external' (actor-audience) from the 'internal' (actor-actor) functions of metalanguage on the stage. The rhetorical structure of the dialogue is considered in Serpieri (1979) as a clash of underlying cultural models.

Handke (1970) reflects on linguistic strategies, particularly the author's, and their effects on the audience.

SPEECH ACTS, CONVERSATION RULES, DISCOURSE ANALYSIS

Austin (1962) is the classic exposition of speech-act theory. The fullest and most accessible introduction is Searle (1969). Searle (1975a) and Searle (1975b) elaborate and modify this account. A number of essays on the subject are collected in Searle (1971). Linguistic approaches are expounded in the excellent anthology Cole and Morgan (1975), in Sadock (1974) and in Lyons (1977).

Applications of speech-act theory to literary discourse may be found in Ohmann (1971, 1973) (with extensive discussion of drama), Levin (1976), Searle (1975c) and Gale (1971). Pratt (1977) attempts a full-scale speech-act theory of literature. Dramatic representation is discussed in these terms in Urmson (1972).

The original formulation of conversation rules occurs in Grice (1967). A linguistic formalization is attempted in Gordon and Lakoff (1971). Some politeness rules are expounded in Lakoff (1973). See also Lyons (1977).

The rules for turn-taking and the general organization of conversation are the concern of a number of American sociologists. See in particular Yngve (1971), Schegloff and Sacks (1973), Sacks *et al.* (1974), Jefferson (1972) and Goffman (1975).

Different methods of discourse analysis are outlined in Sinclair and Coulthard (1973), Coulthard (1977) and Labov and Fanshel (1977).

'Pragmatics' in general as a branch of logic and linguistics is outlined in Van Dijk (1977). A literary pragmatics is proposed by Van Dijk (1976a) and Schmidt (1976). The closely related field of text grammar is treated in Van Dijk (1972). Petöfi (1975), Petöfi and Rieser (1973) and Dressler (1977).

ACTION, POSSIBLE WORLDS AND THE LOGIC OF FICTION

The classic essay in the logic of action is Von Wright (1968). Accessible treatments are found in Rescher (1966), Danto (1973) and Van Dijk (1977). The applicability of action theory to fiction is argued by Van Dijk (1975).

A useful and highly readable introduction to the theory of possible worlds in modal logic and philosophy is given in Bradley and Swartz (1979). Hughes and Cresswell (1968) give a more technical version. Important essays in possible-worlds semantics include Hintikka (1967) and Kripke (1971, 1972). Interesting, if conflicting, accounts are offered in Chisholm (1967), Lewis (1973), Plantinga (1974) and Stalnaker (1976). In recent years, various attempts have been made to extend the theory to fictional worlds: see Woods (1974), Pavel (1975) and Eco (1978, 1979). Two issues of *Versus* (1977, 1978a) are dedicated to the elaboration of a semiotic theory of possible worlds. Of particular interest here is the logical approach to dialogue in Runcan (1977).

Enjoyable introductions to the logic of fiction and drama are given in Gale (1971), Urmson (1972) and Searle (1975c).

BIBLIOGRAPHY

Abel, Lionel (1963) *Metatheatre: A New View of Dramatic Form*. New York: Hill and Wang.

Abercrombie, D. (1968) 'Paralanguage', *British Journal of Disorders of Communication*, 3, 55–9.

Alter, Jean (1975) 'Vers le mathématexte au théâtre: en codant Godot', In Helbo (1975d), 42–61.

Alter, Jean 'Decoding Mnouchkine's Shakespeare (A Grammar of Stage Signs)', in Issacharoff and Jones (1988), pp. 75–85.

Alter, Jean (1990) *A Socio-Semiotic Theory of Theatre*. Philadelphia: University of Pennsylvania Press.

Alternberd, Lynn, Lewis, Leslie L. (1966) *A Handbook for the Study of Drama*. New York: Macmillan.

Antinucci, Francesco (1974) 'Sulla deissi'. *Lingua e stile*, LX, 2, 223–47.

Argelander, Ronald (1973) 'Scott Burton's Behaviour Tableaux'. *The Drama Review*, 17, 107–13.

Argyle, Michael (1974) *Bodily Communication*. London: Methuen.

Aron, Thomas (1968) 'Bérénice et Ariane: à la recherche de critères de littérarité'. *Linguistique et littérature* (special number. *La Nouvelle Critique*), 122–7.

Artaud, Antonin (1938) (trans.) *The Theatre and Its Double*. New York: Grove Press, 1958.

Aston, Elaine (1995) *An Introduction to Feminism and Theatre*. London and New York: Routledge.

Aston, Elaine (1996) 'Gender as Sign System: The Feminist Spectator as Subject', in Patrick Campbell, ed., *Analysing Performance: A Critical Reader*. Manchester: Manchester University Press, pp. 56–69.

Aston, Elaine and Savona, George (1991) *Theatre as Sign System: A Semiotics of Text and Performance*. London and New York: Routledge.

Austin, Gayle (1990) *Feminist Theories for Dramatic Criticism*. Ann Arbor: University of Michigan Press.

Austin, John L. (1962) *How to Do Things with Words*. London: OUP.

Barker, Donald (1976) 'A Structural Theory of Theatre'. *Yale/Theatre*, 8, 1, 55–61.

Barthes, Roland (1964a) (trans) *Elements of Semiology*. London: Cape, 1967.

Barthes, Roland (1964b) (trans) 'Literature and Signification'. In *Critical Essays*. Evanston: Northwestern U.P. 1972, 261–7.

Barthes, Roland (1966) (trans.) 'Introduction to the Structural Analysis of Narration'. In *Image, Music, Text*. London: Fontana, 1977, 79–124.

Bateson, Gregory (1972) 'A Theory of Play and Fantasy'. In *Steps to an Ecology of Mind*. London: Intertext, 177–93.

Belsey, Catherine (1985) 'Disrupting sexual difference: meaning and gender in the comedies', in *Alternative Shakespeares*, John Drakakis, ed. London: Methuen/Routledge, pp. 166–190.

Benjamin, Walter (1963) (trans.) *Understanding Brecht*. New York: N.L.B., 1973.

Bennett, Susan *Theatre Audiences: Theories of Production and Reception*. London: Routledge, 1990.

Bennett, Tony (1979) *Formalism and Marxism*. London: Methuen.

Benveniste, Émile (1966) (trans.) *Problems of General Linguistics*. Miami: University of Miami Press, 1970.

Bentley, Eric (ed.) (1968) *The Theory of the Modern Stage*. Harmondsworth: Penguin.

Bernard, Michel (1976) *L'Expressivité du corps*. Paris: Delarge.

Bettetini, Gianfranco, and De Marinis, Marco (1977) *Teatro e comunicazione*. Florence: Guraldi.

Biblioteca Teatrale (1978) 20: *Dramma/spettacolo: studi sulla semiologia del teatro*.

Birch, David (1991) *The Language of Drama: Critical Theory and Practice*. London: Macmillan.

Birdwhistell, Ray L. (1971) *Kinesics and Context: Essays on Body-Motion Communication*. Harmondsworth: Penguin.

Bogatyrev, Petr (1938a) (trans.) 'Les Signes du théâtre'. *Poétique*, 8 (1971), 517–30.

Bogatyrev, Petr (1938b) (trans.) 'Semiotics in the Folk Theatre'. In Matejka and Titunik (1976), 33–49.
Bogatyrev, Petr (1940) (trans.) 'Forms and Functions of Folk Theatre'. In Matejka and Titunik (1976), 51–6.
Bogatyrev, Petr (1973) (trans.) 'Semiotica del teatro populare'. In Jurij Lotman and Boris Uspenskij (eds), Ricerche semiotiche. Turin: Einaudi.
Bonomi, Andrea (1979) Universi di discorso. Milan: Feltrinelli.
Bouissac, Paul (1968) 'Volumes sonores et volumes gestuels dans un numéro d'acrobatie'. In Langages (1968), 128–31.
Bouissac, Paul (1973) La Mesure des gestes: Prolégomènes à la sémiotique gestuelle. The Hague: Mouton.
Bouissac, Paul (1976a) Circus and Culture: A Semiotic Approach. Bloomington: Indiana U.P.
Bouissac, Paul (1976b) 'Circus Performances as Texts: A Matter of Poetic Competence'. Poetics, 5, 101–18.
Bradley, Raymond, and Swartz, Norman (1979) Possible Worlds: An Introduction to Logic and its Philosophy. Oxford: Blackwell.
Brainerd, B., and Neufeldt, V. (1974) 'On Marcus Methods for the Analysis of the Strategy of a Play'. Poetics, 10, 31–74.
Brecht, Bertolt (1964) Brecht on Theatre. Ed. John Willett. London: Eyre Methuen.
Brook, Peter (1968) The Empty Space. Harmondsworth: Penguin.
Brušák, Karel (1938) (trans.) 'Signs in the Chinese Theater'. In Matejka and Titunik (1976), 59–73.
Burke, Kenneth (1945) A Grammar of Motives. Berkeley: University of California Press.
Burns, Elizabeth (1972) Theatricality: A Study of Convention in the Theatre and in Social Life. London: Longman.
Burns, Elizabeth, and Burns, Tom (eds) (1973) Sociology of Literature and Drama. Harmondsworth: Penguin.
Caine, Cindy S. A. M. (1970) 'Structure in the One-Act Play', Modern Drama, 12, 390–8.
Calderwood, James L. (1969) Shakespearean Metadrama. Minneapolis: University of Minnesota Press.
Cameron, Kenneth M., and Hoffman, Theodore J. C. (1974) A Guide to Theatre Study. 2nd ed. New York: Macmillan.
Campeanu, Pavel (1975) 'Un Rôle secondaire: le spectateur'. In Helbo (1975d), 96–111.
Carlson, Marvin A. (1984) Theories of the Theatre: A Historical and Critical

Survey, from the Greeks to the Present. Ithaca: Cornell University Press.(expanded edition)

Carlson, Marvin A. (1989) *Places of Performance: The Semiotics of Theatre Architecture.* Ithaca: Cornell University Press.

Carlson, Marvin A. (1996) *Performance: A Critical Introduction.* London: Routledge.

Carnap, Rudolf (1947) *Meaning and Necessity.* Chicago: Chicago U.P.

Case, Sue Ellen (1988) *Feminism and Theatre.* New York and London: Routledge.

Cherry, Colin (1961) *On Human Communication.* New York: Wiley.

Chisholm, Roderick M. (1967) 'Identity through Possible Worlds: Some Questions'. *Noûs,* I, 1, 1–8.

Cole, Peter, and Morgan, Jerry L. (eds) (1975) *Syntax and Semantics. 3: Speech Acts.* New York: Academic Press.

Corti, Maria (1976) (trans.) *An Introduction to Literary Semiotics.* Bloomington: Indiana U.P., 1978.

Corvin, Michel (1971) 'A propos des spectacles de R. Wilson: Essai de lecture sémiologique'. *Cahiers Renaud-Barrault,* 77, 90–111.

Corvin, Michel (1973) 'Approche sémiologique d'un texte dramatique: *La parodie* de A. Adamov'. *Littérature,* 9, 86–100.

Coulthard, Malcolm (1977) *An Introduction to Discourse Analysis.* London: Longman.

Culler, Jonathan (1975) *Structuralist Poetics.* London: Routledge.

Danto, Arthur C. (1973) *Analytical Philosophy of Action.* Cambridge: CUP.

Davidson, Donald, and Harman, Gilbert (eds) (1972) *Semantics of Natural Language.* Dordrecht: Reidel.

Davitz, J. L. (1964) *The Communication of Emotional Meaning.* New York: New York U.P.

Davy, Kate (1976) 'Introduction'. In Foreman (1976), ix–xvi.

Deák, František (1976) 'Structuralism in Theatre: The Prague School Contribution'. *The Drama Review,* 20, 83–94.

Degrés (1978) 13: *Théâtre et sémiologie.*

De Man, Paul (1973) 'Semiology and Rhetoric'. *Diacritics,* Fall, 27–33.

De Marinis, Marco (1975) 'Problemi e aspetti di un approccio semiotics al teatro'. *Lingua e stile,* X, 2, 343–57.

De Marinis, Marco (1978) 'Lo spettacolo come testo (I)'. In *Versus* (1978a), 66–104.

De Marinis, Marco (1979) 'Lo spettacolo come testo (II)'. In *Versus* (1979), 3–31.

De Marinis, Marco (1984) 'L'esperienza dello spettatore. Fondamenti per una semiotica della ricezione teatrale', *Documenti di Lavoro*, Università di Urbino, 138–139 (Serie F), pp. 1–36.

De Marinis, Marco (1985) 'Theatrical Comprehension: A Socio-Semiotic Approach', *Theatre*, XV, 1, pp. 5–20.

De Marinis, Marco (1989) 'Dallo spettatore modello allo spettatore reale: processi cognitivi della ricezione teatrale', *Versus*, 52–53, pp. 81–98.

De Marinis, Marco (1992) *The Semiotics of Performance*, translated by Áine O'Healy. Bloomington: Indiana University Press (tr. of *Semiotica del teatro: L'analisi testuale dello spettacolo*. Milan: Bompiani, 1982).

De Toro, Fernando (1988a) 'Text, Dramatic Text, Performance Text', *Degrés*, 56, g-g10.

De Toro, Fernando (1988b) 'Theatre and Film: A Semiotic Approach to their Specificity', in *Theatre and Television*. Amsterdam: International Theatre Bookshop, pp. 179–196.

De Toro, Fernando (1988c) 'Towards a Socio-Semiotics of the Theatre', *Semiotica*, 72, 1–2, pp. 37–70.

De Toro, Fernando (1989a) 'Toward a Specification of Theatre Discourse', *Versus*, 54, pp. 3–20.

De Toro, Fernando (1989b) 'Theatricality or Theatricalities? Towards a Notional Definition', *Theater Three*, 6, pp. 12–13.

De Toro, Fernando (1991) 'Toward a New Theatrology', *The Canadian Journal of Drama and Theatre*, 1, 2, pp. 47–58.

De Toro, Fernando (1995) *Theatre Semiotics: Text and Staging in Modern Theatre* trans. John Lewis, revised and edited by Carole Hubbard. Toronto: Toronto University Press (translation of *Semiotica del Teatro: del Texto a la Puesta en Escena*, Burenos Aries: Editorial Galerna, 1987).

Dinu, Mihai (1968) 'Structures linguistiques probabilistes issues de l'étude du théâtre'. *Cahiers de linguistique théorique et appliquéee*, 5, 29–46.

Dinu, Mihai (1972) 'L'Interdépendence syntagmatique des scènes dans une pièce de théâtre'. *Cahiers de linguistique théorique et appliquée*, 9, 55–69.

Dinu, Mihai (1974) 'La Stratégie des personnages dramatiques à la lumière du calcul propositionnel bivalent'. *Poetics*, X, 147–59.

Doat, J. (1941) *L'Expression corporelle du comédien*. Paris: Librairie théâtrale.

Dodd, William (1979a) *Misura per misura: La trasparenza della commedia*. Milan: Il Formichiere.

Dodd, William (1979b) 'Metalanguage and Character in Drama'. *Lingua e stile*, XIV, 1, 135–50.

Dolan, Jill (1988) *The Feminist Spectator as Critic.* Ann Arbor: The University of Michigan Press.

Dressler, Wolfgang U. (ed.) (1977) *Trends in Textlinguistics.* Berlin: de Gruyter.

Ducrot, Oswald, and Todorov, Tzvetan (1972) *Dictionnaire encyclopédique.* Paris: Seuil.

Durand, Régis (1975) 'Problèmes de l'analyse structurale et sémiotique de la forme théâtrale'. In Helbo (1975d), 112–21.

Duvignaud, Jean (1963) *Sociologie du théâtre: Essai sur les ombres collectives.* Paris: P.U.F.

Duvignaud, Jean (1965) *L'Acteur: Esquisse d'une sociologie du comédien.* Paris: P.U.F.

Eco, Umberto (1976) *A Theory of Semiotics.* Bloomington: Indiana U.P. (London: Macmillan, 1977.)

Eco, Umberto (1977) 'Semiotics of Theatrical Performance'. *The Drama Review,* 21, 107–17.

Eco, Umberto (1978) 'Possible Worlds and Text Pragmatics: Un drame bien parisien'. In *Versus* (1978a), 5–72.

Eco, Umberto (1979) *Lector in Fabula: la cooperazione interpretativa nei testi narrativi.* Milan: Bompiani.

Efron, David (1941) *Gesture, Race and Culture.* The Hague: Mouton, 1972.

Elam, Keir (1977) 'Language in the Theater'. In *Sub-stance* (1977), 139–62.

Elam, Keir (1978) 'Appunti sulla deissi, l'anafora e le trasformazioni nel testo e sulla scena'. In Serpieri *et al.* (1978), 97–128.

Elam, Keir (1983) 'Much Ado about Doing Things with Words (and Other Means): Some Problems in the Pragmatics of Theatre and Drama', *Australian Journal of French Studies,* xx, 3, pp. 261–77 (reprinted in Issacharoff and Jones [1988]).

Elam, Kier (1984) *Shakespeare's Universe of Discourse: Language-games in the Comedies.* Cambridge: Cambridge University Press.

Elam, Kier (1985) ' "Understand me by my signs": On Shakespeare's semiotics', *New Theatre Quarterly,* I,1, pp. 84–97.

Elam, Kier (1989) 'Text Appeal and the Analysis Paralysis: Towards a Processual Poetics of Dramatic Representation', in Fitzpatrick (1989a), pp. 1–26.

Elam, Kier (1996) ' "In What Chapter of his Bosom?": Reading Shakespeare's Bodies', in Terence Hawkes, ed., *Alternative Shakespeares, Volume 2.* London: Routledge, pp. 140–163.

Elam, Kier (2000) 'Language and the Body', in Ann Thompson, Lynnette

Hunter e Lynne Magnusson, eds., *Shakespeare's Dramatic Language*, London, Arden Shakespeare.

Elsom, John (1988) 'Criticism: 1. European', in Martin Banham (ed.), *Cambridge Guide to World Theatre*, Cambridge: Cambridge University Press.

Empirical Research in Theater. The Center for Communication Research, Bowling Green State University.

Ertel, Evelyne (1977) 'Éléments pour une sémiologie du théâtre'. *Travail théâtral*, 28/29, 121–50.

Esslin, Martin (1987) *The Field of Drama*. London: Methuen.

Fabbri, Paolo (1968) 'Considérations sur la proxémique'. In *Langages* (1968), 65–75.

Finter, Helga (1983) 'Experimental Theatre and Semiology of Theatre: The Theatricalisation of Voice', *Modern Drama* 26, pp. 501–17.

Fischer-Lichte, Erika (1987) 'Performance as an Interpretant of the Drama', *Semiotica* 64, 3–4, pp. 197–212.

Fischer-Lichte, Erika (1993) *The Semiotics of Theater*, trans. Jeremy Gaines and Doris L. Jones, Bloomington: Indiana University Press (*Semiotik des Theaters*, Tübingen: Gunter Narr Verlag, 1983).

Fitzpatrick, Tim (1986) 'Playscript Analysis, Performance Analysis: Towards a Theoretical Model', *Gestos*, 2, pp. 13–28.

Fitzpatrick, Tim (1989a) (ed.) *Altro Polo. Perfomance: From Product to Process*. University of Sydney.

Fitzpatrick, Tim (1989b) 'The Dialectics of Space-Time: Dramaturgical and Directorial Strategies for Performance and Fictional World', in Fitzpatrick (1989a), pp. 49–111.

Fitzpatrick, Tim (1995) 'Shakespeare's Exploitation of a Two-door Stage: *Macbeth*', *Theatre Research International* 20:3, pp. 207–30.

Fitzpatrick, Tim (1999) 'Stage Management, Dramaturgy and Spatial Semiotics in Shakespeare's Dialogue', *Theatre Research International* 24, 1, pp. 1–22.

Fitzpatrick, Tim and Millyard, Wendy (2000) 'Hangings, Doors and Discoveries: Conflicting Evidence or Problematic Assumptions?', *Theatre Notebook* 54, 1, pp. 2–23

Foreman, Richard (1976) *Plays and Manifestos*. Ed. Kate Davy. New York: New York U.P.

Fortier, Mark (1997) *Theatre/Theory: An Introduction*. London: Routledge

Foucault, Michel (1971) *The Order of Things: An Archaeology of the Human Sciences*, trans. Alan Sheridan. London: Tavistock.

Frye, Northrop (1957) *Anatomy of Criticism*. Princeton: Princeton U.P.

Gale, R. M. (1971) 'The Fictive Use of Language'. *Philosophy*, 46, 324–40.

Garvin, Paul L. (ed.) (1964) *A Prague School Reader on Esthetics, Literary Structure and Style*. Washington: George-town U.P.

Genot, Gérard (1968) 'Caractères du lieu théâtral chez Pirandello'. *Revue des études italiennes*, XIV, 8–25.

Giglioli, Pier Paolo (ed.) (1972) *Language and Social Context*. Harmondsworth: Penguin.

Goffman, Erving (1959) *The Presentation of Self in Everyday Life*. New York: Doubleday.

Goffman, Erving (1961) *Encounters*. Harmondsworth: Penguin, 1972.

Goffman, Erving (1967) *Interaction Ritual*. New York: Doubleday.

Goffman, Erving (1974) *Frame Analysis*. Harmondsworth: Penguin.

Goffman, Erving (1975) *Replies and Responses*. Urbino: Centro di Semiotica e di Linguistica, Working Papers 46 47.

Goodlad, J. S. R. (1971) *A Sociology of Popular Drama*. London: Heinemann.

Gordon, David, and Lakoff, George (1971) 'Conversational Postulates'. In Cole and Morgan (1975), 83–106.

Gregory, Michael and Carroll, Susanne (1978) *Language and Situation: Language Varieties and their Social Contexts*. London: Routledge.

Greimas, A. J. (1966) *Sémantique structurale*. Paris: Larousse.

Greimas, A. J. (1968) 'Conditions d'une sémiotique du monde naturel'. In *Langages* (1968). (Also in Greimas (1970), 49–91.)

Greimas, A. J. (1970) *Du sens*. Paris: Seuil.

Greimas, A. J. and Courtès, J. (1978) *Sémiotique: Dictionnaire raisonné et comparé*. Paris: Hachette.

Greenblatt, Stephen (1980) *Renaissance Self-Fashioning*. Chicago: University of Chicago Press.

Greenblatt, Stephen (1987) 'Towards a Poetics of Culture', *Southern Review*, pp. 3–15 (reprinted in H. Aram Veseer, ed., *The New Historicism*. New York and London: Routledge, 1989, pp. 1–14).

Greenblatt, Stephen (1988) 'Fiction and Friction', in *Shakespearean Negotiations: The Circulation of Social Energy in Renaissance England*. Oxford: Clarendon Press, pp. 66–91.

Grice, H. P. (1967) 'Logic and Conversation'. In Cole and Morgan (1975), 41–58.

Grice, H. P. (1968) 'Utterer's Meaning, Sentence-Meaning and Word-Meaning'. In Searle (1971), 54–70.

Groupe μ (1970) *Rhétorique générale*. Paris: Larousse.

Guarino, Raimondo (1978) 'Per una definizione del dramma: proposte e problemi dalla narratologia alla tipologia testuale'. In *Biblioteca teatrale* (1978), 75–113.

Guiraud, Pierre (1969) 'Temps narratif et temps dramatique: le récit dramatique'. In *Essais de stylistique*. Paris; Klincksieck, 151–73.

Guiraud, Pierre (1971) (trans.) *Semiology*. London: Routledge, 1975.

Gullì Pugliatti, Paola (1976) *I segni latenti: Scrittura come virtualita in King Lear*. Messina and Florence: D'Anna.

Hall, Edward T. (1959) *The Silent Language*, New York: Doubleday.

Hall, Edward T. (1966) *The Hidden Dimension*. New York: Doubleday.

Hammond, Brean (1984) 'Theatre Semiotics: An "Academic Job Creation Scheme"?' *Interface*, 2, pp. 78–89.

Hamon, Philippe (1972) 'Pour un statut sémiologique du personnage'. In *Poétique du récit*. Paris: Seuil, 1977, 115–80.

Handke, Peter (1970) 'Nauseated by Language (Interview with Arthur Joseph)'. *The Drama Review*, 15, 56–61.

Havránek, Bohuslav (1942) (trans.) 'The Functional Differentiation of the Standard Language'. In Garvin (1964), 3–16.

Hawkes, Terence (1977a) *Structuralism and Semiotics*. London: Methuen.

Hawkes, Terence (1977b) 'That Shakespeherian Rag'. *Essays and Studies*, 22–38.

Heath, Stephen, Maccabe, Colin, and Prendergast, Christopher (eds) (1971) *Signs of the Times: Introductory Readings in Textual Semiotics*. Cambridge: Granta.

Helbo, André (1974) 'Prolégomènes à la sémiologie théâtrale: une lecture de *Port Royal*'. *Semiotica*, 11, 359–73.

Helbo, André (1975a) 'Le code théâtral'. In Helbo (1975d), 12–27.

Helbo, André (1975b) 'La représentation dans le récit'. In Helbo (1975d), 28–32.

Helbo, André (1975c) 'Pour un proprium de la représentation théâtrale'. In Helbo (1975d), 62–72.

Helbo, André (ed.) (1975d) *Sémiologie de la représentation*. Brussels: Complexe.

Helbo, André (1985) 'Approches de la réception. Quelques problèmes', *Versus*, 41, pp. 41–48.

Helbo, André (1987) *Theory of Performing Arts*. Amsterdam: John Benjamins.

Herman, Vimala (1995) *Dramatic Discourse: Dialogue as Interaction in Plays*. London: Routledge.

Hinde, R. A. (ed.) (1972) *Non-Verbal Communication*. Cambridge: CUP.

Hintikka, Jaakko (1967) 'Individuals, Possible Worlds and Epistemic Logic'. *Noûs*, I, 1, 33–62.

Hjelmslev, Louis (1943) (trans.) *Prologomena to a Theory of Language*. Madison: University of Wisconsin Press.

Hodgson, Terry (1988) *The Batsford Dictionary of Drama*, London, Batsford.

Honzl, Jindřich (1940) (trans.) 'Dynamics of the Sign in the Theater'. In Matejka and Titunik (1976), 74–93.

Honzl, Jindřich (1943) (trans.) 'The Hierarchy of Dramatic Devices'. In Matejka and Titunik (1976), 118–27.

Hornby, Richard (1977) *Script into Performance: A Structuralist View of Play Production*. Austin: University of Texas Press.

Hughes, G. E., and Cresswell, M. J. (1968) *An Introduction to Modal Logic*. London: Methuen.

Ikegami, Yoshihiko (1971) 'A Stratificational Analysis of the Hand Gestures in Indian Classical Dancing', *Semiotica*, IV, 365–91.

Ingarden, Roman (1958) (trans.) 'The Functions of Language in the Theatre'. Appendix, *The Literary Work of Art*. Evanston: Northwestern U.P., 377–96.

Interazione, dialogo, convenzione: Il caso del testo drammatico, Bologna: Clueb, 1983.

Interface (1984) *Semiotics and Theatre: 1983 Alsager Seminar.*

Issacharoff, Michael (1981) 'Space and Reference in Drama', *Poetics To-day*, 2,3, pp. 211–24.

Issacharoff, Michael (1988) 'Stage Codes', in Issacharoff and Jones (1988), pp. 59–74.

Issacharoff Michael and Jones, R. F., eds. (1988) *Performing Texts*. Philadelphia: University of Philadelphia Press.

Jaffre, Jean (1974) 'Théâtre et idéologie, note sur la dramaturgie de Molière'. *Littérature*, 13, 58–74.

Jakobson, Roman (1960) 'Linguistics and Poetics'. In Thomas A. Sebeok (ed.), *Style in Language*. Cambridge, Mass.: MIT Press, 355–77.

Jakobson, Roman (1971a) *Selected Writings. II: Word and Language*. The Hague: Mouton.

Jakobson, Roman (1971b) *Coup de l'œil sur le développement de la sémiotique*. Bloomington: Research Center for Language and Semiotic Studies, Indiana University.

Jakobson, Roman, and Halle, Morris (1956) *Fundamentals of Language*. The Hague: Mouton.

Jansen, Steen (1967) 'Sur les personnages dans *Andromaque*'. *Orbis Litterarum*, 22, 77–87.

Jansen, Steen (1968a) 'Esquisse d'une théorie de la forme dramatique'. *Langages*, 12, 71–93.

Jansen, Steen (1968b) 'L'Unité d'action dans *Andromaque* et dans *Lorenzaccio*'. *Revue Romane*, III, 1, 16–29.

Jansen, Steen (1973) 'Qu'est-ce qu'une situation dramatique?'. *Orbis Litterarum*, XXVII, 4, 235–92.

Jansen, Steen (1977) *Appunti per l'analisi dello spettacolo*. Urbino, Centro Internazionale di Semiotica e Linguistica, Working Paper 68.

Jansen, Steen (1978) 'Problemi dell'analisi di testi drammatici'. In *Biblioteca teatrale* (1978), 14–43.

Jauss, Hans Robert (1970) *Literaturgeschichte als Provokation*. Frankfurt: Suhrkamp.

Jefferson, Gail (1972) 'Side Sequences'. In David N. Sudnow (ed.), *Studies in Social Interaction*. New York: Free Press, 294–338.

Jeffrey, Richard C. (1965) *The Logic of Decision*. New York: McGraw.

Joseph, B. I. (1951) *Elizabethan Acting*. London: OUP.

Kaisergruber, D., Kraisergruber, D., and Lempert J. (1972) *Phèdre de Racine: pour une sémiotique de la représentation classique*. Paris: Larousse.

Katz, Jerrold J. (1972) *Semantic Theory*. New York: Harper and Row.

Kempson, Ruth M. (1977) *Semantic Theory*. Cambridge: CUP.

Kernodle, George R. (1944) *From Art to Theatre: Form and Convention in the Renaissance*. Chicago: University of Chicago Press.

Key, M. R. (1975) *Paralanguage and Kinesics*. Metuchen, NJ: Scarecrow.

Kirby, Michael (1973) 'Ontological-Hysterical Theatre'. *The Drama Review*, 17, 5–32.

Kirby, Michael (1976) 'Structural Analysis/Structural Theory'. *The Drama Review*, 20, 51–68.

Kittang, A. (1975) 'Action et langage dans Lorenzaccio', *Revue Romane*, X, 1, 33–49.

Kobernik, Mark (1989) *Semiotics of the Drama and the Style of Eugene O'Neill*. Amsterdam: J. Benjamins.

Koch, Walter (1969) 'Le Texte normal, le théâtre et le film'. *Linguistics*, 48, 40–67.

Kott, Jan (1969) 'The Icon and the Absurd'. *The Drama Review*, 14, 17–24.

Kowzan, Tadeusz (1968) (trans.) 'The Sign in the Theatre'. *Diogenes*, 61, 52–80.

Kowzan, Tadeusz (1975) *Littérature et spectacle*. The Hague: Mouton.

Kowzan, Tadeusz (ed.) (1976) *Analyse sémiologique du spectacle théâtral*. Lyon: Centre d'Études et de Recherches Théâtrales, Université de Lyon II.

Kripke, Saul (1971) 'Semantical Considerations in Modal Logic'. In Leonard Linsky (ed.), *Reference and Modality*. London: OUP, 53–72.

Kripke, Saul (1972) 'Naming and Necessity'. In Davidson and Harman (1972), 253–355.

Kristeva, Julia (1968a) *Sémiotikè: Recherches pour une sémanalyse*. Paris: Seuil.

Kristeva, Julia (1968b) 'Le geste, pratique ou communication?' In *Langages* (1968), 64–84. Reprinted in Kristeva (1968a).

Kristeva, Julia (1970) *Le Texte du roman: approche sémiologique d'une structure discursive transformationelle*. The Hague: Mouton.

Kristeva, Julia (1977) 'Modern Theater Does Not Take (A) Place'. In *Sub-stance* (1977), 131–4.

Kuchta, David (1993) 'The Semiotics of Masculinity in Renaissance England', in James Grantham Turner ed. *Sexuality and Gender in Early Modern Europe: Institutions, Texts, Images*. Cambridge: Cambridge University Press, pp. 233–46.

La Barre, Weston (1964) 'Paralinguistics, Kinesics and Cultural Anthropology'. In Sebeok *et al*. (1964), 191–220.

Labov, William, and Fanshel, David (1977) *Therapeutic Discourse: Psychotherapy as Conversation*. New York: Academic Press.

Lakoff, Robin (1973) 'The Logic of Politeness; or, Minding Your P's and Q's'. *Papers from the Ninth Regional Meeting of the Chicago Linguistic Society*, 292–305.

Langages (1968) 10: *Pratiques et langages gestuels*.

Langages (1969) 13: *L'Analyse du discours*.

Langer, Susanne K. (1953) *Feeling and Form*. New York: Scribner's.

Laqueur, Thomas (1990) *Making Sex: Body and Gender from the Greeks to Freud*, Cambridge, Mass.: Harvard University Press.

Larthomas, Pierre (1972) *Le Langage dramatique*. Paris: Colin.

Laver, J., and Hutcheson, S. (eds) (1972) *Face to Face Communication*. Harmondsworth: Penguin.

Leech, Geoffrey (1974) *Semantics*. Harmondsworth: Penguin.

Levin, Samuel R. (1976) 'Concerning What Kind of Speech Act a Poem is'. In Van Dijk (1976b), 141–60.

Levitt, P. M. (1971) *A Structural Approach to the Analysis of Drama*. The Hague: Mouton.

Lewis, David K. (1973) *Counterfactuals*. Oxford: Blackwell.

Lodge, David (1977) *The Modes of Modern Writing*. London: Edward Arnold.

Lotman, Yuri M. (1972) (trans.) *La struttura del testo poetico*. Milan: Mursia.

(English trans. *Analysis of the Poetic Text*. Ann Arbor: Michigan U.P., 1976.)

Lotman, Yuri M. (1973) (trans.) 'La scena e la pittura come dispositivi codificatori del comportamento culturale nella Russia del primo Ottocento'. In Lotman and Uspensky (1973), 277–91.

Lotman, Yuri M. (1981) "Semiotica della scena", *Strumenti critici*, 15, 1, pp.1–29.

Lotman, Yuri M., and Uspensky, Boris a. (1973) *Tipologia della cultura*. Milan: Bompiani.

Lyons, John (1977) *Semantics*. Cambridge: CUP.

McLuhan, H. Marshall, and Carpenter, Edmund (eds) (1960) *Explorations in Communication*. Boston: Beacon Press.

Magli, Patrizia (1979) 'The System of the Passions in Eighteenth Century Dramatic Mime', In *Versus* (1979), 32–47.

Mahl, George, and Schulze, Gene (1964) 'Psychological Research in the Extralinguistic Area'. In Sebeok *et al.* (1964), 51–124.

Malinowski, Bronislaw (1930) 'The Problem of Meaning in Primitive Languages'. Supplement to C. K. Ogden and I. A. Richards, *The Meaning of Meaning*. 2nd ed. London: Routledge, 296–336.

Marcus, Solomon (1975) 'Stratégie des personnages dramatiques'. In Helbo (1975d), 73–95.

Marotti, Ferruccio (1974) 'Per un'analisi dei teatri orientali: la codificabilità del "gestuale"'. In *Letteratura e critica: studi in onore di Natalino Sapegno*. Rome: Bulzoni.

Matejka, Ladislaw, and Titunik, Irwin R. (eds) (1976) *Semiotics of Art: Prague School Contributions*. Cambridge, Mass.: MIT Press.

Metz, Christian (1971) (trans.) *Language and Cinema*. The Hague: Mouton, 1974.

Miller, Jonathan (1972) 'Plays and Players'. In Hinde (1972), 359–72.

Minonne, Aurelio (1979) 'Il codice cinesico nel 'Prontuario delle pose sceniche di Alamanno Morelli'. In *Versus* (1979), 48–79.

Moles, Abraham (1958) (trans.) *Information Theory and Esthetic Perception*. Urbana: University of Illinois Press, 1966.

Mounin, Georges (1969) Introduction à la sémiologie. Paris: Les Editions de Minuit.

Mukařovský, Jan (1931) (trans.) 'Tentativo di analisi del fenomeno dell' attore'. In Mukařovský (1966), 342–9.

Mukařovský, Jan (1932) (trans.) 'Standard Language and Poetic Language'. In Garvin (1964), 17–30.

Mukařovský, Jan (1934) (trans.) 'L'arte come fatto semiologico'. In

244 BIBLIOGRAPHY

Mukařovský (1966), 141–8. (English trans. in Matejka and Titunik (1976).)

Mukařovský, Jan (1966) (trans.) *Ill significato dell' estetica*. Turin: Einaudi, 1973.

Mullaney, Steven (1988) *The Place of the Stage: License, Play and Power in Renaissance England*. Chicago: University of Chicago Press.

Nojgaard, Morten (1978) 'Tempo drammatico e tempo narrativo: saggio sui livelli temporali ne *La Dernière Bande* di Beckett'. In *Biblioteca teatrale* (1978), 64–74.

Norris, Christopher (1985) 'Post-structuralist Shakespeare', in John Drakakis (ed.) *Alternative Shakespeares*. London: Methuen, pp. 47–66.

Ohmann, Richard (1971) 'Speech, Action and Style'. In Seymour Chatman (ed.), *Literary Style*. London: OUP, 241–54.

Ohmann, Richard (1973) 'Literature as Act'. In Seymour Chatman (ed.), *Approaches to Poetics*. New York: Columbia U.P., 81–107.

Osmond, Humphry (1957) 'Function as the Basis of Psychiatric Ward Design'. *Mental Hospitals* (Architectural Supplement), 23–9.

Ouaknine, Serge (1970) '"Prince constant": étude et reconstruction du déroulement du spectacle', in *Les voies de la création théâtrale*, Vol I, ed. JeanJacquot. Paris: CNRS, pp. 33–129.

Pagnini, Marcello (1970) 'Per una semiologia del teatro classico'. *Strumenti critici*, 12, 122–40.

Pagnini, Marcello (1976) *Shakespeare e il paradigma della specularità*. Pisa: Pacini.

Pagnini, Marcello (1978) 'Riflessioni sulla enunciazione letteraria e in particolare sulla comunicazione a teatro'. In Serpieri *et al.* (1978), 171–81.

Pavel, Thomas G. (1975) 'Possible Worlds in Literary Semantics'. *Journal of Aesthetics and Art Criticism*, 34, 2, 165–176.

Pavis, Patrice (1976) *Problèmes de sémiologie théâtrale*. Quebec. Les Presses de l'Université du Québec.

Pavis, Patrice (1978) 'Remarques sur le discours théâtral'. In *Degrés* (1978).

Pavis, Patrice (1980a) *Dictionnaire du Théâtre*. Paris: Editions Sociales.

Pavis, Patrice (1980b) 'Vers une esthétique de la reception théâtrale. In V. Bourgy and R. Durand (eds) *La Relation théâtrale*. Lille: Presses de L'Université de Lille.

Pavis, Patrice (1981) 'Problems of a Semiotics of Gesture', in *Poetics Today* (1981).

Pavis, Patrice (1981) 'Semiology and the Vocabulary of the Theatre', *Theatre Quarterly* 10, 40, pp. 74–8.

Pavis, Patrice (1982) *Voix et images de la scène*. Lille: Presses Universitaires de Lille.

Pavis, Patrice (1983) 'Production et réception au théâtre: la concretisation du texte dramatique et spectaculaire', *Revue des sciences humaines*, LX, 189, pp. 51–88.

Pavis, Patrice (1985a) 'La réception du texte dramatique et spectaculaire: les processus de fictionnalisation et idéologisation', *Versus*, 41, pp. 69–94.

Pavis, Patrice (1985b) 'Theatre Analysis: Some Questions and a Questionnaire', *New Theatre Quarterly*, 1 (2), pp. 208–12.

Pavis, Patrice (1988) 'From Text to Performance', in Issacharoff and Jones (1988), pp. 86–100.

Pavis, Patrice (1998) *Dictionary of the Theatre: Terms, Concepts, and Analysis* tr. Christine Shantz Toronto, University of Toronto Press (tr. Of *Dictionnaire du théâtre*, 2nd edition, Paris: Editions Sociales, 1987).

Peirce, Charles S. (1931–58) *Collected Papers*. Cambridge, Mass.: Harvard U.P.

Petöfi, Janos S. (1975) *Vers une théorie partielle du texte*. Hamburg: Buske.

Petöfi, Janos S., and Rieser, hannes (eds) (1973) *Studies in Text Grammars*. Dordrecht: Reidel.

Pfister, Manfred (1988) *The Theory and Analysis of Drama*, tr. John Holliday. Cambridge: Cambridge University Press.

Pilbrow, Richard (1970) *Stage Lighting*. London: Studio Vista.

Plantinga, Alvin (1974) *The Nature of Necessity*. London: OUP.

Polieri, Jacques (1971) *Scénographie, sémiographie*. Paris: Denoel-Gonthier.

Poetics Today (1981) Issue (2, 3) on 'Drama, Theater, Performance'.

Pratt, Mary Louise (1977) *Toward a Speech Act Theory of Literary Discourse*. Bloomington: Indiana U.P.

Prieto, Luis (1966) *Messages et signaux*, Paris: P.U.F.

Rastier, François (1971) 'Les Niveaux d'ambiguïté des structures narratives'. *Semiotica*, III, 4, 289–342.

Rescher, Nicholas (ed.) (1966) *The Logic of Decision and Action*. Pittsburgh: Pittsburgh U.P.

Rescher, Nicholas (1975) *A Theory of Possibility*. Pittsburgh: Pittsburgh U.P.

Revzina, O. G., and Revzin, I. I. (1971) 'Expérimentation sémiotique chez E. Ionesco (*La Cantatrice chauve* et *La Leçon*)'. *Semiotica*, IV, 3, 240–62.

Revzina, O. G., and Revzin, I. I. (1973) 'On Marcus' Descriptive Model of Theatre'. *Cahiers de linguistique théorique et appliquée*, X, 1, 27–31.

Revzina, O. G., and Revzin I. I. (1975) 'A Semiotic Experiment on Stage:

The Violation of the Postulate of Normal Communication as a Dramatic Device'. *Semiotica*, XIV, 3, 245–68.

Ruffini, Franco (1974a) 'Semiotica del teatro: ricognizione degli studi'. *Biblioteca teatrale*, 9, 34–81.

Ruffini, Franco (1974b) 'Semiotica del teatro: la stabilizzazione del senso. Un approccio informazionale'. *Biblioteca teatrale*, 10/11, 205–39.

Ruffini, Franco (1978) *Semiotica del testo: l'esempio teatro*. Rome: Bulzoni.

Runcan, Anca (1977) 'Propositions pour un approche logique du dialogue'. In *Versus* (1977), 13–26.

Rutelli, Romana (1978) 'Due frammenti di *Romeo and Juliet*: la manifestazione metalinguistica e paralinguistica della deissi'. In Serpieri *et al.* (1978), 92–6.

Rutelli, Romana (1979) *Romeo e Giulietta: L'effabile*. Milan: Il Formichiere.

Sacks, Harvey, Schegloff, Emanuel A., and Jefferson, Gail (1974) 'A Simplest Systematics for the Organization of Turn-Taking in Conversation', *Language*, 50, 696–735.

Sacksteder, William (1975) 'Elements of the Dramatic Model'. *Diogenes*, 52, 26–54.

Sadock, Jerrold M. (1974) *Toward a Linguistic Theory of Speech Acts*. New York: Academic Press.

Saussure, Ferdinand de (1915) (trans.) *Course in General Linguistics*. London: Fontana, 1974.

Schaeffer, Pierre (1975) 'Représentation et communication'. In Helbo (1975d), 167–93.

Schechner, Richard (1969) *Public Domain*. New York: Bobbs-Merrill.

Schechner, Richard (1973) 'Drama, Script, Theatre and Performance'. *The Drama Review*, 17, 5–36.

Schechner, Richard, and Mintz, Cynthia (1973) 'Kinesics and Performance'. *The Drama Review*, 17, 102–8.

Schefer, Jean-Louis (1969) *Scénographie d'un tableau*. Paris: Seuil.

Scheflen, Albert E. (1973) *Body Language and the Social Order: Communication as Behavioural Control*. Englewood Cliffs, NJ: Prentice-Hall.

Schegloff, Emanuela. and Sacks, Harvey (1973) 'Opening up Closing'. *Semiotica*, VIII, 4, 289–327.

Schmidt, Herta (1973) *Strukturalistische Dramentheorie*. Kronberg: Scriptor.

Schmidt, Herta and Van Kesteren, Aloysius eds. (1984) *Semiotics of Drama and Theatre*. The Hague: John Benjamins.

Schmidt, Siegfried J. (1976) 'Towards a Pragmatic Interpretation of "Fictionality"'. In Van Dijk (1976b), 161–78.

Scotto di Carlo, Nicole (1973) 'Analyse semiologique des gestes et mimiques des chanteurs d'Opéra'. *Semiotica*, IX, 4, 289–317.

Searle, John R. (1969) *Speech Acts: An Essay in the Philosophy of Language*. Cambridge: CUP.

Searle, John R. (ed.) (1971) *The Philosophy of Language*. London: OUP.

Searle, John R. (1975a) 'Indirect Speech Acts'. In Cole and Morgan (1975), 59–82.

Searle, John R. (1975b) 'A Taxonomy of Illocutionary Acts'. In K. Gunderson (ed.), *Language, Mind and Knowledge*. Minneapolis: University of Minnesota Press, 344–69.

Searle, John R. (1975c) 'The Logic of Fictional Discourse'. In *New Literary History*, 6, 319–32.

Sebeok, Thomas A. (to appear) *Semiotics*. Harmondsworth: Penguin.

Sebeok, Thomas A., Hayes, Alfred S., and Bateson, Mary C. (eds) (1964) *Approaches to Semiotics*. The Hague: Mouton.

Segers, Rien T. (1978) *The Evaluation of Literary Texts*. Lisse: The Peter de Riddler Press.

Segre, Cesare (1969) (trans.) *Semiotics and Literary Criticism*. The Hague: Mouton, 1973.

Segre, Cesare (1974) 'La funzione del linguaggio ne *L'Acte sans paroles* di S. Beckett'. In *Le strutture e il tempo*. Turin: Einaudi, 253–74.

Segre, Cesare (1981) 'Narratology and Theatre', *Poetics Today*, II, 3, pp. 95–104.

Semiotica (1978) 24: *Face-to-Face Interaction*.

Serpieri, Alessandro (1978a) *Otello: l'Eros negato. Psicoanalisi di una proiezione distruttiva*. Milan: Il Formichiere.

Serpieri, Alessandro (1978b) 'Ipotesi teorica di segmentazione del testo teatrale'. In Serpieri *et al.* (1978), 11–54.

Serpieri, Alessandro (1979) 'Retorica e modelli culturali nel dramma'. In *Il Modello della cultura e i codici*. Genoa: GJES, 146–63.

Serpieri, Alessandro, *et al.* (1978) *Come communica il teatro: dal testo alla scena*. Milan: Il Formichiere.

Serpieri, Alessandro, *et al.* (1981) 'Toward a Segmentation of the Dramatic Text'. *Poetics Today*, 163–200.

Serpieri, Alessandro (1985) 'Reading the Signs: Towards a Semiotics of Shakespearean Drama', in *Alternative Shakespeares*, ed. John Drakakis, London: Routledge, pp. 119–143.

Serpieri, Alessandro et al. (1981) 'Towards a Segmentation of the Dramatic Text', *Poetics Today*, 2, 3, pp. 163–200.

Serpieri, Alessandro (1988) *Nel laboratorio di Shakespeare: Dalle fonti ai drammi*. Parma: Pratiche (4 vols.).

Short, Mick (1981) 'Discourse Analysis and the Analysis of Drama', *Applied Linguistics* II, 2, pp. 180–202.

Shukman, Ann (1977) *Literature and Semiotics: A Study of the Writings of Yu. M. Lotman*. Amsterdam: North-Holland.

Simonson, Lee (1932) 'The Ideas of Adolphe Appia'. In Bentley (1968), 27–50.

Sinclair, J. MCH., and Coulthard, R. M. (1973) *Towards an Analysis of Discourse Analysis: The English Used by Teachers and Pupils*. London, OUP.

Slawinska, Irena (1959) 'Les Problèmes de la structure du drame'. In *Stil- und Formprobleme in der Literatur*. Heidelberg, 108–13.

Slawinska, Irena (1978) 'La semiologia del teatro *in statu nascendi*: Praga 1931–1941'. In *Biblioteca teatrale* (1978), 114–35.

Souriau, Étienne (1950) *Les Deux Cent Mille Situations dramatiques*. Paris: Flammarion.

Stalnaker, Robin (1976) 'Possible Worlds'. *Noûs*, 10, 65–76.

States, Bert O. (1983) 'The Dog on Stage: Theater as Phenomenon', *New Literary History*, 14, 2, pp. 373–88.

States, Bert O. (1985) *Great Reckonings in Little Rooms: On the Phenomenology of Theatre*. Berkeley: University of California Press.

Stern, Daniel N. (1973) 'On Kinesic Analysis'. *The Drama Review*, 17, 114–31.

Styan, J. L. (1971) *Shakespeare's Stagecraft*, Cambridge: CUP.

Sub-stance (1977) 18/19: *Theater in France: Ten Years of Research*.

Szondi, Peter (1956) *Theorie des modernen Dramas*. Frankfurt: Suhrkamp Verlag.

Thomas, Johannes (1973) 'Quelques aspects de l'analyse du drame'. *Orbis Litterarum*, XXVIII, 319–31.

Todorov, Tzvetan (1968) 'Introduction'. *Communications*, 11: *Le Vraisemblable*, 1–4.

Trager, George L. (1958) 'Paralanguage: A First Approximation'. In Dell Hymes (ed.), *Language in Culture and Society*. New York: Harper and Row, 274–88.

Ubersfeld, Anne (1968) 'Structures du théâtre de A. Dumas père', *Linguistique et littérature* (special number: *La Nouvelle Critique*), 146–56.

Ubersfeld, Anne (1977) *Lire le théâtre*. Paris: Éditions Sociales.

Urmson, James O. (1972) 'Dramatic Representation'. *Philosophical Quarterly*, 22, 333–43.

Vaina, Lucia (1977) 'Les Mondes possibles du texte'. In *Versus* (1977), 3–12.

Valesio, Paolo (1977) ' "That Glib and Oylie Art" Cordelia and the Rhetoric of Anti-rhetoric'. *Versus*, 16, 91–117.

Van Dijk, Teun A. (1972) *Some Aspects of Text Grammars*. The Hague: Mouton.

Van Dijk, Teun A. (1975) 'Action, Action Description and Narrative', *New Literary History*, 6, 273–94.

Van Dijk, Teun A. (1976a) 'Pragmatics and Poetics'. In Van Dijk (1976b), 23–58.

Van Dijk, Teun A. (ed.) (1976b) *Pragmatics of Language and Literature*. Amsterdam: North-Holland.

Van Dijk, Teun A. (1977) *Text and Context: Explorations in the Semantics and Pragmatics of Discourse*. London: Longmans.

Veltruský, Jiři (1940) (trans.) 'Man and Object in the Theater'. In Garvin (1964), 83–91.

Veltruský, Jiři (1941) 'Dramatic Text as a Component of Theater'. In Matejka and Titunik (1976), 94–117.

Veltruský, Jiři (1942) 'Construction of Semantic Components'. In Matejka and Titunik (1976), 134–44.

Versus (1977) 17: *Théorie des mondes possibles et sémiotique textuelle.*

Versus (1978a) 19/20: *Semiotica testuale: mondi possibili e narratività.*

Versus (1978b) 21: *Teatro e semiotica.*

Versus (1979) 22: *Teatro e comunicazione gestuale.*

Von Wright, Georg Henrik (1968) *An Essay in Deontic Logic and the General Theory of Action*. Amsterdam: North-Holland.

Wardle, Irving (1992) *Theatre Criticism*. London: Routledge.

Watson, O. Michael (1970) *Proxemic Behaviour: A Cross-Cultural Study*. The Hague: Mouton.

Wilson, Richard and Dutton, Richard, eds. (1992) *New Historicism and Renaissance Drama*. London: Longman.

Woods, John (1974) *The Logic of Fiction: A Philosophical Sounding of Deviant Logic*. The Hague: Mouton.

Yngve, Victor H. (1971) 'On Getting a Word in Edgewise'. *Papers from the Sixth Regional Meeting of the Chicago Linguistic Society*, 567–78.

INDEX

Abercrombie, D. 71
absurdist drama 94
academic canonization 201
accessibility 92–3, 96, 97
acoustic space 40
actant 114–22; model 114–19
action 108–13; description 110;
    discourse 113; sentences 113
action and time: dramatic 105–13
actor–audience persuasion 81
actor's codes 75–8
Actor's Studio 76
Aeschylean tragedy 127
aesthetics: judgements 197–8;
    justification 39
Aesthetics of the Art of Drama (Zich)
    4–5
Agamemnon 37
agent 109
aktualisace (foregrounding) 15–16
alienation effect 15, 200
All My Sons (Miller) 128–9

Alsager Seminar on Semiotics and
    Theatre (1983) 199, 201–2, 209
Alternberd, L.: and Lewis, L. L. 131
analogousness 20
analytic criteria 167–8
anaphora 137–40, 172; signal
    65
Anglo-Saxon theatre 201
antagonist 110
Antinucci, F. 129–30
antithesis 161–2
Antony and Cleopatra
    (Shakespeare) 95–6
Appia, A. 61, 75
Aristotle 109, 124
Artaud, A. 62, 65
assumption 125
Aston, E. 215; and Savona, G.
    207–8, 209
*Attempted Structural Analysis of the
    Phenomenon of the Actor, An*
    (Mukarovsky) 4–6

audience 213; activity 79; signals
  86–7
Austin, G. 214
Austin, J. L. 68, 143–4, 145, 147, 148
author 98

background: counterfactual 92
Bald Soprano (Ionesco) 94–5, 159
Barthes, R. 17, 39, 108, 216
Bateson, G. 78
Beckett, S. 14, 23, 92, 132–3
Behaviour Tableaux (Burton) 60
Bene, C. 39
Benjamin, W. 62
Bennett, S. 213
Bennett, T. 15
Bentley, E. 61
Benveniste, É. 129, 130; distinction
  131–2
Berkeley University 217
Bernhard, S. 21
Birch, D. 212
Birdwhistell, R. L. 63–5, 66
body-motion communication
  62–70
body-to-body: dialectic 58; space 57
Bogatyrev, P. 6, 8–9, 10, 11, 57
Bond, E. 96
Bread and Puppet Theatre 10
Brecht, B. 15–16, 38, 40, 68, 200
Brechtian theatre 8, 68–9, 77
Broadway 84
Brook, P. 50, 84, 200
Brušák, K. 7, 12
Burns, E. 8, 57, 81
Burton, S. 60

Caesar and Cleopatra (Shaw) 95
Caird, J. 200, 209
calculus: dramatic 114

Cameron, K.: and Hoffman, T. 59
Carlson, M. 202–3, 213
Carroll, S.: and Gregory, M. 162–3
Case, S.-E. 214
cause-and-effect relationship 17
channel 169
Chaplin, C. 5, 14
character: subworlds 102–5
Cherry Orchard (Chekhov) 92
Chinese theatre 7, 10, 12, 69, 79–80
Chomsky, N. 206
chronological time 106
circulation of energy 218
closet semiotics 193–221
co-reference 137–40; rules 137
co-text 135–42
code 31, 43–78; and subcode
  46–50; system 43–5
codified gestures 12
coherence 166; proairetic (action)
  166; referential 166; rhetorical
  and stylistic 167; semantic 82,
  167; text 165–7
collaborators 110
column scheme 168–73
Comédie Française 76
commedia dell'arte 48, 75
commissives 151
communication 1; body-motion
  62–70; dramatic 123–5;
  elementary 31; model 31–4, 35;
  non-aesthetic 38; signification
  28–9; spectator–performer 86–7;
  theatrical 27, 28–87
communicational circuit 33
communicative cooperation 159
competence: dramatic 88; semiotic
  124
complex action 112
connotation 8–10

Constant Prince (Grotowski) 201
contemporary theatre 76
context 125–35; constraints 70–1;
   theatrical 34; types 125–6
context-of-utterance 125, 134
conversation: analysis 211; rules
   155–60
conversational implicature 155–62
cooperative principle 155–6
correlational rules 44
Corvin, M. 42–3
costume 22–3
counterfactual worlds 99
cowboy spectator 80
Craig, W.J. 12, 14
critics: newspaper 196; theatre 199
Culler, J. 83
culture: codes 47, 173; materialism
   215–16; and paralinguistic
   features 71–2; poetics of 217;
   power 212–13; signification 9
cybernetic machine 34
Czechoslovakia 4

Daniel, S. 215
Danto, A. C. 109
Davitz, J. L. 72
de Man, P. 150
de Marinis, M. 205, 206–7, 213
de Saussure, F. 2, 5
de Toro, F. 198, 203–4, 208
declarations 152
decodification 83–6
decoding 38
deconstruction 203
deep structure (Chomsky) 206
deictics: orientation 168, 169;
   strategies 131–5; verbal 23–4
deixis 23–4, 125–31, 139; spatial 131;
   text 139–40

denotation–connotation dialectic 9
Derrida, J. 216
destination 31
determinism 191
diagram 19
dialogic exchange 82
dialogue: dramatic 123
diegesis 100
directives 151
director-theorists 62
disambiguation 129
disattendance factor 80
discontinuity 40
discours 131–2
discourse 3, 39–41; action 113;
   coherence 166; dramatic 123–89,
   162–5; everyday 162–5; generic
   typology 152–3; non-academic
   197; object of 136–7; plot 118;
   pragmatic 132; theatre 39, 137;
   time 106; topic/object of 170;
   typology 152; universe of 135–42
display 27
disseminations 215–21
Doctor Faustus 11, 153
Dodd, W. 86
doings 109
Dolan, J. 215
dominance-subordination 133
drama: model 114–22;
   representation 102; score 168
dramatic world: actualization
   99–102; construction 88–105;
   creation 125
dramatis persona 114–22; status
   119–20
dramatological analysis 167–89
Ducrot, O.: and Todorov, T. 135
dynamic world 128
dynamism 105–7

Early Morning (Bond) 96
Eco, U. 22, 26, 47, 49, 93
Edward II (Marlowe) 145–6
Elizabethan era 21; drama 218;
  public playhouses 211
Elsom, J. 196–7
Endgame (Beckett) 132–3
England 217; city gent 24;
  playhouse 60; theatre 85
enterprise: semiotic 1–2
epistemological orientation 98
Esslin, M. 199, 209
ethnomethodology 211
European drama criticism 196–7
Every Good Boy Deserves Favour
  (Stoppard) 148–9
everyday discourse 162–5
explicit performance 171
expressives 151–2
extensions 203–15

fabula 107–8
fantasy worlds 105
Faust 11, 153
feminism 214; spectatorship 215;
  theory 215
figures: implicatures 155–62
Fischer-Lichte, E. 204, 205, 206
Fitzpatrick, T. 211
flashbacks 107
floor-appointment control 164–5
foregrounding 14–17, 15–16
Foreman, R. 16, 39, 69
Fortier, M. 203
Foucault, M. 216, 217, 219
France 76
Frye, N. 120

Gale, R. M. 154
gender 214

general kinesic continuum 45–6
generative capacity 10
German theatre 205; tradition 200
gestural fallacy 63–4
gesture 23, 62, 64–70
Ghosts (Ibsen) 139
Gielgud, J. 74
Goffman, E. 78, 79, 82, 135, 165
Graeco-Roman ethical base 48
grammar 114
Greek 65
Greek tragedy 127
Greenblatt, S. 217–18, 219, 220
Gregory, M. and Carroll, S. 162–3
Greimas, A. J. 114, 118, 121–2
Grice, H. P. 150, 155, 160
Grotowski, J. 201; Theatre
  Laboratory 76

Hall, E. T. 50, 56, 58
Hamlet (Shakespeare) 68, 84, 103,
  104, 111, 120, 127, 159, 168
Hammond, B. 201
Hamon, P. 119, 120–1
Handke, P. 8, 98, 142
Happy Days (Beckett) 92
Havránek, B. 15
Heartbreak House (Shaw) 126
Henry IV (Shakespeare) 160
Henry VI (Shakespeare) 137
Herman, V. 211–12
hermeneutics 74
higher-order actions 109, 111
histoire 131
historical time 106–7
histrionic subcodes 76
Hjelmslev, L. 9, 142
Hochhuth, R. 95
Hodgson, T. 202
Hoffman, T.: and Cameron, K. 59

Honzl, J. 11, 14, 21, 25, 127, 132
horizon of expectations 85
horoscope 116
Hymes, D. 124

Ibsen, H. J. 139
iconic identity 20
iconism 18–22
ideology 206, 214, 217
idiolect 49
illocution 68, 144, 168, 170;
  -perlocutionary interaction 153;
  classes 151–2; force indicators
  150; perlocutionary strategy 148;
  purity 164
image 19
implicatures: figures 155–62, 171
index (indices) 19, 22–3
indexical symbols 22
Indian theatre 62
information: dramatic 88–9; and
  reference 135–6; theatre 34–9
informational intensity 164
institutionalizations 201–3
intentions 110
interaction 110
intercommunication 33–4
intertextual relations 83–6
intertextuality 191
Ionesco, E. 94–5
irony 160

Jakobson, R. 24–5, 74, 127, 134, 140
Japanese Noh theatre 10, 24, 48
jargon-laden text 208
Jones, I. 60–1
Jonson, B. 60–1, 81
Jumpers (Stoppard) 138–9

Ka Mountain (Wilson) 21

Kabuki theatre 48
Kantor, T. 38
kinemes 63
kinemorphs 63
kinesics: components 62; factors
  62–70; marker 66; paradigms 64
Kirby, M. 40
Kott, J. 20
Kowzan, T. 17, 42–3, 45, 71, 209
Kripke, S. 100
Kristeva, J. 64–5, 84
Kuchta, D. 220

laboratory: semiotic 194
Langer, S. K. 60, 80
language: as action 142–3;
  dramatic 123, 221; poetic 16;
  social theory 212
Laqueur, T. 219
Latin America 204
Laughton, C. 74–5
law: semiotic 44
Le Grand Magic Circus 84
Levi-Strauss, C. 201
Lewis, D. K. 90, 102
Lewis, L. L: and Alternberd, L. 131
lexemes/isotopies/semantic
  paradigms 173
lighting 75
linguistics 16, 63; messages 40
listener 124–5, 169
literary theory: non-theatrical 202
literature 26
logic: dramatic 88–122
logical coherence 166
Lotman, Y. 61, 85, 121, 194, 210, 218
Lyons, J. 36, 121, 130, 131, 139

Macbeth (Shakespeare) 105–6, 108,
  111–12, 115–16, 118, 154, 211

McLuhan, M. 40
mainstream theatre 200
Malinowski, B. 164
manner: maxim of 156
Marlowe, C. 145–6
Marx, G. 8
Measure for Measure (Shakespeare) 21
medieval theatre 58
Merchant of Venice (Shakespeare) 77
message 31, 39–41; theatrical 33, 36
metalanguage 140–2, 172; meditative 141
metalogisms 161
metaphor 15, 19, 24–6
metatheatrical functions 81
metatheatrical superstructure 142
metatheoretical discourse 205
methodology 210
metonymy 24–6
Metz, C. 39
micro-segmentation 168
Miller, J. 69, 74, 128–9
mimesis 100, 101
mobility 204
modality/propositional attitudes 171
model performance 190
modern theatre 57
Moles, A. 33, 36, 40
monologuing 165
Moscow Arts Theatre 74
Mounin, G. 29, 43
Mukarovsky, J. 4–5, 6, 10, 204
Mullaney, S. 213–14

narratology 114; approaches 167
narratorial guides 100
native tradition 217

naturalistic theatre 82
Neoplatonic model 220
New Criticism 217
newspaper critics 196
Noh theatre 24
non-academic discourse 197
non-aesthetic communication 38
nonexistent worlds 102
Norris, C. 216

object-language 140–2
obscurity 210
Occupations (Griffiths) 157
Oedipus Rex 84
Offending the Audience (Handke) 98, 142
Ohmann, R. 145, 147, 152
one sex theory 219–20
Oriental theatre 12, 34
Osborne, J. 154
Osmond, H. 58
ostension 26–7
Othello (Shakespeare) 139, 148
Ouaknine, S. 201
out-of-frame activity 79
overcoding 47–8, 70

Pagnini, M. 42
painting 61
parakinesic signal 65–6
paralinguistic devices 24, 154
paralinguistic features 59–60, 70–5
paraphrase 108
Pavel, T. 94
Pavis, P. 20, 65, 202, 208, 213
Paxton, S. 70
peasant theatre: Russia 57
Peirce, C. S. 2, 18–22, 24
People Show, The 37
performability 191

performance: continuum 43;
explicit 171; hierarchy 14–17;
model 190; opacity 77; spatiality
60; text 3, 190–1
performative verbs 151
performer: –audience transaction 2;
–spectator bond 29; –spectator
distance 59; body 220
perlocutionary effect 171
phantasma-oriented deixis 132
phenomenology: of drama 215–21
photograph 19
Pilbrow, R. 75
Pirandello, L. 98, 113, 141–2
pitch variations 75
Play (Beckett) 23
play-within-the-play 81
playhouses: Elizabethan 211
plot 107–8, 111; discourse 118; time
106
poetic language 16
poetics 1–3; of culture 217
polyfunctionality 205
post-semiotics 193–221; theory 194
post-structuralism 195, 202, 203,
221
posthumous semiotics 193–221
pragmatic discourse 132
Prague School 4–5, 17, 204, 205
Prague structuralism 4–17
Pratt, M. L. 41
presence 86
proairetic (action) coherence 166
propositional attitudes 103–4
Propp, V. 114
protagonist 110
proxemics 50–62; modalities 56–7
pseudonarrative past 134
psychological traits 119
publishers 196

Pugliatti, P. G. 191
purpose 109
Pygmalion (Shaw) 141

quality/quantity maxims 155–6

Rainier, Y. 70
redundancy 38–9
referential coherence 166
reflexivity 101
relation: maxim of 156
Renaissance: drama 217; stage 81;
theatre 58
representation 13, 34
representatives 151
representatum 13
Rescher, N. 92, 99
resistant spectator 215
Restoration stage 80
reviewers 198
Revzina, O. G.: and Revzin, I. I. 95,
160
rhetorical figures 160–2
rhetorical and stylistic coherence
167
Richard II (Shakespeare) 10, 98
Richard III (Shakespeare) 113
Rivals (Sheridan) 141
roles 118
Royal Shakespeare Company
199–200
Ruffini, F. 30
Russell, B. 103–4
Russia 6; formalists 107, 203;
peasant theatre 57; theatre 57, 61;
tradition 200

Saint Joan (Shaw) 135–6
Sartre, J. P. 47
Savona: and Aston, E. 207–8, 209

scenic metonymies 25
Schechner, R. 38, 60, 70, 84
Searle, J. 100, 147–8, 149, 151
Segers, R. T. 85
segment 169
self-characterization 135
semantic coherence 82, 167
semantic relations: vertical 41
semanticization 37
semilogical agenda: hidden 195
semiotics: function 173; moment
  194; terminology 197; types
  193–221; upgrading 195
semiotization 6–8, 18, 26
sequences 109
Serpieri, A. 102, 127, 130, 132, 161,
  210
setting 109
sexuality 219–20
Shakespeare, W. 17; see also names
  of individual plays
Shakespearian tragedy 85
Shaw, G. B. 95, 126, 135–6, 141
Shepard, S. 162–3
Sheridan, R. B. 141
Sherlock Holmes 91
sign 5–6; artificial 17–18; natural
  17–18; systems 24;
  transformability 10–11;
  typologies 17–27
sign-vehicles see signified/signifier
  (sign-vehicles)
signal: anaphoric 65; audience
  86–7; equiprobability 36;
  information 36–7, 40;
  parakinesic 64, 65–6
signification 1; communication
  28–9
signified/signifier (sign-vehicles) 5,
  6–7, 9–11, 37

signifying modes 27
Simonson, L. 75
situation 125
Six Characters in Search of an Author
  (Pirandello) 98
sjuzet/fabula distinction 107, 132
social semiotics 212
social status 124–5
social traits 119
sociofugality 58
sociopetality 58
Souriau, É. 114, 118; functions
  114–17
space 213; acoustic 40, 75; body-to-
  body 57; fixed-feature 56;
  informal 56, 58; meanings 50–62;
  semi-fixed-feature 56; virtual 60
Spanish 203
spatial continuum 58
spatial deixis 131
spatial semiotics 211
spatialization of time 131
speaker 124–5
spectator 59, 215; –performer
  communication 86–7; –spectator
  communication 87; cowboy 80;
  interpretation 85–6; resistant
  215; subworlds 102–5
speech act 142–54; analysis 151; full
  154; on stage 153–4; theory 143,
  203; types 143–53
speech events 154
spoken action 113, 147
stage 50; –audience distance 59;
  representation 13; semiotization
  7–8
Stanislavsky, K. S. A. 72, 76–7
States, B. O. 215
stereotypes 25
Stern, D. N. 63, 66, 70

stimulus-response model 29
Stoppard, T. 138–9, 148–9
story 107, 111
structuralism 114; Prague 4–17
Styan, J. L. 130, 209
stylistic rules 48
subcodes 48; histrionic 76
subindices 22
subjective-objective continuum 13
subworlds: character 102–5;
    spectator 102–5
suspension 111–12
symbol 19–20, 24
synecdoche 24–6
syntax 121; orderliness 163–4;
    systems 56
synthesis 33
Szondi, P. 106

Taming of the Shrew (Shakespeare)
    81
technical systems 75
teleological structure 110–11
Tempest, The (Shakespeare) 23
temporal levels 105–7
tense 169
terminological tradition 34
text 39–41; ambiguous 41;
    coherence 165–7; deixis 139–40;
    dramatic 3, 131–5, 190–1; jargon-
    laden 208; performance 3, 190–1;
    segmentation 41–3, 131–5; and
    sexuality 219–20; spatio-
    temporal structure 41
textuality 162–7
textualization 218–19
theatre: communication 27, 28–87;
    competence 46, 78–87; context
    34; critics 199; discourse 39, 137;
    message 33, 36; nineteenth-

century 57; sign 4–17; systems
    43–78
Theatre Semiotics (de Toro) 198
Theatre as Sign System (Aston and
    Savona) 207–8, 209
theatrical frame 78–83
theatricality 10, 48
Times 197
Tindemans, C. 196
Todorov, T. 83; and Ducrot, O. 135
Tooth of Crime (Shepard) 162–3
topic/object of discourse 170
tragedy 109; Aeschylean 127
Trager, G. L. 71
trans-world identity 95
transcodification 13, 75–8
transmitters 38
Twelfth Night (Shakespeare) 97

undercoding 49
United States of America (USA) 76,
    217; White House 24
universe of discourse 135–42
Urmson, J. O. 92, 97, 112

Van Dijk, T. A. 105, 108, 110, 126
Veltrusky, J. 6, 7–8, 13–14, 15, 25
verbal communication 142
Verfremdungseffekt (alienation
    effect) 15, 200
verisimilitude 83
verse 168
Vertical Mobility 16
Victorian melodrama 48
vocal idiosyncrasies 72–3, 74
vocalic features 71

Wardle, I. 197–8
Weiss, P. 95
West End 84

Western bourgeois theatre 57
Western drama 124
Who's Afraid of Virginia Woolf
(Albee) 104–5
Wilder, T. 105–6

Wilson, J. D. 129
Wilson, R. 42, 70, 200,
217

Zich, O. 4–5, 14